THE GERMAN YOUTH MOVEMENT 1900–1945

The German Youth Movement 1900—1945

An Interpretative and Documentary History

Peter D. Stachura,
University of Stirling

St. Martin's Press
New York

St. Martin's Press, Inc., 175 Fifth Avenue, New York, NY 10010
Printed in Hong Kong
First published in the United States of America in 1981

ISBN 0–312–32624–6

Library of Congress Cataloging in Publication Data

Stachura, Peter D.
  The German youth movement, 1900–1945.
  Bibliography: p.
  Includes index.
    1. Youth movement—Germany—History.
I. Title.
HN19.S77   324'.3   80–14527
ISBN 0–312–32624–6

Contents

Preface

My interest in the wider German Youth Movement stems from my earlier investigation of the Hitler Youth, and in this sense, the present study has followed on from this source. However, I am grateful to Marianne Calmann for convincing me that an interpretative analysis of the Youth Movement was a feasible proposition, though the format of this book is certainly rather different from the kind she initially envisaged.

The many problems encountered during the research for this work over the last four years or so could not have been overcome without the courteous and knowledgeable assistance of the staffs of the various archives and libraries I consulted: the Bundesarchiv Koblenz, particularly Dr Rainer F. Raillard; the Bayerisches Hauptstaats-archiv: Allgemeines Staatsarchiv and Geheimes Staatsarchiv, both of Munich; the Institut für Zeitgeschichte, Munich; the Institute of Contemporary History and Wiener Library, London; and last but not least, the Archiv der Deutschen Jugendbewegung at Burg Ludwigstein. I should like to specially thank Dr Winfried Mogge, director of the latter, for his friendly and expert guidance.

My archival research in Germany was made possible by generous awards made to me by the Social Science Research Council and the Deutscher Akademischer Austauschdienst, which were much appreciated.

Professor Michael H. Kater read parts of my manuscript and provided perceptive criticisms which I was grateful to receive. Responsibility for what I have written is, of course, entirely mine.

Stirling, January 1980   PETER D. STACHURA

List of Abbreviations

AHS	Adolf-Hitler-Schule
BA	Bundesarchiv Koblenz
BDJ	Bund deutscher Jugendvereine
BK	Bund deutscher Bibelkreise
BdM	Bund deutscher Mädel
BHSA, ASA (*or* GSA)	Bayerisches Hauptstaatsarchiv, Allgemeines Staatsarchiv (*or* Geheimes Staatsarchiv)
DDP	Deutsche Demokratische Partei
DJ	Deutsches Jungvolk
DNVP	Deutschnationale Volkspartei
DVP	Deutsche Volkspartei
ERVWJ	Evangelischer Reichsverband weiblicher Jugend
FJ	Freie Jugend Deutschlands
FSJ	Freie Sozialistische Jugend Deutschlands
HJ	Hitler-Jugend
JADJB	Jahrbuch des Archivs der deutschen Jugendbewegung
KJD	Katholische Jugend Deutschlands
KJD (Communist Youth)	Kommunistische Jugend Deutschlands
KJMV	Katholische Jungmännerverband Deutschlands
KJVD	Kommunistischer Jugendverband Deutschlands
KLV	*Kinderlandverschickung*
KPD	Kommunistiche Partei Deutschlands
NA	National Archives, Washington, D.C.
NSDAP	Nationalsozialistische Deutsche Arbeiterpartei
NSDStB	Nationalsozialistischer Deutscher Studentenbund
NSS	Nationalsozialistischer Schülerbund
NSLB	Nationalsozialistischer Lehrerbund

RAJJV	Reichsausschuss der jüdischen Jugendverbände
RFB	Rotfrontkämpferbund
RJF	Reichsjugendführung
RVEJMB	Reichsverband der Evangelischen Jungmännerbünde Deutschlands
SAJ	Verband der Sozialistische Arbeiterjugend Deutschlands
SAJD	Syndikalistisch-anarchistische Jugend Deutschlands
SPD	Sozialdemokratische Partei Deutschlands
SPJ	Sozialistische Proletarierjugend
SS	Schutzstaffel
USPD	Unabhängige Sozialdemokratische Partei Deutschlands
VAJV	Verband der Arbeiterjugendvereine Deutschlands
VJJVD	Verband der jüdischen Jugendvereine Deutschlands
VKJJVD	Verband der Katholischen Jugend- und Jungmännervereine Deutschlands

Introduction
Youth and History

Historians of modern Germany have in recent years displayed a greater awareness of the importance of the younger generation in helping to determine the nature of society and politics in that country. The youthfulness of the National Socialist movement and the widespread support it attracted before and after 1933 from young Germans are well-known features of Germany's historical development in the twentieth century. Interest in youth's historical role has partly grown out of the intensive examination of the 1871–1945 era in German history, whereby scholars have subjected institutions and social classes of every type to rigorous scrutiny, and partly from an expanding concern with youth as a distinct group in society by sociologists, educationalists, psychologists and social anthropologists, as well as by historians. Certainly, neither the younger generation nor the youth movement in Germany enjoyed such popularity in academic circles before the end of the Second World War.

The student disturbances at many European universities during the last decade significantly contributed to the reawakened study of the youth sphere, causing scholars to analyse the status and influence of youth against the background of European history since 1815. From such analyses resulted a compendium of generational theory which sought to explain the historical role of youth in its own right, and, in addition, a sophisticated framework of generationally related concepts such as the birth cohort, political socialisation, and youth's crisis of identity.[1] Generational stress is frequently accentuated as the mainspring of youth's activist temperament, while the genesis of this modern phenomenon is usually traced to the German student societies (*Burschenschaften*) of the early nineteenth century, and passing through a series of stages until culminating in the radical student movements of the 1960s and 1970s.[2] The nineteenth-century German historian Wilhelm Dilthey, in his essay 'Novalis' (1865), was the first to investigate systematically the problem of social generations. His embryonic deductions were later extended and refined by others, particularly after 1918 by the Spanish philosopher José Ortega y Gasset and the German sociologist Karl Mannheim.[3] In more recent times, Lewis S. Feuer's controversial work *The Conflict of Generations* (1969) has added a further dimension to the debate by postulating an intrinsically negative view of the historical role of revolutionary minded youth. On the other hand, Herbert Moller, utilising a demographic explanatory model, makes a more positive assessment of the revolutionary impulse of youth and its capacity to act as a potentially powerful force for constructive change in the historical process.[4] Friedrich Heer has in fact gone much further, in stating that the whole of civilisation has been created by youthful endeavour channelled through organised movements of the younger generation from the beginning of time to the present.[5]

In any event, there is much to be said for the hypothesis that the Industrial Revolution and the unprecedented scale and rapidity of change it set in motion made generational conflict inevitable.[6] The social and economic dislocations of the industrial age were complemented in a sense by the emergence of different forms of ideological and intellectual influence which paved the way, in the case of youth, for unequivocal and sometimes violent articulation of their fears, frustrations and ambitions. The nineteenth century witnessed, therefore, the birth of the 'Youth Revolution', and before 1900 most of the major characteristics of this phenomenon had already been manifested: youth's elastic capacity for idealism and commitment, romantic nationalism, militancy, rejection of the adult world and parental values, and Bohemian-type withdrawal from the mainstream of society, invariably expressed in a back-to-nature outlook. By 1914 youth had made its presence felt in noteworthy fashion in politics, the arts, literature, and the world of ideas. Correspondingly, about the same time adolescence was discovered as a stage of life, and Freud evolved his theory of Oedipal conflict between fathers and sons. Oscar Wilde summed up the emergence of youth in striking, if somewhat exaggerated, vein when he exclaimed, 'Youth! Youth! There is Absolutely Nothing in the World but Youth!'[7] While this new advance of youth in Europe was a minority movement before the First World War, it turned into a large-scale rebellion of the younger generation after 1918. In the post-war period youth came fully into its own in many respects and exercised a vital influence on European events during those turbulent and unhappy decades before 1939. In Germany, youth's prominence as an organised and clearly defined group crystallised around the establishment and subsequent proliferation of the youth movement.

The youth movement in Germany incorporated a variety of heterogeneous, complex elements, which creates major difficulties for anyone trying to generalise about its development. This is especially the case when, as in the present study, the term 'youth movement', is used generically. That is to say, the term is not exclusively related here to the autonomous sector of the movement, but is understood to include also the so-called youth-tutelage organisations of political, paramilitary, and confessional youth — those associations which were by and large under adult supervision. It must be considered wholly misleading to discuss the millions of organised German youths during the years 1900–45 simply on the basis of the independent sector, which, after all, was composed almost entirely of one social class — bourgeois youths — and which, in the Weimar era at least, numbered no more than 60,000 members, or less than 1 per cent of organised youth. Moreover, the independence from adult control and interference of the Wandervogel, Free German Youth, and Bündische Youth — the principal stages of the free youth development — may have been exaggerated.[8] There is no denying, however, that the Wandervogel and its successors in the autonomous stream set the pace and standard by which German youth, regardless of the kind of group they were part of, measured their activities and objectives. One shrewd historian of the independent youth movement has stated that it was 'in its own way a microcosm of modern Germany',[9] but the youth movement as a whole often left an indelible mark on its members. Many prominent politicians, artists, intellectuals and other notable figures in German public life who were born between, roughly, 1890 and 1920 have testified to the importance of their experiences in a youth group for the later shaping of their personal, social and political attitudes. These include such figures as Hermann Hesse, Max Scheler, Paul Tillich, Adolf Reichwein and even notorious National Socialists such as Rudolf Hoess, Commandant of Auschwitz; Heinrich Himmler, Reichsführer of the SS; Adolf Eichmann, who was responsible for the deportation of hundreds of thousands of Jews to extermination camps; and Baldur von Schirach, head of the Hitler Youth. In addition, those not so conspicuous, such as thousands of teachers, civil servants and social workers, felt a profound attachment to the values and ideals inculcated by their particular youth association.

The significance of the youth movement within the broader

perspective of modern German history extends further, however, than its impact on its individual members. The youth movement had a role to play in such areas as youthful socialisation, social welfare, cultural innovation and educational reform. At the same time, it acted as a vehicle for the younger generation's protest against institutional pressures, notably those emanating from the parental home, school, and church. The movement's symbolic position in the emancipation struggle of social and ethnic minorities within and outside Germany should also not be underestimated.[10] Particularly during the Weimar Republic, the youth movement collectively enjoyed a degree of prestige which spread far beyond the orbit of youth. It was, therefore, a highly complicated phenomenon for which a fundamental explanation has to be sought not merely within the confines of a theory of generational antagonism. Only if the techniques of different disciplines of the political sciences are applied will the youth movement become comprehensible to a satisfactory extent.

It cannot be said that existing literature on the youth movement has fully faced up to all central problems concerning its inner meaning and character. This is particularly evident in works directed towards the independent sector, since interpretations of what the Wandervogel and Bündische Youth really amounted to reveal considerable variance. In one respect, this situation is not altogether surprising, because even contemporaries could not agree. For Gustav Wyneken, the autonomous youth movement was primarily an educational and cultural expression, while Hans Blüher, the first historian of the Wandervogel, controversially emphasised its homoerotic nature.[11] Later historians have also shown the same divergence of opinion. George L. Mosse is convinced of the dominant *völkisch* (racist) – nationalist flavour of the movement, but both Armin Mohler and Klemens von Klemperer see it as part of the so-called Conservative Revolution.[12] Jakob Müller, who has written perhaps the most fundamental post-war study of the independent youth movement, has refined the latter view by underlining the place of the Wandervogel and its heirs in reformist–idealistic neoconservatism.[13] Others, such as Harry Pross and Howard Becker, have depicted them, but especially Bündische Youth, as the reactionary precursors of National Socialism.[14] Most post-war commentators would agree, however, that the independent youth movement had a positive, and in some ways far-reaching, impact on a number of crucial spheres, including education.

Another salient problem relating to literature on the youth

movement is the large number of studies which have been written by former members or close sympathisers of it. The majority of the most prominent authors in this field have or had a youth movement background; such is the case with, for instance, Werner Kindt, Karl O. Paetel, Gerhard Ziemer, Rudolf Kneip, Karl Seidelmann, Walther Gerber, Hans Wolf — all from the independent Youth Movement — and Johannes Schult (Socialist Youth) and Walter Laqueur (Jewish Youth). This situation largely explains why literature dealing with the youth movement but dating from before 1933 is too often rather abstract and too readily assumes that the reader is acquainted with basic facts. Also, these early works rarely attempt a comprehensive picture of the youth movement, being more inclined to advocate sectional viewpoints of specific youth groups. The result is a literature which when not downright polemical or propagandistic is fragmentary and of limited value. Works published after 1945 by former members of the independent youth movement in particular sometimes attain a high level of scholarship, but too many of them are little more than impressionist, subjective chronicles of personal experiences. There is, furthermore, an unmistakable propensity in them towards dogmatism and self-justifying apologetics in view of the controversy over the role of the youth movement *vis-à-vis* National Socialism and the Third Reich. The early volumes of the principal publication of the official centre of the youth movement, at Burg Ludwigstein, the *Jahrbuch des Archivs der deutschen Jugendbewegung*, frequently contained material of this variety.

It has been argued, moreover, by authors with a youth-movement background, that no one who was not a member of it can write adequately about any aspect of the movement.[15] They contend, with more justification, that the independent youth movement was a uniquely German phenomenon which had no parallels in other countries, even in those where youth groups did take root.[16] They further stress that the intrinsic substance and ethos of the movement cannot be properly understood by reference to printed documentary sources, since it was not noted for its literary qualities. What mattered, according to this argument, was the experience (*Erlebnis*) and the emotional commitment felt by all members.[17] It would be wrong, however, to conclude that objectively minded scholars applying conventional methods of historical inquiry are, if they did not actively participate in it, somehow unfit to analyse the youth movement or any other organisation which has played a significant role in modern German history. After all, National Socialism, also a uniquely German phenomenon, has been the subject of much valuable and incisive comment by both German and non-German scholars who were not associated with it. In fact, it is probably more valid to say that former members of the youth movement cannot be expected to possess the necessary degree of detachment and critical awareness in dealing with an evaluation of it. Hence, only comparatively recently has a critical historiography of the youth movement begun to emerge from the pens of scholars who have no axe to grind and who are prepared to delve into available primary sources. Admittedly, a large proportion of such material was either confiscated by the National Socialists once in power, or lost or damaged during the war by a combination of Hitler Youth vandalism and Allied bombing, but at least there is a basis on which historians can build.[18]

Historians of the pre-1933 youth movement have to solve the basic dilemma of what kind of approach to make in trying to assess it. The very diversity and lack of a consistent philosophy or ideology in the youth movement make it virtually impossible to treat uniformly as a self-contained, integrated entity. This is the main reason why a detailed, comprehensive and scholarly history of the entire youth movement remains to be written. Instead, scholars have concentrated to date on a wide range of different means of evaluation, which may be summarised as follows.

(1) Detailed monographs on individual youth groups, such as those by Helmut Grau, Barbara Schellenberger and Antje Vollmer.[19] Works of this genre provide relevant and worthwhile information and insights but generally add only a small piece to the complex mosaic that was the youth movement. Moreover, they only reach an exiguous readership of specialists in the field. It should be noted that outside Germany the number of specialists on the youth movement is even smaller,

(2) Biographical studies of leaders and personalities of the youth movement. These are relatively few in number and tend to focus on the better-known names, such as Gustav Wyneken or Romano Guardini.[20]

(3) Documentary collections and reference works, of which there have been some distinguished examples in recent times, notably by Werner Kindt.[21]

(4) Collections of essays by various authors on specific themes of the youth movement. These are normally of good standard and based to some extent on original research.[22]

(5) Autobiographical studies by former members. These are invariably of poor quality and unreliable as authentic historical records, especially if a political or ideological slant is added. Alfred Kurella's book is a case in point.[23]

(6) General accounts of particular segments of the youth movement. This type of study has increasingly attracted scholars since the late 1950s, and as a result a fairly large number of solid works have been produced. Among these should be cited Walter Laqueur's penetrating analysis of the independent youth movement, Felix Raabe's meticulously researched sketch of Bündische Youth, Karl Seidelmann's informative narrative of the Boy Scouts, and Jakob Müller's revisionist study of the independent youth movement up to 1924.[24] Books of comparable scope, if not always quality, have been written on denominational and political youth organisations. Complementing particularist studies of this type are those dealing with individual aspects or problems of the youth movement. Seidelmann's examination of the collective mentality in the independent sector and Paetel's sociological analysis of the youth movement's leadership are instructive examples.[25]

(7) Broadly conceived and interpretative studies which are designed to provide a synthesis of the whole development of the youth movement, including the Hitler Youth. The only author to have seriously attempted such a synthesis, and then from a decidedly partisan stance, has been Luise Fick.[26] Her book was patently designed to serve the propagandistic and ideological purposes of the Third Reich, and as such must be considered highly unsatisfactory. A few more recent books, such as those by Laqueur and Pross, have included discussion of post-1933 events, but only as a tailpiece, in effect, to their main theme of the independent youth movement.

The present book aims to break new ground, therefore, by scrutinising every important branch of the German youth movement from its beginnings at the turn of this century to its effective demise in 1933 and its replacement by the Hitler Youth during the years 1933–45. This is an interpretative synthesis of an extremely diversified but distinctively cultural orientation in the broadest sense. It is hoped to convey the essential flavour of organised German youth during this eventful period by an investigation of its most vital aims, ideals and problems, as well as by a consideration of significant points of debate raised by students of the youth movement. In short, this study does not try to give a detailed history of the movement, nor does it represent an attempt at an exhaustive sociological or psychohistorical treatise. It is to be understood as an exercise in historical exposition and assessment. As such, the book is largely meant to inform a broadly academic readership with a serious interest in twentieth-century German history. It is hoped that it will also serve as a point of departure for further research into the youth movement.

The material for this study has been drawn from both secondary and primary sources. The vast but qualitatively inferior literature produced by the youth movement has been consulted — though, of course, not in its entirety — as have the writings, which have been appearing with increasing regularity since 1945, on different branches of the youth movement. Use has also been made of new archival sources for discussion of the Hitler Youth.

In Part I the major denominational and political youth associations of the 1900—33 period are considered, as well as the independent groups, while the overall contribution of the youth movement to the development of German society and politics before the advent to power of the National Socialists is also assessed. In Part II the organisation which took the place of all these groups after 1933, the Hitler Youth, is the focus of attention. A satisfactory, scholarly general history of the Hitler Youth during the Third Reich has yet to be written.[27] Previous works by Arno Klönne, Werner Klose and Hans-Christian Brandenburg have furnished a wealth of useful detail on many Hitler Youth activities without, however, succeeding in integrating their factual narratives into an appealing conceptual framework.[28] Our understanding of the innate dynamics of the Hitler Youth within a totalitarian governmental system therefore remains superficial. More recent accounts of the Hitler Youth have hardly enhanced our knowledge. Erich Blohm, a former member of the Hitler Youth, has written an unashamed apologia for the organisation,[29] while another ex-member, Hansjoachim Koch, has produced a careless, discursive work clearly meant for an un-sophisticated popular market.[30] The present study does not aim to fill this obvious gap in the historiography of the Hitler Youth, for a full history of the group lies outside its terms of reference. What is presented here is an evaluation of some of the more significant events and features of the Hitler Youth's position as the official youth organisation of National Socialist Germany. These include the Hitler Youth's responsibility for organising German youth within its own ranks and for instilling it with the National Socialist *Weltanschauung*. This form of activity raises in turn vital questions about the Hitler Youth's standing as an authentic youth organisation, its success in attracting the younger generation to the swastika, its educational priorities, and its function during wartime.

The documentary section at the end of the book includes extracts from statements, programmes, regulations and the like which were important not only for the evolution of the youth movement, but which also illustrate something of its pulse-beat. The documents are therefore to be viewed as an essential supplementary aid to the analytical survey in the main text.

Part I
1900 — 1933

1 Wandervogel to Free German Youth

The appearance of an independent youth movement in Germany around the turn of the twentieth century was by no means an isolated event. The Wandervogel was very much a product of wider concerns and uncertainties in bourgeois life which were coming to the surface at that time. Germany's uneven and rapid industrialisation process during the second half of the nineteenth century and the relative lateness of her political unification resulted in a welter of social and political tensions which, particularly after Bismarck's fall as Chancellor in 1890, caused an inherent weakness and instability in the governmental system. As the long-established social and political attitudes of the middle and upper classes came under considerable strain, the feudalistic ruling elite around Kaiser Wilhelm II sought through a programme of naval expansion and *Weltpolitik* to contain the rising tide of discontent within an anachronistic system. The advance of socialism and the labour movement in particular engendered great alarm among the propertied classes, who tended to exaggerate the revolutionary and anti-statist capacity of the Left. By 1900 Germany was one of the leading industrial and military nations in the world, but underneath the glitter of power and might the reality at home of a pressing need for fundamental social and constitutional reform seriously preoccupied the semi-autocratic monarchial state. By 1914, when all diversionary efforts to solve the internal crisis had failed, the Kaiser and the social groups, including the broad range of the middle classes, which had rallied to him (*Sammlungspolitik*) had decided that an offensive war was the last remaining expedient whereby their grandiose plans for European and world hegemony as well as their hopes of preserving the *status quo* in Germany itself could be realised.[1]

Deep foreboding about the future had become a salient feature of the German bourgeoisie as early as the 1880s. They increasingly felt that their social and economic status was being undermined by the new forces and values of urban–industrial society. At the same time as they felt threatened from below by the working class, the middle classes were confronted by an upper-class conservative reaction and more and more felt themselves helplessly squeezed between two major, conflicting ideologies. By about 1900 their anxieties had reached crisis point. This outlook of self-doubt and pessimism was reflected in the growth of militant right-wing political movements such as the various anti-semitic parties and the Pan-German League, and also in the works of writers such as Thomas Mann, Julius Langbehn and Paul de Lagarde, all of whom exercised an important influence on the Wandervogel. Lagarde in particular showed understanding for the way in which Imperial Germany stifled the natural idealism of youth[2] and believed that youth alone could save Germany from irrevocable decline. Langbehn's best-selling novel *Rembrandt als Erzieher* (1890) effectively caught the discontented and rebellious mood of many younger Germans and was widely read in the Wandervogel. In a sense Langbehn's confusedly articulated revolt against bourgeois modernity was acted out by the youth movement.[3]

The Wandervogel was an expression of German middle-class anti-urban and anti-industrial attitudes and thus formed part of the campaign against modernism (*Kulturkritik*) in all spheres of German public life – a campaign that was well underway by 1900.[4] Anti-modernism was not, of course, confined to Germany. Throughout industrial Europe similar expressions of unrest were evident: for example, in Britain they could be heard from Chesterton and D. H. Lawrence, in Russia from Dostoyevsky and Aksakow, in France from Sorel and Barrés, and in Italy from Pareto and Mosca. Despite a veneer of peace, prosperity, and belief in progress, a definite *fin de siècle* psychosis was produced which eventually sought emancipation from a humdrum, materialistic reality in the First World War. The Wandervogel was clearly a manifestation of this essentially bourgeois cultural malaise, while on another level it was linked to new developments in the sciences and arts. There was a probing criticism of established standards, assumptions and codes of conduct. Chiliastic needs and calls to action replaced rational systems of thought. Positivism, scientism and rationalism were all attacked. Foremost in laying the groundwork for a revolution in man's conception of his world were Freud in psychology, Weber in sociology and Einstein in physics. The intellectual revolt was also present in literature and painting – in the movements of cubism, futurism, abstract art and expressionism. The early expressionists above all had much in common with the first generation of Wandervogel members. They came from a similar middle-class background and were born at roughly the same time (c. 1880).[5] Expressionism also arose in protest at the vacuity of life, and like the youth movement was idealistic and regressive at the same time. Its protest was directed against intellectualism and bourgeois hypocrisy, but was as aimless as the early Wandervogel.[6] By 1900, youth in general was thrusting itself forward throughout Europe as a new dynamic element in society, demanding recognition in its own right, and determined to assert its own specific personality. Other hitherto submerged or underprivileged social groups were also stirring at this time, as exemplified by the rise of feminist organisations in Germany and elsewhere.

The Wandervogel arose spontaneously as a movement of youthful protest against the stuffy and constricting conventions of late Wilhelmine society. It reflected an acute boredom with contemporary society, and this was basically caused by the failure of the technological age and urban culture to offer youth either emotional satisfaction or moral inspiration. The demands of youth's spirit were not being met. There was a pervasive uniformity, artificiality and feeling of estrangement about German urban life, and the Wandervogel, an urban-based movement in origin and during its subsequent evolution, constituted a form of opposition to it. The Wandervogel rejected the straitjacket into which so much of German social intercourse had been thrust with the arrival of the industrial era. The depersonalised ethics of mass society repelled it. Youth in Germany was not regarded as a station of life in itself but simply as a transitional stage, an integrated junior section of a society dominated and controlled by adults through the major institutions of parental home, school, and church. Denied scope for self-expression and self-realisation in natural ways, the younger generation were expected to behave and conduct their lives as miniature versions of their elders – an attitude shown, for example, in the imposition of adult sartorial tastes and other habits on children of all ages. The Wandervogel spoke out for a younger generation which was resentful of an overbearing adult society and which wanted to show that it was a distinct entity with its own needs and objectives, and capacity to shape its own life.[7] This is not to say, however, that the Wandervogel nursed a hostility towards parents, teachers and others in authority. Adults played an important sponsoring and advisory role in the

Wandervogel, especially during its early stages, and individual adults were conspicuously to the fore in its activities throughout its history.

The Wandervogel was not a revolutionary movement seeking to destroy the social fabric root and branch. It sought rather a modification of this fabric in a way which would permit youth more freedom and opportunity to exercise its initiative independent of adults. None the less, the presence of generational conflict was powerful, and by 1900 was sharpened by the erosion of the ties which had formerly bound together the family unit.[8] This development has been ascribed to the growing mobility and heterogeneity of industrial society in the nineteenth century, which had as its principal casualties not only the family but also the local community.[9] The consequent degree of social flux removed old traditions, thus making it easier for youth to criticise their parents. With the decline in the status of the family, the authority of the father began to be less secure and hence more vulnerable to criticism or even rejection by his children. This generational tension may also have had something to do with changing occupational prospects in industrial society. New careers opened up for youths in areas unknown by their fathers. Another theory is that this conflict may have been caused, in part at least, by the failure of fathers to develop politically meaningful concepts which could be passed on.[10] In any case, the crisis of the family was most pronounced among certain middle-class social categories, such as civil servants, teachers and other white-collar workers, who fell under serious threat from industrialisation and its effects. In view of their crisis of identity around 1900, it is not too remarkable that many of the youths who found their way into the Wandervogel came from this social and occupational background.[11]

From the beginning, there was no organised political impetus behind the Wandervogel, however much a political vacuum in Germany had to do with provoking it. The purpose of the early Wandervogel was intrinsically humanitarian. It sought, through a passionate commitment to rambling and hiking in the countryside and to the untrammelled delights of Nature, to bring the younger generation back to the purer foundations of a society in which human bonds would be restored to their rightful place of priority over machines, factories, materialism, and the impersonalia of urban civilisation.[12] The upsurge of the Wandervogel was an indictment, therefore, of industrial Germany and its value system. The sociologist Ferdinand Tönnies brought the clash between traditionalism and modernism into sharp focus through his definition of *Gesellschaft* (industrial society) and *Gemeinschaft* (rural – agrarian society).[13] He argued that *Gesellschaft* represented a form of social association dominated by cold intellectualism, self-interest, and rationalism, while *Gemeinschaft* signified a social community regulated by inner feelings, spontaneity, friendship, warmth and emotion. The latter was clearly superior and, according to Tönnies, was better suited to the Germans. In his view, *Gesellschaft* was the despised product of an un-German liberal industrial society. The purpose of the youth movement in this respect was serious and clearly constituted something much more than merely a form of romantic escapism. The Wandervogel was a genuine social movement of profound idealism. It wanted to create a realm of youthful endeavour based on new forms of group loyalty and leadership, which should then furnish the basis of a better, more civilised, more humane society. It aimed to counter the sense of frustration, alienation, and loneliness which mass industrial society induced, and to re-establish the personal identity of individual man who had become a cog in a huge, bewildering machine age.[14] Jacob Burchhardt was only one of many observers who expressed awareness of the dangers of that period when he asked whether individual freedom could survive in a world of faceless uniformity.[15]

Because of its definite motivation and because also of the specific conditions in Germany which created the atmosphere in which it was born, the Wandervogel was a peculiarly German phenomenon. Although it had precursors of sorts in the groups organised by *Turnvater* Jahn and in the student fraternities of the early nineteenth century, the Wandervogel is more recognisable as part of that amorphous but significant movement usually referred to as the Conservative Revolution. A neo-romantic phenomenon directed against the ideas of the eighteenth-century Enlightenment and the French Revolution, the Conservative Revolution generally attracted middle-class people who were dissatisfied with industrial society and virtually everything associated with it, and who wanted to reconstruct society on traditionalist foundations. The Wandervogel shared many of the ideas of this irrational movement. Like it, the Wandervogel sought solace and inspiration in the past, or, more specifically, in an idealised medieval Germany in which, it believed, the *Volk* was untainted by modern impurities, in which human relationships were uncomplicated and honest within a mythical national community (*Volksgemeinschaft*). Unwilling or unable in its early stages to face its own time or the future, the Wandervogel consciously encouraged the cult of the past.[16] The wandering scholar of the Middle Ages became its most powerful image and ideal. Where its knowledge of the past was sketchy or unsure, the Wandervogel filled the gap with romantic myths and fantasies. The absence of a plan or programme of action in the movement was quite deliberate, for it arose without having any precise political or ideological objective. The contrived air of aimlessness about its activity was an expression of the Wandervogel's sense of release from dull routine, and of its craving for simplicity, genuineness and spontaneity. It was in many ways, particularly at the outset, consciously non-intellectual in the broadest sense. Primitivism, sentimentalism and feeling were at the root of its experience. The idea of the emancipation of youth was explicit in its activity. A new life-style for youth (*Jugendstil*), a veritable generational counter-culture, was sincerely aimed at. In other words, the Wandervogel wanted to provide an alternative society to the soulless efficiency and sterile formality of Imperial Germany. But it was initially at least a very introspective movement, prone to withdrawal and self-imposed isolation from its despised surroundings. To some extent, therefore, the early Wandervogel lived in a make-believe world of romantic utopia, but its world was filled with sufficient pleasure and satisfaction to keep it going forward in search of a precise definition of its identity.

One particular factor which was closely linked to the advent of the Wandervogel was the considerable resentment felt by youth at the mechanical and boring routine of school life. The German educational system, including its universities, enjoyed high prestige throughout Europe in the late nineteenth century for its academic standards and scholarship. Inevitably, however, the industrial era brought new problems to education, as it did in most other sectors of social life. In schools, the whole atmosphere was overladen with drabness, an unnaturally strict and formal relationship between teachers and pupils, and a harsh, military-style discipline. Even school buildings often resembled military barracks. Pupils were caught up in a highly competitive situation in which examinations meant everything, and in a rigid system of teaching where they were looked upon as simply the passive recipients of knowledge. The grammar schools (*Gymnasia*), from which most Wandervogel members came, were old-fashioned and almost totally divorced from contemporary social ideas. They were conceived in terms which allowed no place to the natural and legitimate claims of the children themselves.[17] Even with the concentrated stress on academic attainment, there were no sports or extra-curricular activities to help children cope with the emotional consequences of the competitive system. The schools were organised along authoritarian lines and were designed, in addition to academic pursuits, to act as a bulwark of the imperial system, inculcating patriotism and conservative values. School curricula which were formulated in pre-industrial times were still being taught by teachers who, in many instances, were educationally staid and unenterprising. Obedience, subordination, and uncritical acceptance of rules and regulations were demanded of every pupil. This domineering approach was entirely in keeping, of course, with the spirit of the autocratic, bureaucratic State (*Beamtenstaat*).[18] In short, school was a thoroughly unattractive proposition and by 1900 was obviously in need of fundamental reform. The Wandervogel was opposed to such an archaic institution which made life miserable for so many youngsters.

The 'Wandervogel, Ausschuss für Schülerfahrten' (Committee for Schoolboy Excursions), was formally established on 4 November 1901 in the town hall of Steglitz, a comfortable, middle-class township of 25,000 inhabitants on the outskirts of Berlin.[19] Its creation represented the culmination of several years of informal activity by pupils attending the Steglitz Grammar School. The liberal-minded director of the school, Dr Robert Lück, had encouraged his pupils to undertake excursions outside school hours, but the person who inspired the movement from the beginning and who may be legitimately regarded as its real founder was Hermann Hoffmann-Fölkersamb.[20] Born in 1875 in Strasbourg (Alsace), Hoffmann's family (he only took his mother's name, Fölkersamb, in 1921) subsequently moved to Magdeburg. As a pupil at the city's *Guesickeschule* he began, with the kindly support of his German-language teacher, Dr Edmund Sträter, to organise short trips into the surrounding countryside and later further afield with his brother, Ernst, and some friends. On completing his school-leaving certificate (*Abitur*) in 1894/5, Hoffmann moved to Berlin, where he studied philosophy and then law at the university. He continued as a student to organise hiking trips from his home in Steglitz and soon came into contact with pupils of the local grammar school when, with Dr Lück's approval, he set up a stenography class.[21] From this association developed in 1897 the first wandering group, the schoolboys' association 'Stenographia'. Herein lies the immediate genesis of the Wandervogel. Over the next few years Hoffmann's small group developed the essential characteristics of the later Wandervogel: trips at weekends and during school holidays into the countryside at the least possible cost, sleeping out rough in the open or in a disused barn, eating frugally, wearing gaily coloured shirts, carrying rucksacks, adopting the friendly 'Heil!'(Hail) greeting, and developing close ties of friendship and comradeship. More ambitious excursions were also arranged as the group's self-confidence grew: in 1897 the first large-scale expedition (*grosse Fahrt*) to the Harz mountains; in 1898 to Thuringia and then to the Rhine at Cologne, and in 1899 the memorable 'classical' expedition to the Bohemian Forest.[22] Hoffmann elucidated the significance of the expedition to his group's activity in an important article, written in 1898, called 'Hoch das Wandern!' (Long Live Wandering!). His dealings with the group ended in 1900 when, having finished his degree studies, he took up a post with the German diplomatic mission in Constantinople.[23] Before leaving, however, Hoffmann left a written account of these momentous early years entitled *Aus der frühen Geschichte des Wandervogels* (From the Early History of the Wandervogel), which is arguably the most important source for that period. Hoffmann's deputy, Karl Fischer, was charged with the leadership of the group by Hoffmann himself during a celebrated conversation between the two on the Fichtenberg, outside Berlin, in January 1900 (the *Fichtenberg-Abrede*).[24] Fischer played a leading role in the formalisation of the group in November 1901, along with Wolfgang Meyen, who supplied the name 'Wandervogel',[25] and Wolfgang Kirchbach.

Under the guidance of 'Chief Bachant'[26] Fischer, an inspiring, charismatic, idiosyncratic and domineering leader,[27] the Wandervogel soon spread to other schools in Berlin and subsequently throughout central and northern Germany, especially in Berlin—Brandenburg, Thuringia, Lower Saxony, and Hesse.[28] Its development in southern Germany was retarded by the strong opposition of the Catholic Church and the first group did not appear in Bavaria until 1904.[29] Throughout its history, the Wandervogel remained a predominantly urban, bourgeois and Protestant movement. It attracted very few youths from the aristocracy, the officer corps, the industrial *haute bourgeoisie*, or the working class. Youths from proletarian backgrounds did not have the time, pocket money, or inclination to join in the sort of refined activity promoted by the Wandervogel. Their life and work were altogether rougher and tougher than the relatively comfortable existence of Wandervogel youths. If a Wandervogel group happened to pass through a working-class quarter, it was likely to be physically attacked.[30] The movement recruited in the main from the middle strata of the Protestant bourgeoisie, mainly the new *Mittelstand*, including civil servants, teachers, white-collar workers and professional groups (Bildungsbürgertum). It was, therefore, solidly middle-class rather than lower-middle-class in social composition, as Marxist historians have alleged.[31] Lower-middle-class youths usually joined para-military, nationalist, sports or confessional organisations. The large majority of Wandervogel members were grammar-school boys or university students. Only a very small proportion were Catholic or Jewish.[32] The Wandervogel was, therefore, socially elitist in practice, which contrasted sharply with the classless character its early founders had envisaged and with its much proclaimed notion of a classless *Volksgemeinschaft*. Indeed, the movement made no real attempt at any time to extend and broaden the social categories from which it recruited.

Starting off with about 100 followers in 1901, the Wandervogel grew to 25,000-strong by 1914. Most members were aged between twelve and eighteen, and there were some 800 local branches. The character of the movement also changed substantially with this expansion. At the outset it was little more than a carefree hiking and camping sect, organised loosely into small autonomous groups of seven to twenty members, and markedly isolationist in outlook. Contemporaries took little notice of it, and the Wandervogel reciprocated. It was quite unconcerned in a direct way with the issues of the day, formulated no clear opinions on anything, and appeared content to drift on as a sort of extra-curricular romantic diversion. During these early years, in fact, the Wandervogel was not a properly united organisation at all, but rather a body of individuals with no real sense of purpose. What they did have in common, however, was an inimitable bond of close fellowship and solidarity forged by the universal acceptance of the expedition (*Fahrt*) as the movement's lifeblood. The special significance attached to the expedition in the Wandervogel's activity was deepened under Fischer's leadership. It provided the movement with its own means of identity, for it captured the quintessence of the Wandervogel's emancipatory dynamic and constituted the foundation of its collectivist experience. The expedition was also the Wandervogel's original and permanent contribution to the broad sphere of life reform.[33]

By 1904 the Wandervogel had attracted various personalities who were no longer prepared to accept either Fischer's autocratic style of leadership or his conception of what the Wandervogel should be. In that year occurred the first of many splits and secessions, which became a salient feature of the entire German youth movement. Personality clashes, petty rivalries, and doctrinal disputes were invariably the cause of organisational disruption. Siegfried Copalle and a few colleagues led the break which resulted in the dissolution of the old-style Wandervogel and its replacement by two separate groups, the Steglitzer Wandervogel (Copalle) and Fischer's Alt-Wandervogel. The former wanted to adopt a more intellectual and serious attitude to Wandervogel activities, while Fischer's group continued on a more carefree, uncharted course. The first phase of the Wandervogel's history was terminated by this fragmentation, and before long there were other splits, resulting in the formation of further groups, all of which confusingly retained the name 'Wandervogel' in their title. From this point until the famous Hohe Meissner meeting in 1913, the variegated Wandervogel became a much more serious movement of protest and increasingly conscious of a mission to rejuvenate German society. In lösing its naïve innocence, it was drawn into confrontation with important contemporary issues, on which it was often compelled to formulate a definite viewpoint.

Before long the Wandervogel became the object of approaches by intellectuals, reformers, critics of Imperial Germany, and many organisations which saw in youth a potential ally in their struggle against the putative decline in the country's spiritual and cultural health. Much in evidence were diverse life-reform movements, which perceived in the Wandervogel's animosity towards urban—industrial society a kindred spirit worth bringing within their particular sphere of influence.[34] The youth movement was placed in a difficult situation, because, although it came to share the principal aims of the vegetarian, anti-smoking and temperance groups, which were very active before the war, it was unwilling to renounce its independence, especially when, as in the cases cited, adults were firmly in control. As it happened, the lively debate in the Wandervogel over the merits of alcohol and tobacco led to considerable disruption in 1907 when Hans Breuer and Ferdinand Vetter seceded from the Alt-Wandervogel to form a new group, the Wandervogel, Deutscher Bund.[35] The purist element in the Wandervogel's make-up was also underlined by its condemnation of ballroom dancing, the cinema, and many other recreations of the modern age. These self-imposed restrictions helped, in the Wandervogel's view, to set it apart from urban—industrial culture, and for it to be seen as a part of the prewar renewal movement (*Erneuerungsbewegung*).

The Wandervogel made a notable contribution to life reform in the broadly cultural sphere. Its quest for the genuine in the Germanic past led it to rediscover a long dormant folk tradition in songs, poetry, dances and tales, and to rehabilitate old musical instruments such as the lute and guitar. The Wandervogel initiated a new musical tradition based on a folkish orientation. Siegfried Copalle set up the first Wandervogel orchestra in 1902 in Steglitz, and in 1905 published with Frank Fischer and others the movement's first song-book. Overshadowing these innovations, however, was the publication in 1909 of a comprehensive song-book for the Wandervogel by Hans Breuer. It was called the *Zupfgeigenhansl*.[36] Singing had played an important role in the youth movement from the beginning, and Breuer himself wrote that 'the folk-song is a poetic expression of Wandervogel ideals, a mirror of the German essence . . . a valid expression of the Wandervogel's yearning for Nature and pure humanity'.[37] The originality and simplicity of the folk-songs seemed to be the antithesis of the noisy, confusing, patriotic popular music of that period. Music, including choral singing, which the Wandervogel promoted too, was a reflection of its informal, relaxed, yet vital outlook on life, and another manifestation of its dislike of contemporary German society. The same may be said of its noteworthy involvement in drama and theatre, where it helped to develop new trends, and in the field of graphic art. The works of Fidus (alias Hugo Höppner) depicted a German—Nordic physical culture and the cult of the sun, both of which accurately conveyed the Wandervogel's urge towards identification with the beauty of Nature. Fidus's favourite figure in his works was the male nude body, which also, at a certain level, emphasised the homo-erotic element in the Wandervogel. The life-reform movement in Germany as a whole developed a new interest in the human body as a beautiful object and a large number of organisations dedicated to physical development arose.[38] The painter Rudolf Sievers was also closely connected with the Wandervogel and gathered around him in 1912—13 a group of talented young artists disposed to conveying something of the movement's style in illustrated form.[39] The establishment of primitive youth hostels and the building of meeting-places — usually called *Nester* (dens) — by Wandervogel groups likewise emphasised their strong links with Nature and the countryside, on the one hand, and their independence of adults, on the other.[40] The development of an esoteric Wandervogel language (*Wandervogeldeutsch*), learnt from tramps, peasants and craftsmen encountered on hiking trips and rambles,[41] and of its own distinctively dishevelled sartorial style, underlined its sectarian exclusivity from the rest of society as well as its peculiar cultural orientation. This is not to contend that the Wandervogel was an outstanding cultural movement. It was not. But its revitalising impact on music and other branches of the arts was of enduring importance. There was, therefore, a definite reformist—cultural constituent in the Wandervogel's character. That it amounted to much more than a mere escapist, 'back to Nature' movement is most poignantly illustrated, however, by its contribution to school reform.

Arising in part as a rebellion against the authoritarian school system of Wilhelmine Germany, the Wandervogel put forward its own ideal educational principle, that of the self-education of youth through the collective experience in rambling and hiking. It offered, therefore, an alternative educational ethos, albeit in embryo, to the highly institutionalised rigidity of the school system. But the Wandervogel was not content simply to allow both these concepts to run side by side yet separate from each other. It possessed in time a whole new set of ideas for changing the nature of the schools themselves. From the outset, the Wandervogel's emancipatory personality attracted the interest of reform-minded teachers and educational theorists, including two personalities who were to exert the most influence on the movement in this field, Ludwig Gurlitt and Gustav Wyneken.

Gurlitt, a teacher at the Steglitz Grammar School when the Wandervogel appeared and a dedicated follower of Ernst Haeckel's Monist League,[42] was immediately associated with the youth movement as a member of an advisory council of parents and friends (*Eufrat*) at the school.[43] At that time, Gurlitt was already making a name as an outspoken critic of the school system, advocating a more naturalistic and liberal pedagogy. He frequently clashed with the educational establishment on this account, but continued to demand reform. Gurlitt's influence in Wandervogel circles increased substantially when in 1904 some of his disciples broke away from the parent body to establish a new group, the Steglitzer Wandervogel, e.V.[44] Thenceforth, the movement as a whole began to give more thought to the question of school reform, as urged by Gurlitt. His ideas concerning the self-education of youth and of education towards the whole person explicitly criticised the existing system for failing to develop the full personality of the child, who should be treated as an entity in himself. Gurlitt demanded the development of an inquiring spirit, self-expression, discussion, physical movement, and easier relations between teachers and pupils. In addition, he wanted to reduce the purely academic content of the school curriculum and introduce more vocational and practical subjects. As a way of advancing the individuality of youth, he also, more controversially, suggested the elimination of Christian influence from school life, because he believed that it stifled youth's natural vigour. [45] In time therefore, the Wandervogel came to view education not just as a means of self-realisation, but as a revolutionary instrument of change.

The influence of the Wandervogel's developing ideas on schooling was shown in the private Country Home Schools (*Landerziehungsheime*) set up by Hermann Lietz and others. Lietz acknowledged his debt to the informal approach to education put forward by the youth movement, and most of the teachers in his schools came from the Wandervogel. [46] Lietz's basic idea was to create a form of community life which would encourage the free development of children, individually and socially. Mutual dependence and responsibility of teachers and pupils formed the basis of this experiment. In schools generally, where many former Wandervogel members taught, the idea of leadership as invested in individuals of natural charismatic qualities was derived from a Wandervogel concept. Personality rather than knowledge thus became the major criterion for leadership. Gustav Wyneken, for one, fully supported this concept and introduced it into the school he founded with Paul Geheeb, the Free School Community Wickersdorf, in Thuringia.

Wyneken was at once one of the most fascinating and controversial personalities connected with the independent youth movement, despite the fact that he did not come into contact with it until 1912, after reading Hans Blüher's history of the Wandervogel. [47] Only then did he decide that the movement could be a useful vehicle for disseminating his radical views on youth culture. Wyneken had been an early colleague of Lietz but had quarrelled with him, as he did eventually with most people he knew, and in 1906 went to Wickersdorf. There he developed his notions about youth as a stage of life distinct from adulthood, with its own unique skills and values. [48] Wyneken was vigorously opposed to the existing school system because he believed that it stunted children's natural capacities. Free communication and exchange of ideas characterised the Wickersdorf system. Education was all about leadership, not the ritualistic inculcation of knowledge, Wyneken contended. The key element in his educational philosophy, however, was pedagogical eros – that is, education rested on an erotic bond between the charismatic teacher–leader and the pupils. Wyneken, a homosexual, saw himself as a charismatic leader of youth and as the prophet of a new creed, representing a synthesis of certain trends in German idealism and Hellenism, which he aimed to graft onto the newly discovered social phenomenon of adolescence.[49] He was convinced that children could achieve their full potential only if separated from the normal school and from the family. Only in this manner, he argued, could a veritable 'kingdom of youth' (*Jugendreich*), as desired by the Wandervogel, be attained.[50] Wickersdorf became one of the major focal points of progressive educational theory and practice before 1914 in Germany. Most of its pupils came from wealthy homes, and a significant proportion were Jewish.[51] Wyneken attempted, unsuccessfully, to make his school the intellectual pace-setter of the Wandervogel, even though he never had a concrete following in the movement.[52] He never managed to establish a lasting rapport with the leadership, largely because of his prickly temperament. In most cases he rigidly insisted on the correctness of his views, and he would rarely tolerate debate about them. He was thoroughly convinced of his own destiny as the apostle of the new era of youth. If others differed from him that meant for Wyneken that they had failed to understand the logical implications of his philosophy. Such intellectual arrogance was not calculated to win him friends. But there is no doubt that he exercised a considerable influence on the Wandervogel. Although some of his ideas were extreme, Wyneken brought the aims and ideals of the Youth Movement to bear on the problems of everyday life and aroused a new self-assertiveness among youth. This is where his real value to the Wandervogel lay, because his educational concepts were too elitist for general application. His influence extended into the Weimar period of the youth movement. His belief in youth's mission to redeem Germany and his idea of charismatic leadership both served as a powerful catalyst of change in the ranks of Bündische Youth. The Austrian socialist youth move-ment and indeed the Russian communist youth movement bore traces of Wyneken's thought. On the negative side, on the other hand, his radical pessimism regarding the present, together with his utopian optimism concerning the distant future, contributed to the overall ethical confusion and flight from reality which became notable features of the independent youth movement during the 1920s.[53]

Arising from the broader interest of the Wandervogel in educational reform, particularly the question of co-education, was the related problem of allowing or not allowing girls into the movement. At the beginning, the Wandervogel was a consciously male organisation with a decidedly prudish attitude towards sexuality – the issue of homosexuality notwithstanding.[54] The idea of admitting girls was then hardly entertained. After all, the Wandervogel's stress on the virtues of close companionship among members allowed no scope for female intrusion. In adopting this attitude, the youth movement was no different from the rest of German society. Men and women tended not to mix socially except on a formal basis, and there were many conventions which effectively debarred women from fully participating in public affairs and activities of any kind. However, attitudes began to change slowly, and, as the Wandervogel developed a wider social awareness, some members advocated the inclusion of girls in the movement. In 1907 disagreement over the issue was a major reason for the secession from the Alt-Wandervogel of Ferdinand Vetter and Hans Breuer. Their new group, the Wandervogel, Deutscher Bund, immediately permitted girls to join as full members. Other Wandervogel groups still remained hostile to the idea, but by 1911 all of them had come round to accepting girls on an equal footing.[55] The conservative Alt-Wandervogel none the less insisted that the sexes should not undertake expeditions together.[56] The admittance of girls had been a difficult and painful decision for the Wandervogel to take, and there continued to prevail among many members strong undercurrents of male chauvinism. Indeed, the whole issue came up once again for heated debate after 1918. Until then, relations between male and female members remained platonic and somewhat naïve for the most part, with some groups taking elaborate precautions to safeguard against scandal.

Not unconnected with the girls' problem, and clearly of a more sensitive type, was the question of homosexuality in the Wandervogel, which Blüher brought into the open with the publication of the third volume of the history of the movement in 1912.[57] The author, an active Wandervogel member from 1902 until about 1909,[58] wrote partly out of a spirit of vengeance against those leaders who had criticised and disparaged his hero, Karl Fischer. Using the conceptual framework of Freudian psychoanalysis, Blüher characterised the Wandervogel as an 'erotic phenomenon', based on a

suppressed form of homosexuality which he called 'male inversion'.
The matter of homosexuality had first arisen in the Alt-Wandervogel
through its leader, Willy Jansen, a wealthy Hessian landowner.
Because of his interest in nudism, sun-bathing, gymnastics and
physical culture, Jansen had aroused suspicion in some quarters. One
newspaper report, alluding to his activities, termed the Wandervogel
a 'pederasty club founded by older gentlemen with ulterior
motives'.[59] Jansen weathered the storm, but in 1910 had to resign
from the leadership of his group after he had made public remarks
about permitting homosexuality in the Wandervogel. A group of his
supporters left the Alt-Wandervogel with him to set up a new group
in Hamburg, the Jung-Wandervogel, which openly admitted that as
far as it was concerned the essence of the Wandervogel community
was an erotic bond of friendship.[60] The Jung-Wandervogel subsequently became somewhat notorious for the prevalence of homosexuality in its ranks.[61] On the basis of this and similar episodes, Blüher
convinced himself that homosexuality was being expressed in the
intimate comradeship and general atmosphere of male togetherness
that prevailed in the Wandervogel. He further maintained that the
cult of charismatic leadership as well as the ideal of male physical
beauty in the movement had pronounced homosexual overtones.
None the less, Blüher's interpretation, which held sway in the
historiography of the independent youth movement for many
decades,[62] made no distinction between sublimated eroticism and
overt sexuality. In the varying degrees of homosexual predilection,
openly manifested feelings were confined without doubt to a small
percentage of members, even if some of these were well-known
leaders and personalities of the movement, such as Wyneken and
Jansen. Male eroticism did play some part in the ordinary day-to-day
life of the Wandervogel, but it would be misleading to conclude on
this account that the Wandervogel was a predominantly homo-erotic
movement.

The Wandervogel's increasing involvement with particular issues
of the prewar period was bound sooner rather than later to lead it into
the realm of German politics. As early as 1902, the movement was
approached by the extreme rightist Pan-German League (Alldeutscher
Verband), which wanted to establish a close working relationship
between the two groups. A number of Wandervogel leaders were
special guests at the League's celebration of the summer solstice that
year, and again in 1903, and Karl Fischer, a keen disciple of Lagarde,
was impressed by the League's aims.[63] It is perhaps not too re-

markable that an anti-modernist, reactionary organisation such as the League should have viewed the Wandervogel as a potential ally, for the youth's unequivocal rejection of urban – industrial society and its romantic yearning for the Germanic past was the stuff of which the German far Right was made. Moreover, the goal of a Greater Germany struck a responsive chord among many Wandervogel members. Expeditions to German ethnic minorities (*Volksdeutsche*) in Eastern Europe were undertaken from an early date by them and became a regular feature of their activities before the war.[64] There is no denying, therefore, the Pan-Germanic dimension to the Wandervogel's *Weltanschauung*. The Pan-German League made the mistake of underestimating the youth movement's desire for autonomy from all other groups, particularly from those of a political or confessional complexion. The Wandervogel was essentially non-political and its members were discouraged from becoming involved in party political affairs. It sought to bring about social change not by political means but by developing a new type of individual who would then go into society at large to make the desired changes. Nothing came, therefore, of the League's overtures. Its failure to bring the Wandervogel under its auspices should not disguise the fact that a good number of youths, especially in the leadership, were strongly influenced by right-wing ideas and consequently identified with a certain (*völkisch*) outlook. The Wandervogel as a whole, however, was not racist.

The Wandervogel's acceptance of the notion that it had a cultural mission to fulfil naturally led it to a close identification with a nebulous but deeply held commitment to 'Germanness'. This was expressed, usually with romantic, utopian naïvety, in the cultivation of folkish pursuits and the propagation of 'German' virtues – loyalty, idealism, simplicity, resoluteness and comradeship. The Wandervogel was patriotic, possessed of a genuine love of and devotion to the Fatherland. But it was not a party to the loud, sabre-rattling chauvinism which dominated nationalist sentiment in Germany. The Wandervogel's nationalism was moderate, wholesome and in keeping with its intrinsically humanitarian outlook. Complementing this was its abhorrence of militarism for its own sake, and there is no evidence to show that it actively supported either naval expansion or the Kaiser's ambitious *Weltpolitik* programme. Indeed, the only area of the nationalist ideology into which the Wandervogel was, embarrasingly, drawn was anti-semitism.

Although organised anti-semitism experienced a decline in the late

1900s, resentment against Jews became more diffuse throughout Germany's societal and institutional life. Many organisations paid lip-service to the notion of prohibiting Jews from becoming members, but relatively few, except for those of an extreme rightist persuasion, came out publicly against them. The Wandervogel was little different in this respect from a host of other contemporary groups—principally those of a right-wing disposition. That there were convinced anti-semites in the youth movement, especially in the leadership cadres, is undeniable. Few of them, however, were so disposed in an out-spokenly racist sense. Additionally, it would be erroneous to contend on the basis of this evidence that the Wandervogel was generally a racist and anti-semitic movement.[65] The Jewish question was not openly discussed in Wandervogel circles, in fact, until a few years before the war.[66] Two developments in particular brought the movement face to face with the issue. First, a small group of anti-semitic Wandervogel leaders gained editorial control of an important periodical, the *Wandervogel Führerzeitung*, and began publishing blatantly anti-semitic reports and articles, including a notorious piece in October 1913 by Friedrich Wilhelm Fulda which denied that Jews, as non-Aryans, could be members of the Wandervogel. Secondly, the Zittau (Saxony) branch of the Wandervogel e.V's girls' section rejected in 1913 the application of a candidate for membership because she happened to be Jewish.[67] Both events propelled the Wandervogel uncomfortably into the public limelight and clearly demanded from the leadership a statement of policy regarding the Jewish question. The reaction of individual Wandervogel groups and branches was mixed. The Wandervogel leadership chose to pour water on the controversy by giving out a compromise announcement at Easter 1914. While declining to become involved in the affairs of local branches, even where the exclusion of Jews was taking place, the leaders reaffirmed the movement's previously stated position of neutrality on all political and religious questions. It was a tame and inadequate response which could have done little to enhance the Wandervogel's prestige among fair-minded and moderate segments of German society. With the onus now put firmly on local branches whether or not to admit Jews, the practical outcome was that by the summer of 1914 a large majority of these branches had quickly and informally introduced the 'Aryan paragraph' into their constitutions which effectively restricted membership to non-Jewish Germans.[68] This situation certainly indicated a rightward bias in the Wandervogel's carefully cultivated non-political outlook and revealed the extent to which it had become inadvertently caught up in the growing nationalist euphoria in Germany just prior to the war. None the less, the Wandervogel's neutrality, though shaken under pressure, remained intact. After all, the ordinary rank-and-file members, most of whom had hardly reached the age of mature political reflection, displayed little trace of anti-semitism or any other political sentiment. It is also worth remembering that the number of Jews applying for membership of the Wandervogel was very small[69] – in any case, there were Jewish youth groups to cater for their needs. In a broad context, the Wandervogel's increasing difficulty in maintaining a strictly non-political stance is not too surprising in view of the fact that it was unconsciously susceptible to the fundamental politico-ideological attitudes of the social class from which it recruited, the Protestant *Mittelstand*. This also explains why the Wandervogel reacted so spontaneously and enthusiastically to the declaration of war in 1914. Before that, however, the organisational development of the independent youth movement had taken a significant turn.

The many secessions and splits to which the Wandervogel was vulnerable produced numerous small sects as well as several larger groups, which tended to dominate the movement and shape its overall personality. These were principally the Alt-Wandervogel, led by Karl Fischer until 1906; the Steglitzer Wandervogel, widely regarded as the most intellectually inclined group and one which made a substantial contribution to the Wandervogel's cultural development; the Jung-Wandervogel; the Bund Deutscher Wanderer; and the Wandervogel, Deutscher Bund. There were in addition a number of small student Wandervogel groups founded at various universities, including Knud Ahlborn's Deutsche Akademischer Freischar, set up in Göttingen in 1907, the Akademische Vereinigung Marburg (1912), and its counterpart at Jena (1913). Despite the confusing variety of groups, there existed among their members at large an instinctive feeling of inner solidarity and concomitantly a longing for a united association to encompass all organisations which acknowledged the Wandervogel ethos. A preliminary step was taken in that direction in early spring 1910 when the so-called 'Arolser Treaty' was agreed to by three groups (the Wandervogel, Deutscher Bund; the Bund Deutscher Wanderer; and the Deutsche Akademischer Freischar) whereby they established certain areas of co-operation. The treaty formed the prelude to the first unity conference of the youth movement, held, a few weeks later, on the Sachsenburg, when a committee to co-ordinate the various Wandervogel groups was established. As a direct result, an Association of the German Wandervogel (Verband deutscher Wandervögel) emerged in January 1911 in Leipzig to prepare the way for a unified Wandervogel movement.[70] There were many problems to be overcome, of course, and the process took some time to complete, but two years later, in January 1913, a cohesive association, commonly known as the United Wandervogel (Wandervogel e.V. Bund für deutsches Jugendwandern), was created in Göttingen under the leadership of Dr Edmund Neuendorff. Conspicuously absent from the new group, which had over 20,000 members in 800 branches,[71] was the Jung-Wandervogel and conservative elements of the Alt-Wandervogel.[72] Wandervogel unity was not only partial, but also short-lived, because the war intervened before any substantive meaning had been given to the new, united group. In any event, the United Wandervogel, which managed a precarious existence into the war years, was immediately beset by disagreements over a range of vital issues, among them the relationship of the Wandervogel to the schools and the Jewish question.[73] The reality of unity was still elusive and unsatisfactory, but the dream of having one, large, comprehensive movement stoutly persisted. A more momentous effort to bring this dream to fruition was made later in 1913.

The meeting in October 1913 on the Hohe Meissner, a mountain near Kassel, of several Wandervogel groups and diverse reformist organisations from Germany, Austria and Switzerland[74] is regarded by most commentators as the crowning point of the early history of the independent youth movement.[75] Attended by just under 3000 youths and interested adults, including Max Weber,[76] the meeting was held to mark the centenary of the Battle of Nations against Napoleon in a way which poignantly rejected the exuberantly chauvinistic spirit of celebration in Germany as a whole. This 'First Free German Youth Conference', as it was officially designated, was significant for its inauguration of a new and distinctive phase in the history of the independent youth movement. A loose federation of the groups present was created called Free German Youth (Freideutsche Jugend), whose proclaimed ideal was the autonomy of youth, as expressed in a brief, rather vague, but important statement agreed to by the meeting and known as the Meissner Formula:

Free German Youth, on their own initiative, under their own

responsibility, and with deep sincerity, are determined to independently shape their own lives. For the sake of this inner freedom, they will take united action under any and all circumstances. All meetings of Free German Youth are free of alcohol and smoking.[77]

Mainly influenced by Wyneken but actually authored by Ferdinand Avenarius,[78] this was a dramatic, even revolutionary, proclamation which asserted youth's demand to be recognised as an independent estate entitled to self-determination and responsibility. The Formula encapsulated the quintessence of the Wandervogel spirit and it became a symbol of the free youth movement's sense of mission and freedom as well as acting as an inspiration for the future. The Hohe Meissner meeting signalled in general the beginning of the struggle to achieve a new synthesis between the outlook of the youth movement and the everyday affairs of German life. Thereafter, the movement became much more closely involved in contemporary political, social and religious controversies. Indeed, at the meeting itself the already overtly anti-semitic Austrian Wandervogel unsuccessfully attempted to enlist the support of Free German Youth in its struggle against the enemies of 'Germanness'.[79]

Free German Youth sought to take the 'youth revolution' begun by the Wandervogel a stage further. It was committed to finding new life forms for youth and the rest of society, and to situate the personality of the younger generation firmly within a national community (*Volksgemeinschaft*). Free German Youth was, therefore, in the broadest sense a progressive movement which was trying to develop an alternative way of life to that offered by Wilhelmine society. Despite the inherent optimism with which the organisation set about its task, it still suffered from being an elitist and minority movement without deep roots in German society. Moreover, its basic concepts were incomplete and its practical sense was extremely limited. Consequently, Free German Youth's blandishments to German society lacked conviction to a large extent and a considerable gulf continued to exist between the two entities. Free German Youth represented a more philosophical and intellectual movement than the largely intuitive Wandervogel, but its relevance was still not fully appreciated by non-members. Older followers were keenly aware of Free German Youth's deficiencies and prepared for more activist and direct involvement in society's problems, even though this meant inevitably compromising the movement's original ideal of political and confessional neutrality. Younger members of Free German

Youth, on the other hand, thought more about consolidating what had already been realised by the Wandervogel without being too much concerned about venturing into new spheres of activity.[80]

The loose unity achieved by Free German Youth was quickly disrupted not by generational conflict but by profound differences of opinion between conservative and revolutionary factions within it. Major controversy was sparked off when in January 1914 the organisation was the object of a scathing attack by a Centre Party deputy, Dr Schlittenbauer, in the Bavarian *Landtag* (parliament). He accused Free German Youth of fostering immorality, disrespect towards parents and school authorities, and unpatriotic feeling.[81] The radically minded circle around Gustav Wyneken, and the monthly periodical *Der Anfang*, which propagated his views, were singled out for particularly bitter criticism by Schlittenbauer, and Free German Youth was banned for a short period in Bavaria.[82] Moderate elements in the organisation led by Knud Ahlborn were so disturbed by the public furore which ensued that, as a means of re-establishing Free German Youth's credibility, they succeeded at a meeting in Marburg in March 1914 in having Wyneken and his supporters expelled altogether from the movement. At the same time, the moderates agreed to attenuate the tone of the Meissner Formula and to incorporate in it a clause specifically designed to reassure the older generation, and no doubt the imperial authorities: 'We wish to add to the store of values which our elders have acquired and transmitted to us by developing our own powers under our own responsibility and with deep sincerity.'[83] The unity so painstakingly forged at the Hohe Meissner was now reduced to the lowest possible point without an outright break-up taking place. This state of affairs was further underlined when, at this meeting, the moderates created their own association within Free German Youth.[84] The youth movement had thus been emasculated, but, before the full implications of the situation could be assessed, the outbreak of the First World War overtook everything.

German youth, like other sections of Wilhelmine society, were intoxicated by the jingoism which greeted the announcement of war. The younger generation, casting aside their previous schisms and quarrels, flocked with unqualified enthusiasm to the colours, in order to fight what was widely regarded as a just and defensive war against Germany's jealous enemies. The loyalty of the nationalist and basically middle-class youth-tutelage (*Jugendpflege*) organisations was, of course, guaranteed. These groups, sponsored by political parties, the military authorities, sports and gymnastic associations, vocational and trades bodies and the churches, dated from before the emergence of the Wandervogel. They were set up and directed by adults and had no independently formulated activity. By 1914 some 2 million youths were members,[85] of whom 80,000 were Boy Scouts. The first Scout groups, modelled on the British example, appeared in 1908, and three years later a German Boy Scout Association was set up under the leadership of *Reichsfeldmeister* Major Maximilian Bayer. The Scout movement had a distinctly patriotic and military flavour, with uniforms, strict discipline and paramilitary-style drilling forming an essential part of its character.[86]

By the late 1900s government circles had begun to be concerned about the growing mood of restlessness among German youth, for which the advent of the Wandervogel and working-class youth movements was seen as unmistakable evidence.[87] Official investigations were undertaken, resulting in schemes of social welfare reform for youth, but, unfortunately, the war broke out before anything fundamentally practical had been achieved. The State did intervene, however, to help found a conservative umbrella organisation, the Young Germany League (Jungdeutschlandbund) in 1911, its specific aim being to distract youth from socialism. Led by General Colmar Freiherr von der Goltz, this association sought to provide a patriotically oriented physical and moral education to the many nationalist, paramilitary and right-wing groups under its organisational supervision. Its popularity was such that by 1914 just under half a million youths were involved. The League tried without success to bring the Wandervogel under its control, though a few individual groups of the independent youth movement did eventually affiliate to it.[88] The authorities further demonstrated their interest in youth when, also in 1911, the Prussian Government made available to officially approved (that is, conservative and nationalist) youth-tutelage associations a variety of privileges, such as reduced fares for members travelling on the railways, and special funds. As was to be expected, the League benefited considerably from this legislation, which was again mainly designed to counteract socialist and other allegedly anti-statist influences among youth.[89]

The youth-tutelage groups and the independent youth movement were very different in style and aims, and ties between them were few and unimportant. By 1913/14, however, certain ideas of the Wandervogel, such as that concerning self-education, were beginning to have an impact on the adult-controlled sector of organised youth, thus laying the foundation for a meaningful merger of the two youth cultures after the war. In the meantime, the independent youth movement found no difficulty in matching the faith of the youth-tutelage groups in Kaiser and Fatherland as Germany entered the war.[90]

The reality of the conflict was very rapidly brought home to German youth. At the Battle of Langemarck in Belgium in November 1914, a regiment in which many Wandervogel youths were serving was decimated in a futile act of courage. The battle became a legend in the history of the German Youth Movement, including the Hitler Youth, serving to epitomise the unparalleled idealism and willingness for self-sacrifice of German youth in the national cause.[91] Altogether some 7000 members of the independent youth movement lost their lives in the war, among them such distinguished personalities as Hans Breuer, Rudolf Sievers, Frank Fischer and Ferdinand Vetter, as well as Christian Schneehagen, organiser of the Hohe Meissner meeting, and Walter Flex, author of the celebrated wartime novel so avidly read by the younger generation, *Der Wanderer zwischen beiden Welten* (Wanderer between Two Worlds). Langemarck had in the short-term a sobering effect on the youth movement, and, as it became clear that the war would probably be a protracted affair, old and new differences began to emerge among youth, as they did in Germany generally.

The war years witnessed a sharp politicisation of the independent youth movement, with socialist and internationalist factions appearing alongside those of a nationalist and racist outlook. A fragile semblance of unity was still maintained, however, under the auspices of Free German Youth. The rigours of war forced everyone into greater preoccupation with everyday affairs, resulting from 1916 onwards in a decidedly practical and political bias in the youth movement as regards its role in society. Knud Ahlborn for one energetically intensified the movement's involvement in matters of immediate relevance. Leftist opinion initially organised around the journal *Der Aufbruch*, and had leading spokesmen in Karl Bittel, Ernst Joel and Alfred Kurella. In 1917 they were joined by Wyneken, whose readmittance to the youth movement exemplified its increasingly aggressive spirit. Wyneken's comeback was successful, for until the end of the war he was a powerful figure among the more radical sections of Free German Youth. The Right was represented by the small but influential racist Greifenbund and later by Otger Gräff's Jungdeutsche Bund. Part of the explanation for the continuing rightward shift of some elements of Free German Youth lay in the notable increase in the number of Jews coming into the movement during the war, and, of course, they were invariably attracted to the left-wing enclaves.[92]

Politics was not the only sphere which produced problems for the youth movement. With so many of its older members serving at the front, the movement's leadership soon fell into younger and less experienced hands.[93] A generation gap ensued which seriously undermined the all-important bond of fellowship on which the youth movement rested. The question of the role of girls, whose importance in filling the gap left by males could not be ignored, came up once again for intense debate. Despite differences of opinion on these and other matters, the experience of war ultimately convinced everyone in the youth movement that the old world was corrupt and in need of replacement by a completely new type of society. To meet this post-war challenge, it was also widely acknowledged by members that fundamental change would have to take place in the movement itself, because the war had largely swept away the fabric on which the pre-war Wandervogel and Free German Youth had been built. In preparation for the trials of the post-war era, all factions in Free German Youth gathered together in Naumburg in March 1918 with the aim of recreating a sense of real unity in the movement. The participants agreed that the youth movement would have to be activist and revolutionary if it were to help reconstruct German society. But, just when agreement on united action had been reached, the war ended and Germany was plunged into revolution. The youth movement had to reconsider its position yet again. A new era clearly beckoned.

2 Free German Youth to Bündische Youth

Defeat in the First World War and the sudden collapse of the Hohenzollern dynasty immediately plunged Germany into deep constitutional, political and social crisis in autumn 1918. The old Bismarckian – Wilhelmine order, which had already been creaking dangerously before the war, was finally swept aside amidst widespread disorder. Nothing was certain any more and even some members of the youth movement wondered whether time had run out for them. After all, the Wandervogel and Free German Youth had both to some degree been opposed to Wilhelmine society. But any lingering doubts there may have been about the legitimacy of the youth movement in the new situation were brushed aside as youth began eagerly to discuss the future. What was to fill the vacuum now created became the leading talking-point throughout all sections of German society. All kinds of hopes and fears for the future were expressed during the hectic period between the Kaiser's abdication and the promulgation of the Treaty of Versailles in spring 1919.

Many informed circles, including politicians of all parties, looked to youth for inspiration and even leadership during those gloomy days, while the younger generation itself felt more confident and self-assertive than it had been before. Youth had by now come to be accepted as an entity in itself and concomitantly had begun to earn a certain public esteem and status. There was a prevalent belief in the 'mission' of youth and novels depicting the younger generation proliferated. [1] Reinhold Wulle, the *völkisch* writer and propagandist, coined in 1919 the immortal phrase 'Who has youth, has the future.' [2] Youth was generally excited about what lay ahead and desperately wanted to actively participate in rebuilding Germany. Immediately after the end of the war there was a peculiar atmosphere of expectancy and anticipation among the ranks of the youth movement. Everything and anything seemed within the realms of possibility. Hope, enthusiasm and optimism abounded once the enormity of

Germany's collapse had been absorbed. Youth prepared to propel itself headlong into the unknown with courage, idealism and confidence. In this sense the youth movement was revitalised in 1918. Its influence appeared capable of stretching out beyond the immediate orbit of youth into the political parties, the youth–tutelage organisations and even further afield. The movement seemed like a beacon of hope and a point of reference for many groups in society. Sensing the profound unrest of youth and adults alike, the youth movement soon developed a sharper political awareness.

The fragile unity of Free German Youth which had been re-established in spring 1918 at first appeared capable of withstanding the pressures generated by Germany's misfortunes. It seemed likely that the idea of youth as an independent force committed to shaping the future would provide the inner strength and sense of purpose needed to keep the movement together. But the November Revolution put paid to this cherished notion, for no sooner had the revolutionary wave swept across the country than the various political factions which had surfaced during the war broke ranks with greater zeal than ever before. Free German Youth was torn asunder by passionate political controversy.[3]

The revolution produced disarray and confusion in Free German Youth. The ideas on which the independent youth movement had been constructed were regarded as outdated and irrelevant in the changed situation, but what was to take their place caused bitter argument and division. Most sections of Free German Youth enthusiastically welcomed the revolution as a new opportunity to establish Germany on a socialist, proletarian footing. One spokesman declared that 'the very idea of youth demands that Free German Youth support the revolution, because Free German Youth is revolutionary'.[4] A leftist group in Berlin was more expansive:

> Free German Youth welcomes the revolution as a rebellion against all historical, traditional, social, economic, and national privileges and overlordship. We approve of all measures aimed at unleashing community-building forces and emancipating the human soul. We uphold the idea of the brotherhood of all men as well as the idea of mutual help, which will enable our national comrades and all nations to live according to their own rules, under their own responsibility, and with inner sincerity. To create this kind of state is the task of all youth. Towards this aim, Free German Youth declares itself solidly behind the German proletarian movement.[5]

This was a rather extremist expression of a view widely held among Free German Youth members, with the exception of the small *völkisch*-nationalist wing. The revolution was felt to offer the prospect of a fresh beginning but how to proceed with the details of the future state brought no unanimity. Attitudes quickly hardened and rival groupings emerged. A left-wing revolutionary socialist faction appeared in which Karl Bittel, Alfred Kurella, Karl August Wittfogel and Friedrich Vorwerk were prominent. It demanded the total support of Free German Youth for a thoroughgoing revolution and solidarity with the Bolsheviks in Russia. Strong sympathies were evinced for the fledging Spartakus League and subsequently for the German Communist Party (Kommunistische Partei Deutchlands — KPD), in which Kurella, Bittel and Wittfogel soon became actively involved. Bittel's 'Political Circulars', advocating the cause of radical socialist revolution, were widely read and discussed in Free German circles, and in 1918 Kurella, a follower of Wyneken, published his book *Deutsche Volksgemeinschaft* (German National Community), which argued the case for a socialist, humanitarian, pacifist approach to Germany's problems. Directly opposing the leftists was a right-wing neo-conservative nationalist group led by Frank Glatzel, who, inspired by the late Otger Gräff, called for the new Germany to be based on the principles of nationalism and racist anti-semitism. Sandwiched between these two extremes was a liberal centrist element which was by far the largest but also the weakest of the three groupings. The aim of the centre was basically to uphold the independent youth movement's traditional neutrality in political and religious matters and to stress the autonomy of youth and the concept of self-education. It held firmly to the ideals of Hohe Meissner and strove for a renewal of German society along social, classless lines.[6] Glatzel and his supporters tended not to distinguish this group from the radical left-wingers and pointed out that the centrist leader, Knud Ahlborn, was a member of the Independent Social Democratic Party (Unabhängige Sozialdemokratische Partei Deutschlands — USPD).[7] None of the factions regretted the passing of the old order and, in the apocalyptic atmosphere which accompanied the revolution, talk was of the decline of the Western world (Spengler's book on the theme was published in 1918 and exercised considerable influence in the youth movement) and the coming millennium. In the mood of intense and earnest discussion in youth circles, every conceivable political and social subject came in for rigorous analysis.

In view of the disruption in Free German Youth its leadership decided that everything possible be done to maintain at least some semblance of organisational unity, if only to convince the outside world that the movement was still intact and worthy of serious consideration. A leaders' meeting was convened in Jena at Easter 1919 with the aim of bringing all shades of opinion together and restoring unity of a sort, but little of this was achieved. The meeting committed itself to the ideals of universal brotherhood, the liberty of the individual, the abolition of all class barriers and privilege, and the reconstruction of Germany, but the philosophical niceties expounded on these themes were too vague to provide a working basis for practical co-operation. Consequently the meeting was a failure, and Free German Youth struggled on in somewhat bedraggled fashion. The incoherence of the movement was further emphasised a few months later, in August 1919, when Glatzel set up a temporary organisational structure for right-wing sympathisers in the form of a re-created Jungdeutsche Bund, which set forth its nationalist beliefs in the Lauenstein Declaration:

We young Germans, acting from the strength of our national spirit, want to become individual human beings, and to overcome superficial divisions in order to establish a true national community of all Germans and a German Reich as the foundation and embodiment of our race-conscious life.[8]

To all intents and purposes, the Glatzel-led rightist faction had now separated from the main body of Free German Youth. This was made clear by a meeting of Free German Youth at Hofgeismar in early autumn 1920, when another major attempt was made to hold the movement together.[9] By this time, the leftist elements had become solidly Communist, while the rightists did not bother to appear at all. Discussion at the meeting, the theme of which was 'Russia—Bolshevism—Asia—Germany—Western Europe', was mainly conducted between the centrists and leftists and focused on the problems of introducing the classless society and of Russia. Exchanges became so acrimonious that at one point the leftists were ordered to leave the meeting, and they were readmitted only after delicate negotiations. Although everyone rejected the existing social order and agreed on the necessity for far-reaching political changes in the Weimar system, how such changes were to be devised and implemented brought no agreement. The meeting had at least cleared the air to some extent and had registered the dividing line between the pro-Communists and moderates, but at the same time it confirmed that the unity of Free German Youth was irrevocably lost.[10] With the leftist and rightist factions going their own separate ways, what was left was a remnant still clinging to the middle ground, which was rapidly shrinking amidst the violent upheavals of the early Weimar period. A Free German Association (Freideutscher Bund) was subsequently formed by Knud Ahlborn and Ferdinand Goebel to cater for this diminishing minority and to direct their political allegiance to the Republic, but by 1923 it was obvious that the Free German phase of the independent youth movement was finished. Its principal constituents had departed into other spheres of activity and had no intention of returning. A second meeting at Hohe Meissner in August–September 1923 was arranged by Ahlborn, who hoped the tenth anniversary of the first Free German meeting would somehow rekindle a unifying impulse among the factions, but nothing came of it. Far from recapturing the spirit of 1913, the proceedings only brought into sharper relief the differences endemic in the movement and the gulf which lay between it and the original Hohe Meissner gathering. From this juncture, the youth movement sought a second fresh beginning in 1923.

The Free German phase (1913–23) was a tempestuous and crisis–laden period of the youth movement, which during these years came face to face with urgent problems of society and fully experienced the triumphs and defeats which accompanied Germany's development. The immediate post-war years represented a missed opportunity for the youth movement. Its awakened hopes and plans for the future came virtually to nothing amid internecine strife, which became intense once it was seen that the revolution was limited in scope and achievement, and once the Versailles *Diktat* had dampened confidence in the new State. Allegiance to or rejection of the Weimar Republic emerged as the major source of division in the movement. Just as the early years of the 1920s saw the Republic wracked by problems of every description, producing a deeply fragmented society, so also the youth movement failed to retain its cohesion and disappeared beneath a multitude of warring interests. When it dawned on Free German Youth that solutions to Germany's many problems were not to be had overnight, a good deal of its initial vitality was drained from it and the movement tended to drift along rather aimlessly, hoping to latch onto something concrete on the way. Free German Youth lost its sense of balance, and this was illustrated in extravagant fashion by the exploits of Friedrich 'Muck'

Lamberty's Neue Schar in the Thuringian countryside in 1920–1. Lamberty, a Wandervogel member from Westphalia, was a self-styled saviour who denounced all forms of modernism and preached that a 'revolution of the soul' could come through exotic dancing and exaltation.[11] His small band of youthful followers travelled in Pied Piper style from one town to another in Thuringia calling on the peasantry and citizens to take up their gospel of salvation. Their quasi-religious, semi-sexual ecstasy enjoyed a remarkable but ephemeral success. Lamberty's message was a curious but potent mixture which in calling also for a national community based on mystical fanaticism and free love struck a deep responsive chord among his simple, uneducated audience. His popularity only began to subside when the Neue Schar's sexual promiscuity attracted the attention of the authorities, who until then had been most helpful.[12] After a brief attempt at organising his own commune, Lamberty retired in 1921 to Naumburg (Thuringia), where he set up a craft workshop.

That a semi-lunatic figure such as Lamberty could make a name for himself in this ludicrous fashion bears ample witness to the bewilderment and emptiness felt by ordinary Germans at that time. His activity also serves to underline the youth movement's bankruptcy of worthwhile ideas and solutions to the problems facing society. If all the movement could offer was Lamberty, then clearly it had reached a nadir from which rescue would be extremely difficult. By 1921 Free German Youth had no positive direction, being prone to cranks such as Lamberty and inept interest in oriental religions. On a wider scale, it has been argued that the overall significance of the Lamberty episode was that it marked the transitional point at which the individual flair of the youth movement gave way to the collectivist ideal which dominated its ethos later in the 1920s.[14]

The political involvement of Free German Youth was thoroughly undistinguished. It lacked clear, consistent political conceptions and never knew exactly where it stood *vis-à-vis* nationalism and socialism, the two paramount and divisive ideologies of that period. As a result, Free German Youth members lacked firm leadership, and their attitude to politics remained for the most part inchoate and unrealistic. Any attempt at direct political initiative, from the small Republican Party of Walter Hammer and Fritz von Unruh to the futile efforts of the Young Socialists to launch a social republican party in the name of youth, bore the stamp of amateurs. Similarly, Free German Youth signally failed to make politically meaningful the pacifism and desire for international peace and understanding of many of its members. The movement was simply no match for the heavyweight game of Weimar power politics. Honesty and idealism could take it only so far. Free German Youth's lack of organisational coherence and good leadership as well as the licence it gave to individualism could only have led it before long to dissolution as a unified force.

Even those Wandervogel organisations which had held aloof from Free German Youth before and after 1918 found it impossible to cope adequately with the pressures of the post-war world. On returning from the front, the older *Wandervögel* could hardly recognise the movement they had left behind in 1914.[15] They felt little in common with the younger members who had assumed the leadership in their absence. Many of these veterans consequently lost interest in the Wandervogel altogether and withdrew to get married, take up disrupted studies or pursue a career.[16] Alternatively, they formed their own Wandervogel groups for older devotees, such as the Bund der Kronacher, led by Otto Schönfelder. A small number became involved in politics of different complexions. While a group of *Wandervögel* in Jena went to the assistance of the Soviet Republic in Munich in early 1919, another group joined the Freikorps and later set up their own 'Wandervogel Hundertschaft', which fought against the Poles in Silesia and against the Bolsheviks in the Baltic.[17] If generational conflict was an acute problem between younger and older *Wandervögel*, no less disruptive was the renewed tussle in the movement over the status of female members. Unable to accept girls on equal terms, some sections of the Wandervogel split off to found all-male groups, while some existing groups, such as the Alt-Wandervogel, decided against having girls as members. On top of this, the problem of what role the Wandervogel was to play in the future brought conflicting ideological responses, so that by the early 1920s the Wandervogel, like Free German Youth, was profoundly disunited and no longer the powerful force it had once been. Here too, therefore, the signs were clear that a fresh attempt had to be made to put the independent youth movement on a new footing.

A feeling of bitter disillusionment and exhaustion prevailed in the youth movement by 1923. It had proved palpably unequal to the stringent demands of the 1918—23 period, because it lacked a clear-sighted vision, discipline, leadership and intellectual toughness. Hence, the youth movement eventually wallowed in the confusion of the times, leaving its members as disoriented as any other Germans. Some, realising the futility of trying to work through the organisation, withdrew to their own isolated settlements and self-sufficient communities, where they tried to implement, on a small scale, their notions of a new society.[18] The majority, however, enjoyed no such release from their frustrations and could only hope that somehow the future would bring improvement. The youth movement had not yet fulfilled its mission and time was running out for it.

The disintegration of Free German Youth opened the way for a further phase in the history of the independent youth movement. From 1923 until its destruction by the National Socialists, this was known as Bündische Youth, a name derived from the *Bund* (group), which was central to the movement's ethos during these years. The term 'Bündische Youth' is simply a useful and convenient way of referring to the bewildering variety of youth groups which acknowledged to one degree or another the traditions of the Wandervogel and Free German Youth. The numerous groups, factions and sects constituting Bündische Youth had such a wide diversity of characteristics and attitudes that it is impossible to generalise too much or too far about this final period of the independent youth movement. For every general statement about Bündische Youth an exception can invariably be made with reference to one particular youth association at a certain given time. Individual groups centred very largely around the personality of their leaders, so that changes of leadership or changes in the outlook of leaders led to corresponding adjustments in the attitudes of groups. Moreover, as parts of society, the groups were influenced by the trend of social events and alterations in social taste and customs. These factors inevitably tended to make groups develop along divergent lines, though the differences separating them were often relatively slight and superficial. The propensity towards disruption among the groups was enhanced rather than diminished by the emphasis which they placed on the theoretical basis of their activities. Groups working in the same broad sphere naturally gravitated together, but when they laid different interpretations on similar methods and experiences they were unable to combine. The basing of the various groups on a distinctive philosophical outlook might give them a semblance of completeness in themselves but it rendered them exceedingly vulnerable to internecine strife and disruption, even on arbitrary grounds. The organisation of the individual groups was thus in a state of continual flux, partly because of their own essential idiosyncrasies, and partly because of the social medium in which they operated. Every conceivable type of youth group was to be found in Bündische Youth: political, confessional, paramilitary, nationalist, racist, liberal, democratic, socialist, sports, and even Boy Scout. The sectarian character of the movement meant, therefore, a history of secessions, squabbles, personality clashes and ideological disputes. Each group stubbornly and vociferously maintained and defended its own individuality and autonomy. Amalgamations of several groups into large single units were relatively infrequent, though all groups professed a yearning, as the Wandervogel had done, for one comprehensive and united youth movement. That dream was never fulfilled by Bündische Youth: the establishment of the Deutsche Freischar in 1927 and the Grossdeutsche Bund in 1933 were valiant but ultimately unsuccessful attempts in that direction.

Hermann Mau argued that Bündische Youth was above all a collective experience devoid of coherent development, and therefore lacking a history as such.[19] Any account of Bündische development is therefore, according to Mau, bound to be seriously deficient. His implicit point is that generalisations pertaining to Bündische Youth are useful only within strict limits. But, bearing this qualification in mind, some effort can be made to convey something of the overall nature of the movement and the principal problems confronting it.

Bündische Youth represented a more serious-minded, organised, disciplined, and activist phase in the evolution of the independent youth movement. It was no accident that the soldier replaced the wandering scholar as the ideal type, and, indeed, Bündische Youth was much more male-oriented and self-consciously masculine than either the Wandervogel or Free German Youth had been.[20] In Bündische publications the spirit of the front-line soldier and his deeds was often conveyed in drawings and tales. The definite martial air in the movement was also revealed in the popularity of uniforms, insignia, flags, banners, marching columns and parades among the membership. Even the nomenclature of its rank system betrayed a military influence. Bündische Youth's tougher character was in keeping in some respects with the harsh political and socio-economic climate of the Republic, a climate that promoted similar tendencies among adult organisations of both Left and Right. Youth as a whole progressively radicalised before 1933. In Bündische circles the aimless rambling of the early Wandervogel contrasted in the 1920s with the quest of the younger generation for a new badge of identity, for the opportunity to commit itself to a cause. A sense of the heroic, a need for self-sacrifice, and a feeling of preparation for a decisive time to come ('Der Tag') permeated the Bündische ranks. For many of them the period of talking was over; the moment for action had arrived. How to act and in which direction were the only problems.

Life within Bündische Youth revolved around the group. Whereas the Wandervogel and Free German Youth had not seriously tried to curb the individualism of their followers, in the Bündische movement the collectivist experience within the confines of the group transcended everything else. The group was meant to be a total experience for its adherents, providing for their emotional, spiritual and even moral needs. It was designed to offer a full and genuine life experience in a community bound by comradeship, solicitude and solidarity. Members were expected to owe a deep sense of duty, obligation and loyalty to the group of their choice. The group was, therefore, a closely knit body based on mutual trust and unselfishness, buttressed by the binding force of obedience and discipline. There was tight organisation and a hierarchial, authoritarian structure, although each group was regulated unbureaucratically. Personal communication among its members was essential to the group's smooth and efficient functioning. Charismatic leadership was valued more highly than in earlier phases of the youth movement, for groups were constructed around leaders who led by personal example and force of personality. They were elected by members themselves and were in the position of being no more than first among equals. They were comrades not supervisors, though the essentially anti-democratic leader-principle (*Führerprinzip*) was implicitly recognised.[21] Membership qualifications for group entry were stiff. Aspirant recruits had to go through a system of rigorous tests before being admitted, but once in the group they fully and immediately enjoyed the socialistic fellowship within it. The experience of personal integration into a group was the emotional foundation of its membership, the focal point of the group's existence. Members received their importance not on the grounds of their own individual qualities but on the basis of their ability to integrate themselves into the Bündische community. The group represented the national community (*Volksgemeinschaft*) in miniature, living proof of the indissoluble bonds which tied all Germans together. The group was in a very real way, therefore, the paramount form of social and political life, in which the principles of selectivity and comradeship were brought into organic union. As such, the group was Bündische Youth's answer to the fragmented society of Weimar. It was an alternative to both democratic liberalism and Marxian socialism. The group was regarded as a quintessentially German institution which synthesised in a new form the best features of the new society (*Gesellschaft*) and traditional society (*Gemeinschaft*). For many youths the group assumed an almost mystical, religious significance. As 'a secularised form of a religious order',[22] it at one and the same time authenticated and sanctified the existence of the youth movement.[23] Although some members may have viewed the group as only a cultural or educational, or even religious entity,[24] and others as simply a convenient organisational form, most saw it as an end in itself, believing that it was a means of communal living far superior to anything offered by atomised Weimar society. The group concept was perfectly appropriate to the youth movement's ethos, for it permitted youth to assert their independent status while simultaneously holding out a blueprint for the future form of German society. The concept was progressive and for the youth at any rate embodied the true reality.[25]

The group gave to the youth movement the idea of service (*Dienst*) in an altruistic, national cause. Bündische Youth was more nationalistic and self-consciously German than its predecessors. In its genuine concern for German society as a whole, it had clearly cast off most of the introspectiveness associated with the Wandervogel and developed outgoing attitudes already evident in Free German Youth. The Bündische movement had a mission that was no longer exclusively personal. It was preparing for a struggle in which the stake was Germany's future, and, to be capable of fighting with the necessary strength and skill, the group had to condition the minds and bodies of its members. This notion of serving the national cause was reflected, for instance, in a vocabulary which soon emerged among Bündische youths. Evocative terms such as *Befreiung* (liberation), *Kampf* (struggle) and *Freiheit* (freedom) became common. This was an elitist conception of mission and destiny, because the Bündische movement was openly elitist in character and outlook. Members rather aristocratically felt a responsibility to revitalise their weakened and demoralised Fatherland and to create a new, better society, modelled on the group and embracing class harmony, social justice, peace and dignity. However vaguely formulated its sense of mission was, there is no question about the adolescent sincerity with which Bündische Youth applied itself to the task of national regeneration. It was convinced that it was the *avant-garde* of a spiritual revolution which would eventually transform German society. Thus, to the well-established activities of hiking, camping and hostelling were added a new determined sense of purpose, reinforced by more numerous and better organised expeditions outside the Reich to German ethnic minorities. As regards the East, Bündische Youth saw itself as carrying on the tradition of the Teutonic Knights in safeguarding German values from pernicious Slav influence. A central office (the Mittelstelle für Jugendgrenzlandarbeit) was even established in 1925 to ensure that the Bündische crusade in Eastern Europe would be conducted as effectively as possible, and its expeditions there throughout the 1920s and early 1930s were a salient feature of its activity.[26]

The concept of the group was intimately linked to the elitist and exclusive nature of Bündische Youth, which depicted itself as comprising the most able elements of the nation, almost the natural-born leaders of Germany. As one Bündische leader put it, 'The future and the destiny of our people depends on whether we can again create a leadership cadre. The prerequisite is the existence of spiritual values and strengths. The way forward is through a dynamic selection procedure. Hope rests on the best elements of youth.'[27]

Bündische Youth had no inhibitions about presenting this elitist image to the outside world, and certainly from a numerical and sociological point of view it was a movement for the few and privileged. It recruited almost exclusively from the ranks of grammar-school boys and to a lesser extent university students – the sons in the main of the educated and propertied middle classes: civil servants, teachers, social workers, white-collar workers, professionals and commercial and industrial businessmen.[28] In other words, Bündische Youth remained as bourgeois as both the Wandervogel and Free German Youth had been. With its neo-romantic nationalist outlook, it held little attraction for working-class youths, whose preoccupations after 1918 tended to be directed towards more practical, everyday objectives. Only a few groups, such as Karl Oelbermann's Nerother Wandervogel, had a notable percentage of working-class members.[29] Even within the broad spectrum of the new and old *Mittelstand*, Bündische Youth was hardly a widespread phenomenon, for its membership never exceeded 60,000, or little more than 1 per cent of the total number of organised German youth in the Weimar period.[30] The movement, like its predecessors, remained strongest in north Germany, Saxony, Thuringia and Berlin–Brandenburg, while branching out significantly into Silesia.[31] The predominantly Protestant nature of the independent youth movement was thus retained.

Its elitist, aristocratic approach to contemporary society placed

Bündische Youth firmly in the wider neo-conservative front in the Republic, which stressed the importance of producing a cultivated and trained cadre as the most effective way of bringing about Germany's salvation. Indeed, Bündische Youth was numerically the largest constituent of the Conservative Revolution, and through its group concept furnished one of the most noteworthy theoretical expressions of a 'third force' between socialism and old-fashioned nationalism. The role of the group as the new basis of the State pertained unmistakably to the notion of the corporate State adduced by neo-conservative thinkers. In this sense the group was a corporative entity underpinned by the idea of the nation's indivisibility.[32] Neo-conservative spokesmen were fully aware of Bündische Youth's potential value to their cause. Moeller van den Bruck, despite not being directly connected with the youth movement, exerted substantial influence on it, particularly through his fundamental concept of conservative rejuvenation founded on nationalist, socialist and revolutionary precepts. In his most celebrated work, *Das dritte Reich* (The Third Reich), published in 1923, he praised Bündische Youth as a 'true expression of the will to a new State' and looked on the movement as a microcosm of the future Reich. Stefan George was another whose influence on Bündische Youth was far-reaching and he was in no doubt that it was Germany's best hope for the future.[33] Like the conservative revolutionaries, Bündische Youth sought to bridge the gap separating nationalism and socialism. A revolutionary dimension was added to a nationalism that was not restorative and to a socialism that was not Marxist. A new order of national community based on these two crucial ideas was the neo-conservative ethic subscribed to by Bündische groups.

Central to Bündische Youth's whole sense of being and the vital ingredient of the group as a creative force was the concept of the 'new man'.[34] He was to be moulded within the fellowship of group life as the prototypical new German. The realisation of this new type was the prerequisite for a wholesale restructuring of German society according to Bündische principles. The idea of the 'new man' was never explicitly explained by the movement, and, not unexpectedly, there were varying interpretations of what he actually should amount to. Moderate groups, for example, were keen to endow him with a certain religiosity, while others, especially on the right, were more interested in developing him as a heroic, defiant figure, and happily accepted Ernst Junger's description of the stormtrooper as their ideal: 'he is the new elite of Central Europe. He is of an entirely new breed, cunning, strong, purposeful. He is audacious, battle-hardened and merciless in his demands both of himself and others.'[35]

Most sections of Bündische Youth were generally agreed that, in keeping with their neo-conservative orientation, their man should be non-bourgeois, with a dislike of all conventions normally associated with a middle-class mentality. He would also uphold the strong Bündische principle of being a relentless seeker of the truth and combine the desirable qualities of idealism, honesty, courage, creativity, manliness, integrity and patriotism. He would, moreover, have deep roots in the consciousness of the *Volk*, place the interests of the nation above his own, and embody in a balanced synthesis the best qualities of the Wandervogel, the Boy Scout and soldier.[36]

Of the need for a 'new man' all Bündische groups were in unanimous and hearty agreement. Only if he were created would Germany's slide into perdition be reversed. But different groups and personalities of the movement had a variety of ideas on how their man was to evolve in practice. The task was an intrinsically educational one for the groups ruled out military and political methods. The most suitable educational methods thus had to be devised. From the beginning, therefore, there was a strong inbuilt educational component in the Bündische perspective, which carried important ideological overtones. If the movement were realistically to plan the preparation of a new elite, a good deal of intensive experimentation in the educational sphere would have to be undertaken. This meant that the thrust of Bündische educational work would need to be levelled on a higher plane than the campaigns it mounted against pornography, licence in literature and the cinema, and other modernist fashions. These were direct but limited and transient contributions which had nothing to do with the problem of developing the 'new man'. The educational aspects of Bündische work are, therefore, worth closer examination.

Settlements (*Siedlungen*), work communities (*Werkgemeinschaften*) and labour camps (*Arbeitslager*) became an established and significant feature of Bündische Youth's broader educational experience during the 1920s. A few small settlements, such as the Obstbausiedlung Eden near Oranienburg and a vegetarian settlement at Klingberg in Holstein, had arisen even before the war,[37] but it was only after 1918 that the practice became more popular. The settlements were designed to put the concept of the national community into practice on a limited scale by encouraging friendship within a small, closed group dominated by the ethics of primitive communism. They satisfied youth's desire for direct involvement, the need to be seen actually doing something in pursuit of much discussed aims, and developing a new life-style. Most settlements were self-sufficient, vegetarian and teetotal. Activity was mainly of a manual nature — farming, gardening and craft-making — but too frequently insufficient account was taken of the practical economics of the venture, and many settlements failed altogether within a short time. Among the best known and more successful were the settlements at Habertshof in Schlüchtern (Hesse), set up in 1922 by the Neuwerk Movement and led by Hermann Schafft[38] and Emil Blum, and at Blankenburg under the direction of Hans Koch.[39] Neuwerk's socially progressive and Protestant attitudes were heavily influenced by the theological views of Karl Barth. The group rejected nationalism and capitalism, and was pro-republican, having links with the Social Democratic Party (Sozialdemokratische Partei Deutschlands — SPD), of which some leaders, such as Blum, were members.[40] Neuwerk also had strong connections with the pacifist movement and eagerly worked for Franco-German reconciliation.[41] By 1933 its membership, however, had fallen to a few hundred, and later that year Habertshof was taken over by the Hitler Youth.[42] Out of the settlement came in 1924 an interesting educational innovation, the Rural College (*Heimvolkshochschule*), which under Blum's leadership owed much to Wyneken's inspiration. Its curriculum was slanted towards the creation of the 'new man' according to basic Christian Socialist principles.[43]

  The Bündische idea of labour service (*Arbeitsdienst*) was primarily to introduce urban youth to the special virtues of the *Volk*, which it deemed to exist in pure form only in the countryside unspoilt by industrial contamination.[44] The experience of simple living in a labour camp was reckoned to be useful in conveying to youths drawn from a wide range of social backgrounds the essence of the national community. There was also a powerful motivating ideal of settlement, especially regarding the remoter eastern parts of Germany. Labour service enjoyed considerable popularity later in the Weimar period, above all in rightist circles, as a means of preserving and strengthening racist and patriotic conceptions, and many former Freikorps men established labour camps for this purpose.[45] The first post-war youth groups to recognise the benefits of labour service were Artur Mahraum's Jungdeutsche Orden and the Artamanen movement,[46] but it was the Silesian Jungmannschaft and subsequently the Deutsche Freischar which prosecuted the idea most vigorously in Bündische circles as a whole. A labour camp under the auspices of the Silesian group was set up in Colborn near Hanover in 1925 with the aim of bringing together young workers, students and peasants in preparation for future service to society. The Deutsche Freischar extended this approach at its camps held at Löwenberg (Silesia) in 1928, 1929 and 1930.[47] In the early 1930s labour service was taken up by Weimar governments and several adult organisations with a view to relieving unemployment. This represented, of course, a distortion of the concept originally conceived by Bündische Youth.

In its search for the most appropriate and efficacious methods of implementing the 'new man' ideal, Bündische Youth inevitably became involved in the educational concerns initiated by the Wandervogel, and by and large it succeeded in continuing the youth movement's association with positive and progressive contributions in education, especially as regards school and the adult sphere.

Before 1914, experiments in educational reform had accepted the medium in which the school had to work and the traditional basis on which it rested. After 1918, the efforts of educational reformers were directed by their recognition of the school as an instrument for the reshaping of society, not according to the dictates of State, or church, or school, as previously, but an instrument in the sense that through it the education of the individual and his synthesis in a new social order might be effected.[48] Both in the Bündische movement and throughout the field of educational reform could be discerned a new social idealism purposefully directed towards practical ends. The school-reform movement, which had come to a virtual halt during the war, was presented with a more favourable environment in which to introduce its ideas when an ostensibly democratic system of government was established in 1918/19.

The changes in German education after 1918 were promoted by a combination of reform-movement pressure and the social attitudes of the new era. It was felt that the school system had to be altered in accordance with the new situation, particularly with regard to the provision of equal opportunities without distinction of social class. Because of this, however, education inevitably became involved in politics. Before 1914 the school had assisted in the regimentation of the younger generation in service to the State. The November Revolution freed the school from this opprobrious task, but the value of the school as a training-ground for religious and political partisanship was fully appreciated. Party politics intruded, so that progressive ideas in education were soon supported by the Left, while the *status quo* was defended by the Right. Despite these political entanglements, significant changes did take place in schools as regards organisation, methods and practice, and the influence of Bündische Youth was clearly visible.

Until 1918 the youth movement's influence in education had been largely from outside the system. The new-found freedom of post-war Germany meant not only that original educational ideas fostered by the youth movement were now given scope for expression in schools, but also that henceforth its methods, concepts and idealism had a decisive impact in the system. The drive to reform from without gave way to a more energetic drive from within. At the very outset, however, the experience of Gustav Wyneken indicated that sweeping reforms could not be introduced at one stroke, that it would take time and patience to remodel the schools and extirpate their authoritarian ethos. Wyneken, appointed an adviser in the Prussian Education Ministry in autumn 1918, met with such ferocious opposition from teachers and parents to his plans for radically changing the way schools were administered and the subjects they taught that he was compelled to resign. [49] He was also disappointed in Bavaria, where he was attached to the Education Ministry at the invitation of Kurt Eisner. When Eisner was murdered early in 1919, Wyneken's position became untenable, and, giving up his attempts at reforming the schools, he withdrew from public life. [50] None the less, in the early stages of the Republic, Free German Youth held up Wyneken's school at Wickersdorf as the ideal to which all school authorities and educationalists should aspire. Seminars, debates and plans relating to reform were offered by Free German Youth in considerable quantity as it mounted a sustained attack on the *status quo*. No attempt was made to conceal the view of its left wing that school was an expedient for social and political revolution against capitalist, class-ridden society. [51] Predictably, Free German Youth achieved very little and Wyneken's rebuffs in Prussia and Bavaria did it irreparable harm. But the influence of Wyneken's ideas endured in German youth, serving as a vehicle for change and rebellion in the Bündische movement. His revolutionary pathos, hatred of bourgeois liberalism, and romantic utopianism became fundamentals of Bündische ideology.

During the 1920s a valuable effort was made at democratising the school system, a development wholly consonant with the educational ethos of Bündische Youth and actively encouraged by it, as the progressive Association for Fundamental School Reform (Bund für entschiedene Schulreform) freely acknowledged.[52] Bündische Youth helped to humanise relationships in the classroom between teacher and pupils, to promote the growth of parental participation in school affairs through parent–teacher councils, to encourage more emphasis on musical, cultural and artistic subjects in the curriculum, including the creation of choirs and theatrical societies, and to advocate the cause of gymnastics, physical fitness and sports in the daily life of the school.[53] The school outing (*Wandertag*) was widely introduced in schools under direct youth movement influence, which was also an important factor in the greater interest shown by schools in acquiring rural retreats (*Schullandheime*) for their pupils' enjoyment. The case for extending school holidays was successfully argued by Bündische Youth on the grounds that, to allow further development of their personality, pupils needed a prolonged period of relaxation and recreation away from the school routine. This anthropological truth became widely accepted in schools in the 1920s.[54] In fusing work with play in schools, Bündische Youth, and particularly one of its leaders, Edmund Neuendorff, who was closely involved in this development, was a harbinger of democratic modernity.[55] Another leading personality of the movement, Georg Götsch,[56] was largely responsible for persuading the liberal-minded Prussian Minister of Culture, Carl Heinrich Becker, to initiate in 1923 the Prussian College of Physical Exercise. Becker, an important figure in Weimar education, was also greatly influenced by Götsch in matters of teaching-training methods and by another youth-movement stalwart, Adolf Reichwein,[57] on educational questions in general.

Bündische Youth took up the demand originally made by the Wandervogel for pupils to be given greater latitude for in-dividualistic self-expression in schools and for extra-curricular activities to be regarded as essential elements of the overall educ-ational process.[58] Pupils were encouraged by Bündische spokesmen to participate more fully in the management of schools, though by the late 1920s even limited forms of pupil self-government were exceptional in most areas. Arising from this trend, however limited, Bündische Youth was able to convey to schools the notion, given practical expression within its own ranks, of the teacher's being less of an instructor and more of a leader among equals. Although the mixing of boys and girls within the same organisation was uncom-mon in Bündische Youth, this fact did not prevent it from providing a direct impetus to the idea of co-education in schools. Progress in this

sphere was more obvious in some regions than in others: Saxony and
Thuringia tended to favour progressive innovations in school, thus
reflecting the leftist political complexion of their governments during
at least part of the Weimar era, while traditionally conservative
Bavaria did not.[59]

After 1918 the experimental pedagogical ideas of the youth
movement were implemented most successfully in a number of
specialised institutions: the Community Schools (*Gemeinschaftsschulen*), the Country Home School movement begun by
Lietz, the Pedagogical Academies founded in Prussia by Minister
Becker, and the Folk College (*Volkshochschule*) movement, in which
many former youth-movement members were employed as teachers.[60] The Folk Colleges represented the adult education sector
after 1918, the term being generically used to cover a large variety of
different kinds of institutions, ranging from those offering university
extension courses to residential centres. Adult education became one
of the principal focal points for the new enthusiasm for education
which spread across Germany after the war, and most of its students
came from the lower classes, having had no more than an elementary
schooling. Several Folk Colleges were founded by former
Wandervogel and Bündische members, as were some private
experimental schools, such as Fritz Klatt's Leisure and Education
School at Prerow, Max Bondy's School Community at
Gandersheim, Knud Ahlborn's youth camp at Klappholtal, and Karl
Seidelmann's school at Bad Münder.[61] The influence of Bundische
Youth on adult education in Weimar Germany was considerable, and
even reached into high-powered organisations such the Hohenrodter
Bund, led by Wilhelm Flitner and Eugen Rosenstock.[62] In
general, the number of youth movement members engaged in the
various branches of the teaching profession was substantial, while
some of the most distinguished educational theorists, including
Hermann Nohl, Paul Natorp, Heinrich Heise, Friedrich Wilhelm
Foerster, Theodor Litt and Eduard Spranger came from or stood
close to the youth movement, and carried over to their professional
work ideals instilled there.[63]

The contribution of Bündische Youth to the liberalisation of
education in Weimar consisted not only of the weight it lent to
progressive reforms and its promotion of education as a humanitarian
discipline, but also of its success in affirming the right of school pupils
to be looked upon as a group whose requirements had to be carefully
taken into account if the educational process was to possess any

fundamental validity. Thanks to the efforts of Bündische Youth, the younger generation finally emerged as an entity in its own right in the formation of educational priorities. Hermann Nohl implicitly paid tribute to this contribution when he characterised Bündische Youth as an 'educational people's movement',[64] and Heinrich Roth went further when he identified the unique spirit of the youth movement as the driving force behind the broad educational reform movement of the 1920s.[65]

Complementing this significant contribution to education was Bündische Youth's notable endeavours in the social and cultural spheres. The social concerns and perceptions of both Free German Youth and Bündische Youth have already been stressed, but what practical impact did their theoretical assumptions have on the social environment outside youth circles? For a start, the youth movement signally influenced official thinking on youth welfare and in several instances actually showed the way forward by offering concrete example. After the war some older Wandervogel members who felt alienated by the different atmosphere prevailing in the youth movement found an outlet for their social awareness and aspirations for a better world in the realm of social and welfare work, especially in social education.[66] This entailed responsibilities such as helping the homeless, the underprivileged, the indigent, social misfits, deprived children, orphans, and children from broken homes, as well as giving help and advice to juvenile delinquents. These forms of compassionate and caring activity at the grass-roots level constituted an indispensable support and supplementary aid for statutory measures such as the National Youth Welfare Law (Reichsjugendwohl fahrtsgesetz) of 1922 and the Youth Criminal Code (Jugend-gerichtsgesetz) of 1923. The motivation of the former youth-movement members engaged in such work was mainly humanitarian, though among a few there may have been added a certain degree of religious, ideological or political idealism. Various centres and institutions directly under the influence of the youth movement or staffed by its former members provided an organisational framework for this social work. Among the best known were the Social Work Community of East Berlin, led by Friedrich Siegmund-Schultze; the Educational Home, Lindenhof, led by Karl Wilkers; and the Guild of Social Work.[67]

Social habits in Weimar were affected to some extent, especially during the early 1920s, when the urge for things new was at its height, by the youth movement's naturalistic impulse, which was usually expressed in its rejection of smoking, alcohol and formal clothing, and its encouragement of outdoor sports, physical exercise and gymnastics.[68] The stiff collars of the pre-1914 era became less fashionable in the 1920s as Bündische Youth set the pattern for the wearing of open-necked shirts. The Wandervogel habit of not wearing hats also spread to Weimar society.[69] The youth movement can claim some credit for introducing, especially between the sexes, a more relaxed and spontaneous element into everyday social intercourse, which for so long had been dominated by stiff, artificial conventions.[70] Another worthwhile contribution to the social environment of a different type was the influence of former Wandervogel members Alwin Seifert and August Lemuth in the fields of housing construction and town-planning. The development of smaller and cheaper residential accommodation and of suburban areas on the outskirts of towns and cities were partly the result of youth-movement concepts, while the environmental preservation lobby had its wholehearted support.[71]

Bündische Youth's cultural influence was manifested most lucidly in the fields of music, architecture and drama. The Wandervogel tradition of encouraging folk-songs and dances was maintained and further developed in the 1920s. Walter Hensel founded the celebrated Finkensteiner Singing Movement in 1924[72] and Fritz Jöde helped refine the youth movement's particular form of youth music. The Boberhaus in Silesia, created in 1926 by the Silesian Jungmannschaft with assistance from Minister Becker contributed brilliantly to the progress of folk-music culture,[73] while the Music Home founded and led by Götsch in Frankfurt an der Oder in 1928 is a monument to the youth movement's musical talent, flair and inspiration. A chain of lesser music schools set up by Bündische Youth throughout Germany ensured that its impact in this area was truly nationwide. Its musical efforts were admirably backed up by its sustained commitment to the development of theatrical drama. Martin Luserke probably did more than anyone to popularise this form of artistic enterprise among young and old alike,[74] though not to be overlooked is the role of the Ekkehard Play Troupe, created by the former Freikorps commander and leader of the Schilljugend group, Gerhard Rossbach, which enjoyed considerable acclaim during its performances throughout Germany.

Progressive architects, including the Bauhaus circle in Weimar, acknowledged their debt to the youth movement's spirit and futuristic concepts in their work, and sculptors and graphic artists such as Käthe Kollwitz were inspired to some degree by the youthful style of the movement.[75] Craftsmen belonging to archaic trades received a boost from the movement's devotion to folk culture. Overseeing its involvement in the cultural field was the New German Artists' Guild, which was established in 1919 by Willi Geissler and others as a forum for discussion and exchange of ideas and information among writers, musicians and artists of all kinds who operated in spheres of interest to the youth movement.[76]

In the educational, social and cultural fields it can be readily appreciated that Bündische Youth exerted a reformative and re-vitalising influence. By direct action and example, its members claimed a measure of authority quite disproportionate to their numerical strength. This fact is ample evidence of the importance of the youth movement's role in German society at large. Activities and interests which in their origins had been confined to it became a comparative commonplace. They became part of the total nexus of social activity in Weimar Germany, part of its climate of opinion.[77] The idealism and new perspectives which Bündische Youth was able to pass on to society were unequalled by many other contemporary organisations in Germany. Bündische Youth was at the very nerve centre of emancipatory tendencies among the German people in the early twentieth century.

If Bündische Youth's laudable contribution to educational, social and cultural development is beyond dispute, the nature and extent of its political involvement is highly controversial. The leading question about its political role concerns the magnitude of Bündische responsibility for the rise and final success of National Socialism. The political fabric of Bündische Youth was no less variegated than that of the Weimar Republic in general. Virtually every conceivable shade of ideological outlook was represented in the Republic's political spectrum, and in national (*Reichstag*) elections literally dozens of parties, large and small, competed for support. Bündische Youth contained a similar diversity among its groups. None the less, several general types of youth organisation within the movement are discernible, including a liberal–democratic stream which basically favoured the Republic up to a point, and an extreme nationalist and *völkisch* stream which decidedly did not. There were in addition a number of paramilitary, conservative and national revolutionary organisations which when the political crisis point was reached in the early 1930s could be counted as at least passive supporters of the anti-republican camp. Entirely missing from Bündische Youth was a radical leftist contingent. Pro-communists and revolutionary socialists withdrew from Free German Youth in the early 1920s to join left-wing groups outside the youth movement. Before discussing the political problems of Bündische Youth, some reference to particularly notable individual groups within these broad categories would be appropriate.

The Boy Scout (*Pfadfinder*) movement, which was largely middle class in composition, was a new and conspicuous recruit to the independent youth movement after the war. Forsaking the supervision of adults as well as a chauvinistic and militaristic philosophy, most Boy Scouts after 1918 warmly embraced fundamental free-youth-movement principles in their programme in an attempt to break away from an ethos that in their eyes had been discredited and irrevocably defeated.[78] The peculiarly German type of Boy Scout had become superfluous. In any case, the movement had lost many members, for in 1918 it could muster no more than 20,000. A decisive meeting at Schloss Prunn (Bavaria) in August 1919 paved the way for the Boy Scouts' reorientation towards the youth movement. The change of heart was immediately made evident in the so called *Prunner Gelöbnis* (Solemn Declaration), and in subsequent years the Boy Scout element in both Free German and Bündische Youth was vibrant, constructive and influential. Energetic younger personalities such as Martin Voelkel and Franz Ludwig Habbel, who both set up their own splinter groups before joining forces in the 1800-strong Bund deutscher Neupfadfinder in 1921,[79] supplied a good deal of *élan* and the White Knight Circle in the Neupfadfinder was a driving force for progressive attitudes in Bündische Youth as a whole.[80] The Boy Scouts suffered as much as any other segment of the youth movement from splits and secessions, and by the early 1920s the original Deutscher Pfadfinder Bund (German Boy Scout Association) existed side by side with several other groups. It and most of these other groups acknowledged their adherence to Bündische ideals. In 1925 a merger brought together the progressive groups under Voelkel's leadership in the Grossdeutscher Pfadfinder Bund (Greater German Boy Scout Association), which the following year joined with various Wandervogel groups to form the Bund der Wandervogel und Pfadfinder under Hans Dehmel. This grouping of about 12,000 members represented the 'purist' exponents of the free Bündische tradition and regarded itself as the elite of the movement. In 1927 it was renamed the Deutsche Freischar.[81]

The genesis of the Deutsche Freischar lay in the post-war

reorganisation of the Alt-Wandervogel, which, after losing a substantial part of its membership through resignation and secession, joined with a few other small Wandervogel groups in 1923 to form the Wandervogel deutsche Jungenschaft, or, as it was known from 1924, the Alt-Wandervogel, deutsche Jungenschaft, led by Hans Dehmel and Georg Weber, and then by Ernst Buske. This group constituted the core of the Wandervogel elements in the Bund der Wandervogel und Pfadfinder before it became the Deutsche Freischar.[82] Made up mainly of grammar-school boys and students and led from 1928 by Ernst Buske, the group had 12,000 members in 1929, concentrated in Brandenburg, Saxony and Silesia. The Deutsche Freischar provided stability and prestige to the Bündische movement and its leaders were among the most enterprising and intelligent of the independent youth movement. Unfortunately, the sudden death of Buske in 1930 shook the group fundamentally, and, after several injudicious mergers with other groups, including Admiral Adolf von Trotha's Grossdeutsche Jugendbund, it broke up. A reformed Deutsche Freischar appeared in late 1930 under Helmuth Kittel, but it was a pale shadow of its former self and exerted little influence on the rest of the Bündische world.[84]

The mantle of the Deutsche Freischar as the leading group in Bündische circles was taken over to a certain extent by the Deutsche Jungenschaft (d.j.1.11.) set up by Eberhard Köbel in November 1929 and formally constituted in this form in August 1930. 'Tusk', as Köbel was affectionately known, was one of the most eccentric, dynamic, controversial, egotistical figures thrown up by the Weimar youth culture. He brought new ideas, a new style and a new vitality to Bündische work, and his arresting ideas on graphic art design and foreign, mostly Russian,[85] music left an indelible mark on the movement.[86] 'Tusk' set the highest ambitions for youth and convinced his 2500 followers that they were indeed the *avant-garde* of a new era in which youth and its concepts would pay the decisive role.[87] His influence extended beyond the youth movement, for he and his activities became talking-points in leading social and political circles in Weimar. Köbel failed, however, to realise his dream of uniting all Bündische groups under his command, and in 1931/2 he began to drift from the scene, sullen and resentful at the world's lack of full understanding for his notions. His connections with radical leftist groups led him in April 1932 to join the KPD and to leave the d.j.1.11.[88] During the Third Reich, after having unsuccessfully offered his services to the Hitler Youth, he rejoined the illegal d.j.1.11.

to conduct a relatively effective resistance against the regime until the Gestapo stepped in. 'Tusk' went into exile in Sweden and then Great Britain, returning to East Berlin after the war. He died in 1955.[89]

The extreme right-wing groups consisted most notably of Adler und Falken, Deutsche Falkenschaft, Die Geusen, Schilljugend, Freischar Schill, and the Artamanen. The last was the most important of these. Founded in 1924 by the *völkisch* propagandists Wilhelm Kotzde and Bruno Tanzmann, the Artamanen[90] was originally designed to replace Polish seasonal labour in east German agricultural estates, but soon developed into something rather more grandiose, embracing not only anti-Slavism, but also a 'Blood and Soil' programme and a *völkisch* Pan-Germanism with a practical emphasis on Eastern settlement[91] and labour service.[92] As such, the Artamanen was of all Weimar youth groups ideologically closest to the Nazi Party (Nationalsozialistische Deutsche Arbeiterpartei – NSDAP). Many of its leaders and ordinary members were party members, including Heinrich Himmler, later *Reichsführer* of the SS, Walther Darré, the party's agricultural expert, and Rudolf Hoess, Commandant at Auschwitz, and a fair proportion served in the SS.[93] Indeed, Artamanen ideas later had a considerable influence on SS concepts and practices.[94] One Artamanen leader revealingly remarked in a letter to Hitler on 22 June 1927, 'The first Artamanen group in Limbach in 1924 was schooled in a pure National Socialist sense. . . . Today our relationship is such that the overwhelming part of the Artamanen leadership are members of the NSDAP.'[95] Clearly, therefore, the movement, which had 2300 members in 1929 and some 5000 in 1932/3,[96] was not in the mainstream of the Bündische tradition; it was rather supra-Bündische (*überbündische*). The movement split into several factions in the late 1920s and one such group in Mecklenburg formed the basis of the Hitler Youth's Land Service scheme in 1934.

Most of the other *völkisch* youth groups were ideologically related to National Socialism, particularly Adler und Falken, founded in 1920 by the indefatigable Kotzde, and Die Geusen (at least until 1931/2),[97] but their influence was as limited as the size of their membership.[98] The conservative and paramilitary youth organisations, such as the Jungstahlhelm and Kyffhäuser-Jugend were much larger'but ideologically passive. The small band of national revolutionary groups, including the Pfadfinderschaft Westmark and Wikinger Jungenkorps, which emerged in response to the worsening political and economic situation of the late 1920s and early 1930s, were volatile, committed, but uninfluential.[99] All Bündische groups were members of the cover organisation known as the Reichsausschuss der deutschen Jugendverbände (Reich Committee of German Youth Groups), making up a negligible fraction of its total membership in 1932 of nearly 5 million.[100]

The diversified character of the groups in Bündische Youth preclude any dogmatic generalisations about the movement's political outlook and its relationship with National Socialism. A definitive answer to these questions can only be produced when much more primary research has been undertaken into individual youth groups and regional studies made of their activities. But the ideological and political views which shaped the Bündische *Weltanschauung* can be broadly adumbrated. After all, a vast majority of Bündische members rejected the Weimar Republic, the political parties and parliamentary democracy. One of the few groups which consistently and purposefully campaigned for a non-party socialist democracy within the republican system was the Leuchtenburg Circle, led by, among others, Fritz Borinski. Founded in 1924 and located mainly in Leipzig, this group of no more than 100 members promoted political education and socialism in Bündische circles.[101] It was a lonely and unrewarding battle, however, because, although Bündische Youth pursued a policy of strict neutrality in party politics for most of the pre-1933 period, its striving for a new Reich, a national community, a Greater Germany and a charismatic leader placed it unequivocally in the camp of the 'National Opposition'. The middle-class Protestant youth who predominated in Bündische Youth shared, consciously or unconsciously, directly or indirectly, the same basic articles of faith as their nationalist-minded parents and elders. Moreover, it was the same social groups which eventually formed the bulk of the National Socialist movement and gave Hitler the electoral backing he needed to achieve power in 1933. Was Bündische Youth a recognisable part of this 'brown revolution', as writers such as Harry Pross, Howard Becker, George L. Mosse, Wilhelm Roessler and, more recently, Michael H. Kater, have argued?[102] In fact, in 1933 and shortly afterwards many Bündische spokesmen themselves were at pains to demonstrate that the NSDAP and Hitler Youth were the legitimate and natural extensions of the Bündische movement. From the National Socialist side, Will Vesper subscribed to this hypothesis, regarding the Hitler Youth as the fulfilment in a Hegelian sense of the independent youth movement.[103] On the other hand, the Hitler Youth emphatically repudiated any serious links with Bündische

Youth, though it did admit to learning some useful practices from the Wandervogel.[104] This view is supported to one degree or another by a large group of historians, who, whilst not overlooking faults and deficiencies in Bündische Youth, absolve it of the charge of being a direct precursor of National Socialism.[105] The problem is full of contradictions and diametrically opposing interpretations, but a balanced perspective may be obtained by analysing the political, ideological, organisational and personal factors involved.

Bündische Youth never developed a comprehensive, coherent political programme, despite its intense discussion of politics throughout the 1920s.[106] The movement was not meant to be political. Other aspects of its work, in education for example, took precedence. There was, as a result, a feeling prevalent among members that to become involved in political realities was somehow to abandon the orbit of the youth movement. Its deep-seated romanticism and penchant for retrospective cogitation on an idealised past may also help account for Bündische Youth's inability to reach concrete political decisions or to form definite political attitudes. Its detached concern and vacillating demeanour laid the movement open to accusations of aristocratic dilletantism. Few of its friends would have said it possessed an obvious capacity for hard-headed realism. Only on rare occasions did Bündische Youth descend from its lofty pinnacle to enter the rough and tumble of everyday politics. In 1930 several groups, led by the Deutsche Freischar, helped to establish the liberal, democratic German State Party, (Deutsche Staatspartei), while the same year Heinz Dähnhardt's Jungnationale Bund gave active support to the newly founded Conservative People's Party (Konservative Volkspartei). Both enterprises proved abortive, as did Dr Kleo Pleyer's attempt to organise a 'Bündische Reichschaft' as a new style of political party based on Bündische principles.[107] Thereafter, Bündische Youth retreated once more to the safe periphery of Weimar politics, re-emerging only briefly and ineffectively at the end of 1932 to assist in limited fashion the government of General Schleicher.

Critics contend that a substantial section of Bündische Youth, particularly its *völkisch* wing, shared many of the most fundamental and important concepts which were the essence of National Socialist ideology. In other words, they are convinced that the movement's ideology was so similar to National Socialism that it must be seen as an integral part of the broader development which made the NSDAP's victory possible. Apologists argue that, despite undoubted ideological similarities with National Socialism, Bündische Youth interpreted basic concepts quite differently from the NSDAP. According to this view, ideological correlation with National Socialism was very limited, superficial, even sophistical. One historian has even gone so far as to assert that the neo-conservative Bündische Youth was ideologically incompatible with National Socialism, since Hitler embodied the exact opposite of what it essentially stood for – namely, spiritual and cultural regeneration and the creation of the 'new man'.[108] Both schools of thought have made strong cases, and where to draw the line between them is a complex and delicate undertaking. It is made all the more so because of the partisanship which has intruded into the debate from both sides. There is the unsophisticated Marxist (or neo-Marxist) argument which dismisses virtually all of German bourgeois society before 1933 as fascist, and one historian of this persuasion stretches our credulity beyond reasonable limits by characterising the NSDAP as a crusade against the working class.[109] Such statements betray nothing but blinkered prejudice masquerading as properly quantified historical observations, and in the end do nothing to further our understanding of anything. From an entirely different perspective, the recent debate concerning the extent of continuity in modern German history[110] has produced stimulating ideas which touch directly on Bündische Youth's relationship with National Socialism. But a major reservation about the 'integration' hypothesis so ably adduced by Kater is that it tries to incorporate too much historical experience into its conceptual and empirical framework.[111] Kater claims to have identified the existence of fascist ideas and tendencies in large segments of Bündische Youth before 1933, and he believes that this ultimately conditioned the whole movement for eventual and relatively painless absorption into the Hitler Youth. He goes further when he maintains that this development was the logical outcome of important underlying trends in the independent youth movement from the time of the Wandervogel. Insufficient allowance is made here, it may be thought, for significant nuances in ideological interpretation and emphasis between Bündische Youth and the NSDAP/Hitler Youth. Finally, the existence of hopelessly tendentious publications on the pre-1933 youth movement contributes little to the process of measured and objective evaluation of the subject. The efforts of some former members to rehabilitate and enhance the record and prestige of the youth movement at all costs are in some ways understandable but ill serve authentic historical assessment.[112]

Setting aside these elements of bias, the stronger of the two cases appears to lie at the moment with the apologists. There is good reason to believe that Bündische Youth did understand concepts such as a 'new Reich', 'national community' and so forth differently from the NSDAP. The notion of a new Reich, which was particularly associated with the White Knight Circle, had little in common with the later Third Reich. The Bündische Reich was admittedly a nebulous vision, something representative of an ill-defined neo-romantic yearning for a future State fashioned along the broad lines outlined by Moeller van den Bruck and Ernst Jünger rather than by Alfred Rosenberg or Adolf Hitler. Karl Paetel tries to convey the meaning of this Bündische Reich in these words: 'The New Reich was neither Luther's realm of God nor a political German Reich, though it contained elements of both; rather it was primarily the symbol of the new attitude of a new generation . . . .'[113] At any rate, it was to be a Reich embodying Bündische, not National Socialist, principles. Furthermore, Bündische Youth was entirely different from the NSDAP in the meaning it placed on the concept of a national community. The Bündische version was not designed to include the mass of Germans, only a spiritually prepared sociological elite. The proletariat hardly entered into its calculations at all. In this respect, of course, the Bündische concept simply mirrored the movement's narrow bourgeois orientation. Bündische Youth was not endowed with an informed wider vision or a realistic comprehension of the world beyond its immediate vicinity. It was composed of middle-class youths in sheltered bourgeois surroundings who really did believe that the world revolved around them. As far as they were concerned, the National Socialist version of the national community was too expansive, plebeian and vulgar, the product of a mass society and a consciously mass-based political movement. Between the two concepts there was little common ground. Much the same may be said with regard to the idea of charismatic leadership. The Bündische version was innately educational, while the NSDAP understood it in an abrasively political-cultist way which very much hinged on the presence of Hitler. This was a perversion of the Bündische concept. Similarly, the Bündische myth of soldiers and knights was not imbued with the aggressive political spirit given it by the National Socialists. Bündische Youth dreamt of an impossible utopia in which glorious deeds and acts of bravery were performed by upstanding fighters in the name of human decency and honour. The patriotic element was not totally absent, but it was kept in check by other influences, romantic and divorced from reality as they were. National Socialist militarism was an integral part of its political creed: it was brutal and destructive, as Europe was to discover in the Second World War. The nationalism of Bündische Youth was of the 'new' variety which emerged largely under the auspices of the neo-conservative movement in Weimar. The 'new nationalism' contained elements of Pan-Germanism and anti-semitism, but not to the same degree of intensity or on the same global level as in the NSDAP. The Bündische *völkisch* outlook was mainly cultural and non-political rather than biological-racist. It has even been claimed, somewhat implausibly, that anti-semitism was on the decline during the later 1920s in Bündische Youth.[114] But the important point is that, with the exception of its *völkisch* wing, Bündische Youth did not adhere to the pathological and virulent racial anti-semitism of the National Socialists. In fact, the Jewish question was not discussed very much among the youth, partly because it was not of major concern to them, and partly because there were only a few hundred Jews in the movement anyway, usually in liberal-minded groups such as the Deutsche Freischar.[115] Anti-semitism of a temperate kind was to be found in most right-wing organisations in Germany at that time, and was also evident to a lesser extent in the Centre Party (Zentrumspartei), especially in 1931/2, and other groups of the political middle and left. To equate this often religiously inspired anti-semitism with the Hitlerian type is plainly erroneous.

Bündische Youth was ideologically neo-conservative rather than National Socialist or proto-Nazi. The ideas propagated in the movement cannot be said to have prepared the youths to become, then or later, dedicated followers of Hitler, although they may have allowed them to become reconciled more readily to the Third Reich when it emerged than would otherwise have been the case. The process of adaptation to the regime after 1933 took place, however, under a completely altered set of circumstances, which included a ruthless policy of co-ordination and outright terror tactics. For this reason the question of Bündische resistance to National Socialism should not be considered pertinent to the debate concerning Bündische responsibility for the success of Hitler in 1933. The post-1933 political activities of former Bündische personnel, particularly those who played a prominent part in the regime, should also be considered irrelevant, because again circumstances changed drastically, and many Germans found it impossible to avoid involvement on some scale with the National Socialists.[116] In any event, former Bündische members were to be found in socialist, communist and confessional groups after 1933, so that the diversity of their political involvement tells us comparatively little about their politics before Hitler came to power, and says nothing for the view that their activities in the Third Reich should be seen as the natural culmination of pre-1933 attitudes. Many members and followers of the Social Democratic and Communist movements went over to the NSDAP after 1933, yet there can be no question of their having collaborated with, or prepared the way for, the NSDAP. The same criteria are applicable to the Bündische case.

Bündische Youth's rejection of the Weimar Republic and its value system helped in a small way to undermine the government and create the conditions in which it was finally brought down. In this sense, Bündische Youth had a very limited responsibility for the political chaos in the early 1930s from which the NSDAP benefited most of all. But Bündische Youth, not being an ideological precursor of National Socialism, did not actively or passively promote Hitler's cause. Its responsibility, from an ideological point of view, was no more than that of many other right-wing organisations. An examination of the organisational and personal aspects of the Bündische relationship with National Socialism strengthens this thesis.

We have already noted that the *völkisch* wing of Bündische Youth had close ideological and personal ties with the NSDAP, but this affinity was far from being total. The *völkisch* groups doggedly adhered to the concepts of Bündische elitism and non-involvement in party politics by refusing to surrender their independence to the NSDAP. On only two occasions before 1933 did these groups seriously contemplate the possibility of organisational incorporation into the Party. In 1925/6, the Schilljugend was on the verge of becoming the official youth section of the NSDAP when its leader Gerhard Rossbach finally refused Hitler's offer on the grounds that his group valued its independence too much. In 1929 a determined attempt was made by Baldur von Schirach, then leader of the National Socialist Students' League, to bring together Adler and Falken, Die Geusen, Freischar Schill and Artamanen with the Hitler Youth, whose socialistic outlook he deplored. But the *völkisch* contingent's inherent sense of elitism and dislike of party politics were decisive factors in the collapse of this plan.[117] Thus, even the ideologically committed in Bündische Youth took care to mark out a dividing line between themselves and the NSDAP, though this scarcely mitigates their responsibility for disseminating National Socialist ideals.

Most other parts of Bündische Youth did not even begin to approximate either organisationally or personally to Hitler. There was a small number of pro-National Socialist sympathisers scattered among Bündische members, notably in the Bibelkreise,[118] Grossdeutsche Jugendbund and Freischar junger Nation groups, but the bulk of the membership wanted little to do with the NSDAP and still less with the Hitler Youth,[119] which was the object of their scorn and contempt.[120] The political commitment, fanaticism, populist socialism and sheer rowdiness of the Hitler Youth were comprehensively repudiated by Bündische Youth. The Jung-Wandervogel, for example, dismissed the Hitler Youth, which had been trying hard to establish a basis of co-operation with it, as a 'militaristic mass movement'.[121] For its part, the Hitler Youth, though borrowing certain external forms and practices from Bündische Youth, made it the target for a campaign of vehement denunciation. Both groups were bound to be antagonistic to each other, not only because they were completely difficult types of youth movement, but also because they had conflicting ideas of the wider problems in Weimar Germany and of the ways in which they could be solved.

Movement of personnel from one organisation to another was a salient feature of Weimar political life and no less so in youth circles. It is hardly remarkable, therefore, that the Hitler Youth succeeded in attracting some recruits from the non-*völkisch* sections of Bündische Youth, particularly after late 1931, when the Hitler Youth under von Schirach's direction steered a course more suited to middle-class youth. Although some of these recruits later attained high rank in the Hitler Youth — for instance, Gotthard Ammerlahn became a regional commander (*Obergebietsführer*) — the number of youths involved was insignificant.[122]

In summary, Bündische Youth's links with National Socialism, whether political, ideological, organisational or personal, were too limited to justify the contention that it was a forerunner of the NSDAP and Hitler Youth. Bündische Youth was too isolated in its romanticised ivory tower to show any real engagement in the tough sphere of Weimar politics. Hence, the nature of its political influence on members was generally incoherent, while the extent of that influence on the wider world was inconsequential. The fault of Bündische Youth lay in not recognising the danger posed by National Socialism and, as a result, in not helping to build political resistance to it.[123] The movement may be blamed for not providing the proper kind of moral leadership for its members. Its failure also to promote a more rational approach to problems instead of fostering emotionalism and anti-intellectualism is a serious indictment of the Bündische ethos. It might also have done better to develop a sense of individual responsibility among members. But in these omissions, important as they undoubtedly are, Bündische Youth was not unlike so many other organisations in Weimar Germany. Like them, it was swept along by the force of events, eventually finding itself in the hands of a totalitarian dictatorship whose priorities had in practice little in common with the quintessential Bündische outlook. Confronted in 1933 with a situation to which they had directly contributed comparatively little, the majority of Bündische members simply tried to make the best they could of it — like millions of other Germans, of whatever political or religious disposition. The responsibility of Bündische Youth for Hitler was largely indirect and limited more or less to the same degree as a host of other groups, particularly those which also represented middle-class, nationalist and Protestant Germany. They were all political failures.[124]

3 Confessional Youth: Catholic, Protestant, Jewish

The principal confessional or quasi-confessional youth organisations were those under the auspices of either the Catholic and Protestant (Evangelical) church authorities, or Jewish religious and lay bodies. Collectively these organisations constituted the largest sector of the wider German youth movement, with approximately 2 million members in the 1920s.[1] In both the Catholic and Protestant groups the religious factor was usually dominant, and priests and pastors were conspicuously to the fore as leaders and intellectual mentors. Most of these organisations therefore remained until their dissolution after 1933 youth-tutelage groups – under adult control for the most part. But there were notable exceptions, because after 1918 the independent youth movement began to exert an important influence on the youth-tutelage sector, causing some confessional and even political groups to accept wholly or in part the ethos, ideals and activities of the Wandervogel and its successors. Among confessional associations such as the Catholic Quickborn and the Jewish Blau-Weiss the combination of traditional religious attitudes and the spirit of Hohe Meissner was demonstrated in exemplary fashion. Leading figures such as Romano Guardini on the Catholic side and Wilhelm Stählin on the Protestant were instrumental in harmonising Christianity and Wandervogel ideals and ensured that a special type of confessional youth group would emerge in its own right to add yet another distinctive detail to the colourful mosaic that was the German youth movement before Hitler.

Under the direction and management of the Catholic Church, all kinds of youth associations were established during the last quarter of the nineteenth century, though Catholic youth groups had existed intermittently since about 1640. Apart from those groups which were directly within the ecclesiastical orbit, there were also Catholic sports and vocational youth organisations. By 1914 the number of organised Catholic youth exceeded half a million, making the

Catholic element of the greater German youth movement the second largest after the multifarious sports and gymnastic societies. The Catholic groups were for the most part tightly and centrally organised and somewhat introspectively minded, thus reflecting the defensive attitude that had been induced in the Catholic community in general by years of discrimination and persecution from the Reich authorities, particularly during the *Kulturkampf* in the Bismarckian era. The Church wholeheartedly subscribed to the belief that strength lay in numbers, provided they were effectively co-ordinated, and this outlook left an enduring mark on the entire spectrum of Catholic youth activity.

The first step towards united action came with the establishment of an umbrella organisation in Mainz in 1896, the Verband der katholischen Jugend-und Jungmännervereine Deutschlands (League of Catholic Youth and Young Men's Associations – VKJJVD), which was led by a priest, Dr Josef Drammer. At that time there already existed some 600 individual Catholic youth groups throughout Germany, and most of them now affiliated to the new organisation, which came to fulfil a powerful co-ordinating role in Catholic youth life until its forcible dissolution by the National Socialists. In 1907 a General Secretariat of the VKJJVD was set up in Düsseldorf, and from 1908 until 1926 it was headed by a local priest, Carl Mosterts, one of the most influential leaders in the Catholic youth movement.[2] The organisation supplied a strong, positive impetus to the work of Catholic youth, especially in the religious, educational and social spheres. When Mosterts extensively reorganised it on taking over the leadership from Drammer in 1913, he reaffirmed its objectives in these fields, but added an equally important apostolic and vocational dimension.[3] His unbounded energy, personality, and full-hearted commitment to these tasks led to substantial increases in the VKJJVD's affiliated membership, from 150,000 in 1907 to 350,000 by 1918.[4]

Only very limited contact existed between Catholic youth and the independent youth movement before 1918. Catholic authorities were deeply suspicious of the emancipatory and anti-authoritarian views of the Wandervogel, and the Hohe Meissner meeting was the object of hostile criticism from Catholic quarters.[5] In Bavaria, the Centre Party succeeded in having the Wandervogel banned for a short period, because of its alleged disruptive tendencies.[6] The ecclesiastical hierarchy was ultra-conservative and insisted upon a rigorous form of obedience to those in authority, be they priests, parents or teachers. Catholic youth had no option but to accept this injunction, which allowed no room for Wandervogel concepts of youth autonomy or self-education. However, once the war was over and the Weimar Republic with its generally more liberal values came into being, the situation in the Catholic world underwent some degree of change, which resulted in a slightly more flexible ambience as far as Catholic youth was concerned. Although the power of the hierarchy over the Catholic community was not significantly undermined by the unprecedented political upheavals which took place in Germany after 1918, the influence of Free German and Bündische youth on the Catholics assumed greater proportions. As adult-sponsored youth organisations in general took up the ideals and practices of the independent youth movement to one degree or another, causing many of them to become virtually indistinguishable from, or even to become recognised parts of, Free German and subsequently Bündische Youth, the Quickborn group personified this development among Catholic youth.

The official Catholic attitude to the independent youth movement during the 1920s continued to be highly critical and caused much debate and disagreement among the ranks of youth. The debate focused on issues such as the socially critical and libertarian principles of Bündische Youth, the relationship to authority, and, probably the most contentious of all, the relationship between males and females.[7] Traditional Catholic opinion on these points was diametrically opposed to that prevailing in the independent youth movement, as was freely and defiantly acknowledged from the Catholic side. A report in the Catholic-influenced *Süddeutsche Monatshefte* made this abundantly clear:

> the [independent] youth movement is not a Catholic movement. . . . The Meissner Formula remains alien to Catholic youth since it preaches independence from the authority of the Church. It was inevitable that the youth movement would be opposed by the Catholic Church because it represents a revolt against the norms and values that have been basic to society for thousands of years . . . .[8]

This statement undoubtedly articulated the true feelings of an overwhelming majority of Catholic youth. After all, they had more secure roots than the predominantly Protestant youth who filled the ranks of Bündische Youth. They had, as it were, their own self-contained society within a society, whose definite and established attitudes and practices on a whole range of different aspects of life were a source of certainty and strength. This made Catholic youth resilient and largely immune to the profound discontents in other sections of the younger generation in Weimar Germany. Only a small minority of Catholic youth felt the need to break out of the ghetto mentality in the search for a new meaning to life, bound up in a synthesis of Bündische ideals and Catholicism. The Quickborn group led the way in this venture, and successfully achieved a position that was at the same time independent and critical, and yet part of the Church.

Founded by a priest, Dr Bernhard Strehler, with the assistance of two other colleagues, Fathers Klemens Neumann and Hermann Hoffmann, in Neisse (Silesia) in 1909, the Secondary Schoolboys' Circle (*Gymnasiantenzirkel*), as the group was somewhat anonymously known until the name 'Quickborn' was adopted in 1917, was dedicated more than anything else to promoting the cause of abstinence from alcohol. Development of the group was initially quite slow, but after the war considerable progress began to be made, and by 1921 it had 6500 male and female members organised in over 500 branches throughout Germany, but especially in the traditionally Catholic west and south.[9] A decisive fillip was given to Quickborn's self-confidence by the acquisition in 1919 of Burg Rothenfels, which is situated on the Main and became the focal point of the group's organisational and intellectual activity.[10] Although Quickborn had in its early days revealed a tentative awareness of the Wandervogel, it was not until after 1918 that it began systematically to adopt and cultivate many of the ideas and methods of the independent youth movement. The externals of the Wandervogel, including the peculiar jargon and cult of the mystical, were the first elements to be assimilated into Quickborn life. The heritage of the Catholic Middle Ages — mystery plays, religious folk-songs, rituals and ceremonial — was exploited by the group to create an atmosphere analogous to that prevailing in Bündische organisations.[11] Each of the three priests involved in the leadership contributed his own particular facet to Quickborn's activities: Hoffmann promoted trips and expeditions and indeed anything else which he felt would transform the group into a fully fledged part of the independent youth movement; Neumann encouraged the practice of singing, while Strehler infused an emotional, lively piety which was quite uncharacteristic of German Catholicism in that period. While by no means neglecting the original objectives of combating alcoholism and of serving Christ, Quickborn was guided by Strehler towards a socially critical awareness, which as expected met with disapproval from the Church.[12]

Despite Strehler's position as official leader in the early 1920s, the personality whose influence and charisma dominated Quickborn was the BerlinUniversity professor Romano Guardini. As writer, theologian, and philosopher, Guardini established himself as one of the outstanding figures of the entire Weimar youth scene. His ideas had a powerful impact not only on Quickborn and the rest of the Catholic youth movement, but also on the Church and, indeed, other spheres of secular intellectual life in Weimar Germany.[13] He was determined to bring Quickborn as close to Bündische Youth as possible without endangering its spiritual and religious idealism, and, in the face of substantial opposition from the Church, he achieved this objective.[14] Guardini was attracted by the concept of youth autonomy, the elimination of outside adult interference in the everyday affairs of organised youth, but at the same time he recognised that youth's independence should not assume exaggerated dimensions, as in some sections of Bündische Youth. He enunciated what he called the proper limits to the realm of youth; hence, humility, obedience and respect for authority were fundamental to his outlook. Within Quickborn and other Catholic youth groups which assimilated the spirit of Bündische Youth, this meant in practice that youthful leaders organised the daily routine and activities of their groups while being able to call upon or listen to the advice of parents, teachers and priests. More importantly, Guardini emphasised that members of Quickborn were Catholics first and youth-movement followers only second, and demanded that this scale of priorities be accepted without demur by the group.[15] He even made this point in a well-known public debate with Max Bondy, a member of Free German Youth in 1921, though he also stressed that there was a good deal of common ground between Catholic groups such as Quickborn and the independent youth movement.[16] Guardini certainly ensured that Quickborn was both intellectually and spiritually progressive by contemporary Catholic standards while maintaining a certain distance from total identification with Bündische Youth. In a sense, therefore, the group occupied a no man's land, a limbo between two contrasting types of youth cultures, yet this hybrid position did nothing to impair its creativity or vitality.

Largely under Guardini's guidance, Quickborn helped to evolve new forms of divine service and injected its modernist perspectives into the liturgical movement within the Church. New-style hymns came into wide use as a direct consequence of Quickborn's initiative, and altogether the group could claim to have noticeably increased the richness and meaning of religious experience for youth and adults alike. Furthermore, in the sphere of adult education Quickborn made a special mark. It founded its own adult-education college and encouraged its members to become teachers in this branch of education. Heinrich Kahlefeld and Felix Messerschmid, both former Quickborn members, gained prominence through their work in this field, and Guardini himself exerted a direct and considerable influence.[17]

The development of Quickborn during the 1920s was by no means free of strife. In addition to the pressures emanating from a suspicious and at times openly hostile Church hierarchy were those from sectional interests within the group itself. Notwithstanding its relatively small size, Quickborn embraced several different schools of thought alongside the mainstream led by Guardini. In an organisation as intellectually fertile and as socially diversified as Quickborn, a variety of attitudes on important matters were to be expected, and these were reflected by informal groups ranging from a pacifist circle around Lorenz Fischer to a small *völkisch* clique.[18] In these circumstances, Quickborn unavoidably suffered from a series of secessions, notably in 1925, when outspokenly pro-Bündische members numbering a few thousand split off to form their own group. None the less, when Guardini formally took over as leader of a reformed Quickborn in 1927, a greater degree of organisational and ideological uniformity was imposed, and it continued as a viable and influential unit of some 6000 members in the Catholic youth sector.

Quickborn's status as a kind of Catholic Bündische group was shared, if not quite as illustriously or to the same extent, by a number of other organisations which had solid links with the Church. The most prominent of these were Grossdeutsche Jugend (Greater German Youth); Neudeutschland, Verband katholischer Schüler höherer Lehranstalten (New Germany, League of Catholic Students); Schar der Normannsteiner; Deutsche Pfadfinderschaft St Georg, a Boy Scout troop; Katholische Wandervogel; Kreuzfahrer (Crusaders), wandernde katholische Volksjugend;[19] Jungborn, katholische abstinente Jugend der Werktätigen;[20] and Die Sturmschar. The Grossdeutsche Jugend, set up in 1915 and led by Nikolaus Ehlen, upheld the Franciscan ideals of brotherly love and simplicity, and from this developed a wide-ranging solicitude for the socially deprived as well as a deep commitment to pacifism.[21] In contrast, the much larger Neudeutschland (21,000 members, as opposed to the Grossdeutsche Jugend's 1200 in 1929), an overwhelmingly middle-class group, was from its creation in 1919 by the Archbishop of Cologne, Cardinal Felix von Hartmann, under Jesuit influence, and consequently was more concerned with the rational and intellectual side of Catholic religious life.[22] Its acceptance of Bündische ideals was set out in the 1923 Hirschberg Programme, which proclaimed, 'our goal is the new life-style with Christ', and Neudeutschland's leader from 1921, Johannes Zender, successfully copied Guardini's method of amalgamating Catholic and Bündische principles.[23] Also success-ful on a more modest scale was the Deutsche Pfadfinderschaft St Georg, an amalgam dating from 1929 of several Catholic Boy Scout groups which had sprung up in Wuppertal and Beuthen only the previous year. The militaristic tradition of the German Boy Scout movement and its association with a nationalist, Protestant ethos ensured that its popularity in Catholic areas would always be modest. The St Georg group, ably led by Willi Werner, increased its membership from 2000 in 1931 to some 9000 two years later, but its strong attachment to Catholicism meant that it never formed part of the mainstream Scout development.[24] Altogether, these Catholic groups which claimed Bündische affiliation had a combined mem-bership before 1933 of only 55,000−60,000, an insignificant fraction of organised Catholic youth as a whole.

In 1921 a huge cover organisation, the Katholische Jugend Deutschlands (KJD), was established by the indefatigable Carl Mosterts for all church-sponsored youth groups, and by 1933 there were twenty-eight individual groups, representing 1.5 million youths.[25] The corresponding girls' organisation, the Zentralverband der katholischen Jungfrauenvereinigungen Deutschlands (Central Association of Catholic Girls' Groups of Germany), had 767,000 members.[26] The largest single Catholic youth group was, of course, the VKJJVD with 387,000 members in 1930. When Mosterts died in 1926 it was led by Father Ludwig Wolker, who in 1930 agreed to its being renamed the Katholische Jungmännerverband Deutschlands (Catholic Young Men's Association of Germany − KJMV). The KJMV intensified its religious, educational and charitable work during the early 1930s and was undeniably the major bastion of the

Catholic youth movement. At the same time, the KJMV was constrained by developments in the Weimar Republic to take a political stand.

From the late 1920s politics began to be openly discussed in Catholic Youth periodicals, including the KJMV's *Stimmen der Jugend*. In 1930 the editor of this journal, Georg Wagner, published a comprehensive review of the political views of Catholic youth. It was shown that most of them rejected liberalism and the parliamentary party system.[27] Like the German Catholic community in general at that time, Catholic youth was moving perceptibly to the right, and the idea of a future Greater German Reich was widely favoured. Anti-semitism, albeit of a religious type, also began to rear its head more insistently than before. Certainly, disillusionment with the Republic was rampant among Catholic youth. At its annual convention in Trier in 1931, however, the KJMV stressed that its political attitudes were formulated 'according to the principles of Catholic philosophy, free from party political connections'.[28] Catholic youth as a whole emphatically rejected the totalitarian doctrines of the extreme left and right and relatively few of them joined either the National Socialist or Communist movements. The Church made plain the incompatibility between its Christian teaching and the doctrines of National Socialism and Marxism, and its spokesmen repeatedly advised Catholics not to support the extremist parties in national and local elections.[29] This was good enough for the Catholic youth groups, whose officials and publications combined vigorously to condemn both Hitler and Thälmann, the Communist leader. With the economic depression and political instability continuing to turn Catholic youth away from liberalism, the highpoint of the Weimar crisis in 1932/3 saw them falling into line behind the Church in supporting the then only nominally democratic Centre Party and Bavarian People's Party.[30]

It was perhaps too much to expect that the Catholic youth groups would display much political maturity during the last years of Weimar. After all, they were non-political and their training was far removed from the world of politics. Their decisive and worthwhile contribution came through their finely developed social, religious and cultural perceptions, for which the balanced, intelligent sponsorship of the Church is due considerable credit. The success of the Catholic youth movement in these fields is as incontestable as its political unawareness. Yet Catholic youth can hardly be held responsible in any real measure for the collapse of the democratic order and the ascent of National Socialism. The burden of political failure, however, was weightier among their Protestant counterparts. There was not nearly as much drive on the Protestant side to organise youth. Whereas 32 per cent of Catholic youth aged between fourteen and twenty-five years were in a church-sponsored youth group, only 7 per cent of the corresponding Protestant youth were in a similar position.[31] The various Protestant churches were reluctant before 1918 to become involved in the organisation of youth. For one thing, they were not under the same political and social pressure as the Catholic Church. They were closely aligned to the ruling House of Hohenzollern and clearly constituted a branch of the Establishment. In his struggle with the Catholics, Bismarck had laid the basis for the view that the Second Reich was Protestant. Comfortably ensconced in this throne-altar alliance and representing the dominant majority, the Protestant leadership felt little need actively to encourage youth groups of their own. This changed, of course, when the authoritarian and Prussian edifice of which the Protestant Church was an important part collapsed, amidst the loss of the First World War and the November Revolution.

Protestant youth groups before 1918 did appear independent of the churches, though not usually of individual pastors, and were all under adult supervision. The first noteworthy gathering of loosely orga-nised Protestant groups took place in 1882 at the Hermann Monument in the Teutoburger Forest, which led directly the following year to the formation of the Christlicher Verein Junger Männer in Berlin by Friedrich von Schlümbach. This associa-tion was in fact the German equivalent of the popular American-based Young Men's Christian Association and similarly aimed to foster missionary and social work among youth.[32] The same year a schoolboys' Bible-study group (*Schüler-Bibelkränzchen*) was founded in Elberfeld by Pastor Fritz Mockert and Willi Weigle, a student. Renamed the Bibelkreise in 1915, this group adopted some of the Wandervogel's external forms, such as camping and hiking, without considering itself at that stage part of the independent youth movement. Another Protestant group which later also affected Bündische pretensions was the Bund deutscher Jugendvereine (League of German Youth Associations – BDJ), established in Halle in 1909 though originating from a small circle created in Hamburg in 1896 by Pastor Clemens Schultz.[33] It was principally interested in social and religious work among the community at large, but particularly among young workers and apprentices. Oriented more towards middle-class youth was the Christliche Pfadfinderschaft Deutschlands (Christian Boy Scout Movement of Germany), which, while fully accepting the nationalist – military outlook of the German Scouts before the war, also attempted to bring a degree of Christian idealism into its work. Founded in 1910, this movement was strong in Württemberg and Saxony.[34]

All these groups arose as part of the spiritual revival taking place in Protestant churches during the latter part of the nineteenth century, in which pietist and reformative impulses were predominant. They emerged in response also to the needs of youth in a rapidly changing world in which the onset of industrialisation caused profound problems. In some youth groups the pietist–missionary momentum was uppermost; in others the social–charitable element took precedence. Initially drawing most of its members from the lower middle and artisan classes, the youth groups were also able towards the end of the century to attract increasing support from both the propertied bourgeoisie and the proletariat. By 1914, however, middle-class values dictated the life-style of a majority of groups, with strong emphasis on prayer meetings, educational courses, lectures, and weekend trips and excursions into the countryside.[35] A similar trend was evident among the female youth associations which appeared during the second half of the nineteenth century. Indeed, as early as 1893 a central cover organisation for them was created, the Evangelischer Reichsverband weiblicher Jugend (Protestant Reich Association of Female Youth – ERVWJ). One of the best-known female groups was Guida Diehl's Neuland Movement, which was set up in 1908 and originally dedicated to religious work. It later gained notoriety by becoming one of the first Protestant youth groups openly to sympathise with National Socialism.[36]

The First World War acted as a catalyst in the history of the Protestant youth movement. When the older leaders and members of the groups went off to fight, younger elements came into their own and soon began questioning traditional forms and practices, and even aims.[37] More and more the younger members showed a preference for adopting the style of the independent youth movement, including the ideas of youth autonomy. The political upheavals of 1918–19, which were a traumatic experience for Protestant Germany in particular, brought further tensions between conservative and progressive factions in the youth groups. Breaking-point was often reached, resulting during the early post-war years not only in secessions of younger from older members and the creation of entirely new groups, such as the Bund der Köngener and Bund Christdeutscher Jugend, but also in the direct intervention of the Church leadership in the youth sector for the first time. All these events made for a rather chaotic period for Protestant youth, reflecting of course the deep troubles disrupting the Protestant community at large as it strove to come to terms with a State whose main supporters were the former *Reichsfeinde* (enemies of the Reich), socialists, liberals and Catholics. The concern of the Protestant Church leadership to reorganise its religious and secular activities led it to sponsor a new umbrella association for Protestant youth groups, the Reichsverband der evangelischen Jungmännerbünde Deutschlands (Reich Association of Protestant Young Men's Leagues of Germany), which was founded in Kassel in 1921 under the leadership of a Berlin cleric, Dr Erich Stange. By 1932 it had 265,000 members, compared with 304,000 in the equivalent girls' association, the ERVWJ. Separate from both these associations and often in direct opposition to the ecclesiastical authorities were those Protestant groups which after 1919 accepted the ideals of the independent youth movement. They consequently made up the most interesting and vital section of the Protestant youth movement in the Weimar era.

Attracted to these groups were youths whose questions about the meaning of life and the place of Christian ideals the Protestant churches found difficult to answer. The war had made a deep impression on the wider spiritual perceptions of many Protestant youths. The experience and camaraderie of the trenches had awakened interest in developing a Christian-based national community, while the horrific casualties and suffering involved in the conflict demanded from them a more concrete and realistic relationship to their faith. For some Protestant youths this entailed the adoption of a radical religious outlook which did not fit easily into the thinking patterns of their churches. The problems besetting these youths were debated in lively fashion at countless meetings and conferences during the immediate post-war period and from this source emerged the momentum for the creation of a new type of youth group, which tried to capture the mood of nonconformist Protestant youth. The theme of a celebrated meeting of Protestant academics at Hoheneck (Bavaria) in 1922, 'Renewal of the Church through the Spirit of the Youth Movement', became the guiding principle for them, emphasising the authentic spirit of religiosity in their outlook.[38] As one of their spokesmen, Heinz Dietrich

Wendland, explained, 'the youth movement is inspired by a yearning for the infinite, for the eternal'.[39]

The group most closely identified with the incursion of independent youth movement ideas into Protestant youth was the Bibelkreise, renamed Bund deutscher Bibelkreise (BK) in 1928. From it developed a number of similarly disposed groups in the 1920s, including the Bund der Köngener, but, more importantly, the BK's particular interpretation of the Protestant—Bündische fusion was very influential in this sector of Protestant youth. Latterly led by Pastor Udo Smidt (1930—4), it had about 16,500 members in the mid-1920s and 20,000 in 1933, most of whom were middle-class schoolboys, and was strongest in Berlin, Westphalia and the Rhineland.[40] The Bund der Köngener[41] was set up by the secessionist Württemberg branch of the BK after deciding that it wanted to be free of the pietistic Methodism of the parent body and to develop a deeper attachment to Bündische ideals.[42] Led by Professor Jacob Wilhelm Hauer, who later gained notoriety as head of the pro-Nazi German Faith Movement, the Köngener established branches in several areas, but the bulk of its bourgeois student and schoolboy membership of 700 was located in Swabia, where Eberhard 'Tusk' Köbel was one of its local leaders.[43] From 1927 to 1930 the group was an affiliated member of the Deutsche Freischar, the prominent Bündische organisation.[44]

The only Protestant youth personality who rivalled in any meaningful way the influence and stature of Guardini was Professor Wilhelm Stählin, whose primary involvement from 1922 onwards was with the BDJ, which had over 20,000 members. His aim was to build a free people's church (*Volkskirche*) and a Christian national community, thus continuing the populist appeal of the BDJ's founder, Clemens Schultz. The group had already committed itself to the principles of the independent youth movement in its Magdeburg Declaration of 1919, but Stählin was determined to strike a balance between this orientation and Christian principles in a way which would strengthen its standing among the mainly lower-middle-class and proletarian membership.[45] He was convinced that the broad mass of less privileged youth who had been alienated for so long from what they regarded as a bourgeois church would not be tempted to re-enter its fellowship through pietism and revivalism. Instead, a strong social commitment on the part of the Church was the only way forward, he believed. The BDJ followed this path, and its synthesis of popular socialism and Christianity afforded it a distinctive image which in the early 1930s was sustained by the considerable practical aid given by the group to unemployed young workers.[46]

The Bund Christdeutscher Jugend, founded in 1921 and renamed Christdeutscher Bund in 1927, drew most of its support from the same social categories as the Bund der Köngener and aimed ultimately for a non-denominational, reformed Christianity within a Bündische-style corporative State structure. But its self-conscious elitism, which was encouraged by its leader, Pastor Leopold Cordier, and its liking for abstract theological discussion kept membership down to about 1500 and severely curtailed the group's influence on other Protestant youth.[47] In contrast, the Jugendbund für entschiedenes Christentum (Youth League for Fundamental Christianity), which dated from 1894, exerted a wide appeal, especially in eastern Germany, and had attracted 60,000 members by 1932. Most of these came from a small farming, lower-middle-class or proletarian background.[48] There was a heavy pietistic stress on prayer and religious services, while sporting and educational activities were explicitly repudiated. As one leader put it in 1925, 'We are concerned with questions relating to a lively, fundamental Christianity . . . we desire sincere conversion to God. We are the only Christian youth movement which knows nothing but the Bible, the Bible, and yet again the Bible.'[49] With such an ascetic and uncompromising outlook, the group's popularity is rather incomprehensible, although its very down-to-earth fundamentalism was bound to elicit a response from a certain Protestant mentality which exults in such puritanical zeal.

The pro-Bündische Protestant groups and Church-dominated groups shared several characteristics in the early 1930s which transcended whatever ideological differences separated them. A strong spirit of nationalism and militarism permeated their organisational structures and activities and they recorded a large increase in their memberships[50] – a consequence of the acute anxieties experienced by Protestant youth amidst political and economic collapse in Weimar Germany. Above all, however, the Protestant groups shared a serious political myopia which had catastrophic repercussions for them and the rest of Germany.

The political attitudes of Protestant youth clearly and unmistakably reflected those of their parents and elders. The NSDAP came to power with the support principally of middle-class Protestant Germans, the social background from which most members of the

Protestant youth groups came. These groups accepted the nationalist, anti-democratic, and anti-semitic outlook of the Protestant
Mittelstand. It is interesting to note that before 1933 the Hitler Youth
was much more successful in attracting recruits from Protestant
youth groups than from Catholic ones, and Protestant youth
displayed a far greater susceptibility to National Socialist ideas than
did the Catholics. On the other hand, it is undeniable that virtually all
shades of political opinion were to be found among the Protestant
groups. Moreover, a distinction has to be made between their leaders
and ordinary members; whereas the former tended to look upon
Hitler with scepticism, the latter, who were younger, showed no such
inhibitions.

The Bibelkreise was especially known for its favourable stance
vis-à-vis National Socialism. It tended to admire old-fashioned
Prussianism, discipline, and the concept of a Greater German Reich,
and developed in the first instance strong bonds with right-wing
organisations such as the German National People's Party
(Deutschnationale Volkspartei – DNVP) and Stahlhelm before
coming out in support of Hitler. In 1930 one observer calculated that
70 per cent of BK members were inclined towards National
Socialism, a point not disputed by its leader, Udo Smidt, and many of
them counted as 'Old Fighters' of the party.[51] Other groups, such as
the Christdeutscher Bund and BDJ, though supporting the patriotic
claims of National Socialism, refused to become involved in party
politics like Bündische Youth, and adopted a stance of friendly
neutrality.[52] None the less, almost all parts of the Protestant youth
movement, including the Christdeutscher Bund and BDJ, enthusiastically acclaimed Hitler's assumption of power and issued
passionate declarations of loyalty to the Third Reich, as many official
Protestant spokesmen did. Particularly reprehensible because of the
influence they were bound to exert on the minds of young Protestants
were the brazenly pro-Hitler sentiments of a small minority of
Protestant churchmen.[53] They welcomed Hitler's aim of destroying
the Weimar Republic and its parliamentary system and establishing
in its place an authoritarian Reich dedicated to extirpating 'godless'
Marxism and democracy. It is little wonder, therefore, that Protestant
youth generally failed to develop a positive individualistic attitude to
the realities of pluralist society.[54] They fell back instead on the old
traditions to solve their problems: a euphoric nationalism, an inherent
belief in the mystical qualities of the German *Volk*, and an emotional
anti-intellectualism. Unwittingly, this outlook simply paved the way

for their own eventual destruction. The responsibility of Protestant youth for Hitler is naturally subject to the qualification that the primary blame lies with their tragically misguided elders.

The decline of the Weimar Republic and the concomitant ascent of National Socialism were of special significance for the Jewish community in Germany, and materially shaped the development and character of the Jewish youth movement. The position of Jews in German society underwent considerable change from the time full emancipation was granted in the mid-nineteenth century until the advent of National Socialism. During this period the emphasis in the German–Jewish symbiosis switched from assimilationism to Zionism and the idea of emigration to Palestine. Within the half million or so German Jews many different strands of political and religious thought and affiliation were present. This degree of fragmentation was equally characteristic of the Jewish youth move- ment, whose evolution cannot be separated from the history of German–Jewish relations or from the manifold pressures which were brought to bear on the situation, especially after 1918. The complex historical environment in which it was born and in which it grew to maturity consistently imposed constraints of a peculiar kind on the course of the Jewish youth movement, as did the very heterogeneity of Jewish life and culture itself. Most obviously, this produced a youth movement which was as diversified as the independent German youth movement. Alongside the long-standing assimilationist and religious groups came youth organisations dedicated to Zionism and socialism. The majority of groups were non-religious and tended to be organised along ethnic lines. Ideological differences were, there- fore, compounded by differences in the sociological composition of memberships, thus separating bourgeois from proletarian groups. Once the enormity of the National Socialist threat had been appreciated, these elements of discord became much less important in the experience of Jewish youth groups, as most of them came to realise that the Third Reich did not offer a choice between meaningful assimilation and emigration.

The first phase in the history of the Jewish youth movement during the latter part of the nineteenth century was marked by the emergence of several groups independent of adult control and strongly impressed by the example of the Wandervogel.[55] In fact, the influence of the independent German youth movement on its Jewish counterpart was significant and positive right up until 1933. The independent Jewish groups came into existence alongside established adult-sponsored youth and student associations which had appeared in Breslau in 1886, Heidelberg in 1890 and Berlin in 1892—3 largely in response to the rising tide of anti-semitism and to the decline in liberalism.[56] These events convinced many Jews that the Establishment was resolved to block the full integration of the Jewish community into German society. Organisational activity was thought to offer the best way of enabling Jews to claim their civic rights in full. Assimilationists were against outspokenly Jewish groups which took delight in proclaiming their Jewishness, while Zionist circles took the opposite view, arguing that Jewish youth should have their own organisational identity and rejecting the proposition that the Jewish struggle be conducted within and not intrinsically against German society.

Adult-sponsored youth groups were set up with increasing regularity during the next couple of decades, particularly in Stuttgart, Frankfurt am Main, and Hamburg, and in 1909 Dr Alfred Apfel, a Berlin lawyer, founded a cover organisation, the Verband der Jüdischen Jugendvereine Deutschlands (Association of Jewish Youth Societies of Germany – VJJVD), which by 1913 had 14,500 members belonging to no fewer than 113 affiliated groups.[57] The VJJVD was a youth-tutelage association whose creation owed much to a Jewish masonic lodge, the United Order B'nai B'rith, which believed there was a need for youth clubs to cater for young Jewish commercial employees who often found themselves away from home on business. Although strictly neutral as far as politics was concerned, the VJJVD possessed a powerful liberal and humanitarian flavour and was anti-Zionist before 1914.[58] Not until the VJJVD was well-established did the first independent Jewish youth groups make their appearance, led by the Biau-Weiss, Bund für jüdisches Jugendwandern (Blue-White, League for Jewish Youth Excursions). Set up in Breslau in 1912 by Joseph Marcus, it was initially the youth section of the Jüdische Wanderbund 1907, but very quickly became completely self-sufficient. Branches of Blau-Weiss followed in Berlin, Vienna, Mulhouse and Munich, boosting its membership to about 900 by 1914. The name 'Blau-Weiss' was formally adopted the same year, and Dr Adalbert Sachs, a co-founder of the Berlin branch, was elected leader.[59] Like the Wandervogel, the group rejected bourgeois society and its stiff conventions as well as urban civilisation and materialism. Other ideas and outer forms were also eagerly adopted from the independent German youth movement, including the practice of publishing a monthly periodical, *Blau-Weiss Blätter*, which was edited by Felix Rosenblüth.[60] But Blau-Weiss was also something more than this. It opposed the assimilationist outlook of the older generation, who had prospered since emancipation and who therefore sought to protect and preserve their stake in German society. The members of Blau-Weiss had little sympathy for the liberal and rational world of their parents and instead sought a new set of spiritual and cultural values rooted in their Jewishness. In this respect it emerged in the early phase of its development as a kind of Zionist Wandervogel – that is, cultivating its Jewishness within a Wandervogel framework. Blau-Weiss thus evolved new terms of reference for Jewish youth stung by anti-semitism into rediscovering intrinsic Jewish values. The mystical–philosophical ideas of Martin Buber were also of crucial importance to this quest. Particularly in his thesis of the 'primacy of Judaism', Jewish youth found the answer to the problematical German–Jewish duality.[61]

In seeking to blaze a new trail, Blau-Weiss inevitably met with stout opposition from liberal and orthodox Jewish circles, headed by the pro-assimilationist Central-Verein deutscher Staatsbürger jüdischen Glaubens (Central Society of German Citizens of the Jewish Faith) and also parents, who disliked, apart from anything else, the notion of their sons and daughters tramping about unsupervised in the countryside.[62] Despite these obstacles, the Blau-Weiss example was copied in 1916 by small and loosely structured units of what materialised after the war as the Esra and Kameraden youth groups.[63] The numbers engaged during this early period in the independent Jewish youth movement were patently limited, but at least the foundations had been laid for vigorous expansion after 1918.

Both the VJJVD and the independent groups had arisen basically from the uneasiness of Jewish youth in being confronted by a conflict between their Germanness and Jewishness, and from a search for their own fundamental identity in a period of accelerating crisis. To this desire for inner harmony and self-identification the VJJVD postulated the ideal of a synthesis and a compromise. It produced a rational formula based on the experience of Jewish liberal values. Blau-Weiss, on the other hand, offered a radically different solution to the problem, arguing that the ultimate objective of stimulating Jewish consciousness could only be realised through understanding the German *Volk* and then transporting its ideals to Jews.[64] In other words, by applying the principles of the Wandervogel, Blau-Weiss sought to transform assimilationist Jewish youth into conscious Jews. The whole problematical situation was clarified to a certain extent by the experience of the war years, 1914–18.

The war had a decisive impact on the Jewish youth movement, as it did on the Wandervogel and Free German Youth, though in quite different ways. Many Jews joined the German armed forces, often as volunteers, and appeared as patriotic as anyone. A Blau-Weiss member, Karl Glaser, wrote revealingly that 'we know our love of the Jewish people does not contradict our love of the German Fatherland'.[65] None the less, the war had the overall effect of engendering a Jewish Renaissance among the same Jewish youths who marched off into battle for Kaiser and Fatherland. This transformation can be accounted for in several ways. In the first instance, many of these youths were deeply disillusioned by the degree of bitter anti-semitism they came across among their German comrades at the front, leading them to the conclusion that when the war was ended they would be unable to co-exist with the Germans in a true bond of community. Jewish youth came to believe in the necessity of having a full community in which they and their ideals would be allowed unfettered expression. If this was impossible to achieve in partnership with the Germans, then, so they reasoned, it would have to be an exclusively Jewish community. The assimilationist ethos no longer seemed appropriate for many youths. The Jews also witnessed the example of small nations, such as those in Eastern Europe, achieving freedom and national sovereignty in 1918–19, and wondered why they, also a small national entity, should not achieve as much. The meeting with Jews of Eastern Europe and seeing first-hand evidence of the suffering and humiliation heaped upon them strengthened the growing conviction of many German Jews that their future lay in having their own homeland outside Germany. The Balfour Declaration of 1917, coupled with the despair felt by German Jews at the end of the war, gave further impetus to the drive for Jewish values.[66] In political terms these changes in Jewish thinking were forcefully articulated in Zionism, which after 1918 became a major influence, especially in the Jewish youth movement.

The end of the war saw a new sober and self-critical atmosphere pervading the Jewish youth groups. Blau-Weiss had even begun to forsake its quasi-romantic outlook in 1916 following a crucial national conference in Lochwitz, and by 1918, when it had nearly 3000 members, it had adopted a Zionist orientation with the practical aim of establishing settlements in Palestine.[67] Many prominent leaders of the pre-war era, such as Rosenblüth and Moses Calvary, consequently withdrew from the group. Under the energetic leadership of Walter Moses, Blau-Weiss, which was now strongest in Berlin, Strasbourg and Munich,[68] set up agricultural and artisan vocational centres to train members for their life in Palestine.[69] The influence of the Wandervogel was not totally eliminated, however, as was shown in parts of Blau-Weiss's Prunner Basic Law (*Grundgesetz*), which was promulgated in 1922. The group's elitism, its explicit rejection of East European Jews and the Palestinian working class, led to its eventual isolation in the Jewish community, however, and the complete failure of its settlement projects in 1925. A year later, Blau-Weiss disintegrated altogether.[70] Other groups were also by then, of course, pursuing Zionist aims, including, sooner or later during the 1920s and early 1930s, the Jung-jüdischer Wanderbund, as defined in its 1922 Frankenberger Formula; Kadimah, Ring jüdischer Wander- und Pfadfinderbünde (Kadimah, Circle of Jewish Hiking and Boy Scout Associations); Zofim; Brith Haolim;[71] and Hapoel Hazair. The last two groups also injected a radical socialist idealism into their Zionism.[72] The settlement movement was significantly boosted among these youth groups when in 1922 a German branch of the Hechaluz (Pioneer) was created in Berlin. It was Zionist, working-class and socialist, and set up gardening and agricultural training centres throughout Germany to train recruits for work in Palestinian kibbutzim.[73]

A large number of Jewish youth groups did not immediately follow the Zionist path. Esra was formally constituted in 1918 by Jewish orthodox circles as a consciously anti-Zionist association, and the Reichsverband der Kameraden, Verband jüdischer Wander-Sport und Turnvereine (Reich Association of Comrades, Association of Jewish Hiking, Sport and Gymnastic Associations), formed in 1919, not only acknowledged the Meissner Formula but also pronounced allegiance to the German Fatherland and German national values. It regarded itself as primarily a German and not a Jewish group.[74] It had 1500 members in 1930. The Deutsch-Jüdische Jugend-Gemeinschaft, led by Ludwig Tietz, was founded by the Central-Verein to counter-balance the independently-minded Kameraden, though it too was pro-assimilationist. In due course, however, it also went its own way.[75] The VJJVD suffered a drastic decline in membership during the war, when the eighteen to twenty-five year olds, who were in a majority, were drafted for military service. After 1918 the association was caught up in the wide-ranging debates in Jewish youth circles, but refused to be drawn beyond a continuing devotion to religious and social tasks. Consequently, it lost the support of both the Central-Verein and the Zionists, and its 41,000 membership, which made it the largest Jewish youth group in 1918, dropped off alarmingly until it almost broke up. A shadow organisation limped along for a few years until the association made a remarkable comeback in the late 1920s, primarily as a forum for modernist educational ideas. A second period of decline began in 1930 and membership was reduced to a record low of 6400 four years later. Only then did the VJJVD commit itself to Zionism.[76]

The advance of Zionism and socialism significantly broadened the social basis of the Jewish youth movement. The Blau-Weiss and others recruited in the main from the middle classes, but in the 1920s with the proliferation of pioneer-oriented socialist groups lower-class youths of East European parentage began to join in large numbers.[77] For them the ideals of Bündische Youth meant little, though in all Jewish groups the concept of the group (*Bund*) was accepted and given a Jewish connotation – the creation of a 'new man' who was Jewish.[78]

Jewish youth groups of all shades were grouped under the umbrella Reichsausschuss der jüdischen Jugendverbände (Reich Committee of Jewish Youth Groups – RAJJV) which was established in 1924 with some 30,000 members organised in eleven affiliated groups – almost one third of the total number of Jewish youths in Germany at that time.[79] When Ludwig Tietz became chairman in 1927, the RAJJV began to fulfil a useful co-ordinating function in the Jewish youth movement. A handful of pro-Bündische groups, such as Kameraden, and embracing only 5000 members, were affiliated to the co-ordinating agency for the German youth movement, the Reichsausschuss der deutschen Jugendverbände.[80]

If the 1920s had seen a decisive penetration of Zionist and socialist concepts into the Jewish youth groups, albeit in a non-party political form, the early 1930s witnessed the ascendancy of these concepts and their prosecution with greater enthusiasm than ever before. Many groups previously assimilationist in outlook now had a change of heart and joined the Zionist camp: the most striking example is offered by the Kameraden. In 1932 a small communist element split off to form the Freie deutsch-jüdische Jugend, and an intransigently assimilationist faction grouped in the Schwarze Fähnlein, the nucleus of Hans-Joachim Schoeps's Deutscher Vortrupp, Gefolgschaft deutscher Juden (German Vanguard, German Jewish Followers).[81] The majority of Kameraden, strongly influenced by Buber's philosophy and led by Hermann Gerson, reformed as the 1000-strong Werkleute, Bund deutsch-jüdischer Jugend (Craftsmen, League of German Jewish Youth), which soon promoted emigration to Palestine.[82] Most of its members came from wealthy, *Haute-bourgeois* backgrounds, thus indicating that Zionism had reached into the full spectrum of the Jewish social structure by 1933. Another group unable to bear up under this onslaught was Esra, which collapsed in 1932 when its large Zionist following joined the Brith Hanoar group. With the extreme leftist and assimilationist streams of the youth movement now reduced to virtual impotence, the Zionist-settlement supporters were left to dictate its character and activities. This turn of events stood in stark contrast, of course, to the consensus of opinion among adult German Jews, who, underestimating the strength of National Socialism, steadfastly clung to an assimilationist philosophy.

The National Socialist *Machtergreifung* (seizure of power) inaugurated the final chapter in the history of the Jewish youth movement, as it did for German Jewry at large. In 1933 there were ninety-seven individual Jewish youth groups, which were not subject to the wholesale dissolution of other youth organisations by the Hitler Youth. But there was a spontaneous coming together in the Jewish community, which resulted, first, in a reduction in the number of youth groups through the process of amalgamation, particularly among Zionist groups, and, secondly, in an overall increase in their memberships.[83] After 1933, German Jews developed a new, revitalised self-awareness of being Jews, and observance of religious festivals, for example, steeply increased. Those who insisted on emphasising their German rather than their Jewish identity dramatically declined in number. In the youth movement they now concentrated in a few groups such as the Bund deutsch-jüdischer Jugend, with 5000 members the largest non-Zionist group, led by Martin Sobotker; and Schoeps's Vortrupp, the most active.[84] Schoeps preached a combination of conservative Prussianism and co-operative German Jewishness under the slogan 'Bereit für Deutschland' (Ready for Germany), and aimed to attract those members of dissolved German youth groups who were Jewish, and thus on racial grounds not permitted to join the Hitler Youth.[85] In rejecting both Marxism and western democracy, Schoeps sought to provide a third way between the Zionists and the liberal Jewish establishment by postulating a fusion of *völkisch* Germanness and existential Judaism. In this rather far-fetched quest he received support from organisations such as the Reichsbund jüdischer Frontsoldaten (Reich League of Jewish Front-line Soldiers), but he made little headway with the National Socialist regime.[86]

For a time after 1933, all Jewish youth groups were able to go about their business relatively unhindered, and the Hitler Youth maintained its overlordship through liaising with the RAJJV, which it formally recognised. While trips and camping expeditions went on until about 1937, the emphasis in Jewish youth work lay in the preparation and despatching of members to settlements in Palestine.[87] The youth groups performed in this regard an important role in saving thousands from the terrible fate which lay ahead at the hands of the Third Reich, but at the same time they effectively ceased being a 'youth movement' in the accepted sense of the word. The youthful energy and idealism of the groups were also a source of comfort and inspiration for the Jewish community as a whole as it became more and more isolated from the mainstream of German life. Following the promulgation of the Nuremberg racial laws in 1935, the pressures on German Jews augmented until reaching a climax in the pogroms of November 1938 (*Kristallnacht*). At that point, all Jewish youth groups except the Hechaluz were banned and dissolved. Many members had already left for Palestine by then. For the unfortunate who stayed behind there was the option of organising underground resistance to the regime, as the Herbert Baum circle did,[88] or of simply waiting for further degradation and finally extermination.

The Jewish youth movement played a major part in reversing the process of assimilation in German Jewry and moulding a concrete alternative, the settlement movement to Palestine. It was an astonishing achievement, helped of course by wider political developments in Germany, but none the less remarkable for that. The youth movement's historical role was therefore constructive and of immense significance, particularly as the final outcome was the emergence of an independent Jewish State in Israel.[89] In this context, the movement, measured on its own terms, was undoubtedly one of the most successful strands of the youth movement in Germany before 1933.

The confessional youth movement had a good deal to commend it, especially in relation to the religious and social work of Catholic youth and the contribution made by Jewish youth to the wider revival of German Jewry as a self-conscious ethnic and cultural entity before 1933. Unfortunately, Protestant youth conspicuously failed to reach these pinnacles of achievement, though individual youth leaders and even churchmen honestly tried to accentuate the more positive features of its work. Overshadowing the endeavours of Protestant youth was the intimate association with National Socialism of the older Protestant generation, whose reactionary propensities were hardly attenuated during the Weimar era. Protestant youth was willy-nilly part and parcel of the political and cultural ethos which made Hitler's victory possible. Its presence in the confessional youth sector must be seen, therefore, as pernicious and negative. However, the question of politics intervened more directly and abrasively into the work of the party political youth groups, and they clearly merit attention.

4 Political Youth: Socialist, Communist, Anarchist, National Socialist

The widespread expectations focused on the younger generation immediately after the end of the First World War, and the simultaneous recognition by adults that youth now had to be seen as having its own group identity brought as important repercussions on the political sector of the youth-tutelage organisations as on the independent youth movement. It has already been observed that certain parts of the confessional youth groups readily adopted the forms, ideals and methods of the Wandervogel and Free German Youth after 1918. A similar trend, although on a generally more limited scale, was evident in sections of politically organised youth. In a very broad sense, the whole youth movement in Weimar Germany shared some basic characteristics, such as love of hiking, camping, weekly meetings, friendship and cameraderie; but, of course, a new, more urgent and resolute political element emanating from the upheavals of the 1918–33 period was injected into the arena. Although the mood of German youth after 1918 was more serious and disciplined than before the war, the chief responsibility for the development of political activities on the part of some youth rests with the Weimar parties. Youth groups attached to political parties made their appearance before 1914, but their size and function were unimportant. After the war, however, political youth organisations, especially those connected with the most powerful parties, assumed a larger degree of prominence, and collectively constituted a separate and distinctive stream of the German youth movement.

The early post-war years witnessed a determined effort by most political parties to broaden their appeal to youth and at the same time to create a reservoir of youthful support for the future through the establishment of their own special youth affiliate. Their initiative coincided with a process of politicisation, engendered by war and revolution, in the younger generation, as we have already seen in regard to the independent youth movement. Nationalism and socialism in varying degrees of intensity exerted a strong influence on the young, who strove for commitment and identification with a cause. In particular, the political movements of the extreme Left and Right, with their emphasis on heroic activism and their cult of violence and idealism, benefited from the mentality of many Weimar youths. Both the Communist and National Socialist movements attracted proportionately a higher number of the young than the conservative, liberal or social democratic parties. Both the Centre Party and the SPD had something to build on, for youth groups had been affiliated to them since pre-war days. In 1895 the *Windthorstbünde*[1] were organised by the Centre Party, though they were not at that stage fully fledged political youth groups, since virtually all young Catholics viewed that party as their rightful political home in any case. In 1920 matters were more tightly regulated when the Reichsverband der deutschen Windthorstbünde, also known as Jung-Zentrum, was formally created. The group played a very low-key role in party affairs and was unable or unwilling to assert itself even on issues likely to affect youth. The main weight in Catholic youth work lay in the confessional groups, but this hardly disturbed the Centre Party in a narrow political sense, because of the overwhelming support given to it by Catholic youth as a matter of course. The Jung-Zentrum was consigned, therefore, to a peripheral role, and its membership never exceeded 10,000.[2]

The SPD, on the other hand, was under more pressure to organise its sources of political support after 1918, because of competition for the allegiance of the working class from both the USPD and the KPD. A socialist youth movement emerged in the 1900s and eventually came under party control, but in the early 1920s substantial sections of proletarian youth were impressed by the Wandervogel ethos and consciously strove to combine it with socialism.[3] Hence, although the Sozialistische Arbeiterjugend acknowledged allegiance to the SPD, it was never officially bound to the party, as, for example, the Sozialistische Proletarierjugend was to the USPD or the Kommunistischer Jugendverband Deutschlands (KJVD) to the KPD. The German Democratic Party (Deutsche Demokratische Partei – DDP) experienced a similar problem to the SPD with its youth group. In 1918 the Reichsverband deutscher demokratischer Jugendvereine was founded, but a few years later it became somewhat sceptical of party politics altogether and maintained a certain distance from the DDP, though never deviating from a solidly pro-republican stance.[4] Rather more successful in creating a loyal and tightly-knit youth section were the German People's Party (Deutsche Volkspartei – DVP) and the DNVP. In 1919 a Reichsjugendbewegung of the DVP was established, with the aim of 'developing and deepening by serious endeavour love for the German people and homeland, as well as understanding of things German, fostering good breeding and morals, and strengthening the body. Civic education is our way and a new, strong, greater Germany our aim.'[5] Renamed the Hindenburgjugend-Bund in 1929, when it had 12,000 members, the group played only a modest role in party affairs. In 1922 the DNVP created the Reichsverband der deutsch-nationalen Parteijugendgruppen, from which shortly afterwards evolved the 40,000-strong Bismarckjugend,[6] but, although stead-fastly loyal to the party executive, despite the upheavals and secessions which became such a salient feature of the DNVP's history, the youth group was content to keep its identity safely embedded within the party machine and made little impression on party policy. The NSDAP ventured into the youth sphere the same year as its right-wing rival when Adolf Lenk set up a Jugendbund der NSDAP. The group remained small and under Lenk's weak leadership it failed to be taken seriously by the party. In November 1923 the group was banned, along with the NSDAP, by the authorities, in the immediate aftermath of the Munich *Putsch*. An official youth affiliate of the party did not re-emerge until 1926, when the Hitler Youth came into being.[7]

Politically-oriented youth groups were also connected with a string of paramilitary organisations on both Left and Right, including the pro-republican Reichsbanner Schwarz-Rot-Gold and the nationalist veterans' league, the Stahlhelm, as well as splinter political groupings such as the anarchists. All of them subscribed to the view that their respective attitudes had to have the support of the younger generation if they were to be realised in the long-term. The existence of these youth groups together with those formally tied to political parties meant that the political youth movement in Weimar contained as many varied elements as were to be found in both the independent and confessional movements. Not only were there differences in the ideological outlook and social background of members within the political youth sector, but, further, the groups themselves varied greatly in size, influence and functions. Some were active agents of their party, some were passive. From this complicated picture, however, two segments of political youth activity stand out: first, the working-class youth movement, which was split into Social Democratic, Independent Socialist, Communist, anarchist and even smaller sectarian units; and, secondly, the National Socialist youth movement, which ultimately became one of the largest single political groups. The remainder of this chapter will concentrate on these two principal, though fundamentally different, constituents of the political youth movement.

The genesis of the working-class youth movement lay in the industrialisation process in Germany[8] during the second half of the nineteenth century, which resulted in hundreds of thousands of youngsters being sucked into factory life and allied industries. By 1900 there were just under 1 million male and female workers aged 14 – 18 years.[9] Working conditions for young workers and apprentices were deplorable: low pay, long hours, lack of further educational opportunities,[10] little in the way of recreational periods or holidays, a minimum of legal protection from unscrupulous employers and masters,[11] and badly heated and ventilated factories and workshops – these were the main features of a prosaic, even miserable existence.[12] The rapid advance of the Social Democratic and trade-union movements had not led to any material improvement in the lot of the young worker, because their energies were entirely taken up with larger issues affecting the German working class in general, including reform of the parliamentary and constitutional systems. There was little time or inclination to deal specifically with the problems of the young worker, who like his bourgeois counterpart, was still not regarded as a separate social entity. But the emancipatory aspirations of bourgeois and proletarian youth were essentially different: while the former sought freedom from the socialisation process of the established institutional framework comprising school, family and church, the latter was concerned in the first instance with liberation from the economic exploitation of capitalist employers. Educational and political objectives followed later.[13] The situation was cruelly highlighted with the suicide in 1904 of a 16-year-old Berlin locksmith apprentice, Paul Nähring, who had been driven to this calamitous end by his master's persistent bullying and physical ill treatment.[14] The resultant shock and anger provided the impetus for serious discussions on how to set up an organisation in northern Germany dedicated to the welfare and protection of the young working class. Political motives initially played no part in the deliberations. An example of what to do was furnished by events in southern Germany. In October 1903 a young worker's group was founded in Offenbach by a member of the Austrian socialist youth movement, and in autumn 1904 Dr Ludwig Frank, a Jewish lawyer and later SPD Reichstag deputy, set up a similar organisation in Mannheim, the Verband der jungen Arbeiter. In October the same year, after a good deal of groundwork by Max Peters, a seventeen-year-old Berlin apprentice, the Verein der Lehrlinge und jugendlichen arbeiter Berlins (Association of Apprentices and Young Workers of Berlin) was established, with Helmut Lehrmann as elected chairman.[15] The Berlin group, whose statutes expressly forbade its involvement in politics and religion, aimed to provide a variety of services which it hoped would ameliorate and broaden the life-style of young workers. Of immediate practical benefit was its provision of a complaints office, which gathered information about violations of the industrial code and, where further action was deemed appropriate, arranged the necessary legal assistance. The group also subsequently arranged meetings, lectures and seminars with a view to informing its members about their work and career prospects, as well as to point them in the direction of further education.[16] A certain degree of moral education was also introduced, and the group, like many other contemporary reformist-minded organisations, came out strongly against alcoholism and against smut in literature and the cinema.[17] Observing Prussian legal restrictions on political activity among minors, the group none the less moved within the ideological world of socialism,[18] and, despite much harassment from the police and State authorities,[19] soon established branches in other northern and central German towns and cities, such as Halle, Kiel, Erfurt, Königsberg, Cottbus, Bernau, Rostock and Magdeburg. By early 1906 there were several thousand members.[20]

The development of a working-class youth movement in southern Germany was made easier by the generally more liberal legal atmosphere prevailing there. The political orientation of Frank's group did not have to be concealed, and it was accordingly able to adopt a much more aggressive and anti-militarist tone. It also was fortunate in being able to engage the friendly help of party and union officials. In February 1906 a specially convened conference in Karlsruhe agreed to create a single federation for all south German young workers' groups, the Verband junger Arbeiter Deutschlands, which began publication, under Frank's editorship, of a monthly periodical, *Die Junge Garde*. By 1908 the federation had 4500 members. The northern movement, following yet again the example of the south, set up its own federation in December 1906, the Vereinigung der freien Jugendorganisationen Deutschlands, which had 5400 members within a few years, and started its own publication, *Die Arbeitende Jugend*.[21] The first issue of this periodical immediately set a bold tone: 'Working youth, awake! Cast off the shackles of oppression and intellectual browbeating. . . . Ensure that you are worthy and ready to be a co-fighter with your working-class comrades! The future of the nation rests on the shoulders of working youth . . . .'[22]

The emergence of separate north and south German working-class youth movements occurred completely independently of official backing from the SPD and unions. At the 1904 SPD conference in Bremen, several motions had called for the foundation of a socialist youth group, but had floundered through lack of support.[23] The moderates, who by that time were firmly entrenched in both the party and union executives, stressed the need for unity and centralisation in the labour movement and feared that a separate organisation for youth would frustrate their aim and weaken the collective will of German socialism. This circumspect attitude was born, of course, of the years of struggle for survival against State persecution, which included Bismarck's anti-socialist laws. The SPD liked to regard itself as a self-contained community with an all-embracing philosophy which answered all questions, solved all problems, and provided for all its members' needs from childhood to old age. The spirit of comradeship and solidarity, a feature not uncommon to downtrodden minorities, instinctively grated against any ideas or actions which threatened to split up the movement. It was an article of socialist faith in Germany that strength lay in organised activity under united leadership. There was also the fear among moderates in the party that a youth organisation would belong to the radical camp. They were aware that people such as Klara Zetkin were alert to the potential of youth as a revolutionary force. With this in view, the moderates concluded that there was no place for a separate youth group.[24] Some three years later the party was still opposed to the idea and made little effort to hide its annoyance at the initiative of young workers in the north and south. However, the question of youth welfare in a rapidly industrialising society could not be postponed indefinitely by the SPD. Although a separate youth group was still ruled out by the party, it was by 1908 prepared to consider the foundation of local youth committees to be effectively under joint party and union control.

At this juncture, the Reich Government came, paradoxically, to the aid of the SPD though the new Reich Law of Association (*Reichsvereinsgesetz*), promulgated in 1908. The law extended to the rest of Germany a number of restrictions on political activity which were already in force in Prussia.[25] Section 17 prohibited all young people under the age of 18 years from joining political clubs or attending political meetings of any kind. The law was rightly seen by the socialist movement as a direct repressive measure against the young working class.[26] The State had become increasingly worried by the anti-national and anti-militarist sentiments of young workers and by their susceptibility, between leaving school at 14 years of age and being called up for military service at 20 years, to socialist ideas. How to preserve this category of youth for the 'national' cause was considered by the authorities a task of vital importance. The 1908 law was seen by them as a decisive step towards the fulfilment of that task. The law has also to be understood in the context of considerable State aid in the late 1900s for the establishment and development of organisations like the Jungdeutschlandbund whose patriotism and reliability were above reproach, and for the expansion of the Continuation Schools system, whose objective was 'to gather youth around the flag of duty, partiotism, and fear of God' in order to counter socialism.[27] The double edge of this policy was to crush the incipient socialist youth movement. As it happened, the policy dovetailed perfectly with the increasingly conservative-minded SPD establishment and unions. They had no desire to be caught in contravention of the law. The authorities were not to be given an excuse for intervention against them and thus wreck all that had been patiently built up over the years by the party. The SPD lost little time, therefore, in complying with the 1908 law and in implementing the Robert Schmidt-inspired plan for adult controlled local youth committees.[28] The party congress in Nuremberg in September 1908 drew up the details of the new youth policy. The independently formed Verband der arbeitenden Jugend Deutschlands – an amalgam of the north and south German youth groups of May 1908 – was compelled to dissolve, and before the end of the year the first of the youth committees were set up.[29]

The broad strategy of the party was to provide a framework of support for youth activities of a non-political type with the long-term aim of encouraging youths to join the SPD or a union, or ideally both. The creation of the youth committees meant that the independent phase of the socialist youth movement, which had about

10,000 members in 1908, was over until at least after the war. The youth committees were directed by local party and union officials, who invariably had little conception of youth work and who instead tended to administer them as juvenile appendages of the adult organisations. The stress was on sports, recreational and educational activities. The party's dominant role was further underlined when in 1909 a central body, the Zentralstelle für die arbeitende jugend Deutschlands, was set up under the chairmanship of Friedrich Ebert, the later Reich President, to co-ordinate the work of the youth committees.[30] A new fortnightly newspaper, *Die Arbeiter-Jugend*,[31] was put out under the editorship of Karl Korn and achieved the impressive circulation figure of 108,000 copies in 1914. By that date there were 837 youth committees, embracing 100,000 members scattered throughout Germany.[32] The large majority of them were unskilled young labourers and semi-skilled apprentices employed mainly in manufacturing industry. Despite the impressive increase in membership in just five years, only in the minority of areas where the party's radical faction was in the ascendancy, as in Berlin, and parts of Saxony, Thuringia and Ruhr–Rhineland, was there serious opposition among youth to the loss of its autonomous organisation. The youth question was used as a political football in the power struggle between moderates and leftists in the SPD and the loss of an independent youth group represented another setback for the latter faction. But, encouraged by Karl Liebknecht, Klara Zetkin and Rosa Luxemburg, among others, the more radically oriented youth continued to cherish hopes of regaining their freedom from party control and of changing the emphasis in socialist youth work towards political activity – particularly the fight against militarism and for proletarian revolution.[33] After all, they could argue with justification that the State was showing no relaxation of its antagonism towards the socialist youth movement. The Reich Law of Association was strictly, often overzealously, applied by the authorities. Meetings of the youth committees were carefully watched by the police and sometimes forbidden to take place at all or broken up after they had begun.[34] Moreover, the State's efforts to promote patriotic indoctrination in youth-tutelage groups and educational establishments intensified, thus emphasising more clearly than ever before the class nature of its authority. The success of the SPD in the 1912 *Reichstag* elections encouraged the State to think of more drastic and comprehensive measures to prevent youths from falling under socialist influence. In 1913, for example, the Prussian Ministry of War pressed for the introduction of general compulsory pre-military service for all males aged 15—20 years, and in early 1914 high-level discussions took place on the possibility of a youth training scheme. A few weeks before war broke out, the War Ministry proposed a programme of sports and miscellaneous physical training exercises as a means of strengthening patriotic sentiment among 13—20-year-olds.[35] The war intervened before any of these rather far-fetched plans could be implemented, and under the aegis of the *Burgfriede* (cessation of party strife) domestic tensions temporarily subsided. Peace on the home front was transient, however, and before long serious disruptions shook the SPD and its youth movement.

The SPD supported the call in 1914 for a defensive war against Germany's alleged encircling enemies, and the socialist youth movement responded in patriotic fashion by providing numerous recruits for the armed forces. One of its first casualties was Ludwig Frank, who was killed at the front a few months after the conflict began. *Die Arbeiter-Jugend* carried patriotic articles exhorting its readers faithfully to serve the national cause as the class struggle was postponed. Enthusiasm for the war effort was, however, by no means unanimous among working-class youth. Those under radical influence followed the stridently anti-militarist line of argument propounded by Liebknecht and others and very soon certain groups of socialist youth were busily engaged in the illegal distribution of anti-war propaganda. In the SPD, opposition to the war and the government policy of imperialist annexation culminated in the secession of Marxist elements and the setting up in 1917 of the USPD. Among working-class youth corresponding trends occurred.

The youth movement was quickly debilitated by several developments. Many of its older members were inducted for military service and younger and generally more radically-minded members came to the fore in the organisation. They became increasingly vulnerable to the anti-war propaganda of the Marxists. Resentment was further fuelled by the series of legal restrictions that the State imposed on youth for the duration of the war. Among working-class youth these measures clashed with their new sense of enhanced status, for those working in industry were given unprecedented opportunities to occupy relatively well-paid jobs vacated by older workers who were called up. But the wartime rise in juvenile crime and delinquency reached such proportions that the authorities decided to clamp down heavily. In October 1915, for instance, the sale of alcohol and tobacco to youths under 17 years of age was prohibited under martial law.

Cinemas, dance halls and ice-cream parlours – all traditionally popular meeting places for the young – were declared out of bounds. Further measures imposed curfews and stringent laws against loitering.[36] All this on top of the difficult-enough conditions of war was bound, despite widespread attempts at evasion, to engender discontent, especially among working-class youths with some money in their pockets and nowhere to spend it. That the SPD should be seen collaborating with a government capable of such action naturally increased oppositional views in the party's youth movement. In 1915 oppositional youth elements were already organising at a local level in co-operation with party radicals, and in March 1916 the first move towards co-ordinated action on a national scale was taken with the foundation of the Jugendbildungsverein von Gross-Berlin (Youth Educational Association of Greater Berlin), which had 1500 followers.[37] The group set about preparing a national conference of all anti-war sympathisers in the socialist youth movement. This took place at Jena in April 1916, by which time the oppositional movement embraced 13,000 youths. Liebknecht made most of the running at the meeting and was mainly responsible for the decisions to establish a separate central body of oppositional youth, publish a rival newspaper to the *Arbeiter-Jugend*, which was to be boycotted, and join the Socialist Youth International. The meeting also adopted sharply worded resolutions condemning the war and militarism, and calling for an intensification of the class struggle.[38] The oppositional youth faction was very much a minority in the socialist youth movement and remained so until the end of the war. Ideologically, it was closely aligned with the Spartacists. The authorities were aware of these developments and reacted swiftly and forcefully against the leadership of the oppositional youths.[39] Their newspaper, *Freie Jugend*, was banned just after beginning publication in 1916; many arrests were made by the police; and the draft was employed to hive ringleaders such as Wilhelm Rodominsky, head of the oppositional central office, into the army. Internecine feuds such as that between the Plättner-Becker-Group in Bremen and the Berlin central office further reduced the effectiveness of the oppositional youth movement, though coherent pockets were maintained in Berlin, Thuringia, Bremen and Brunswick.[40]

In 1917 oppositional youths were able to show their colours at various anti-war demonstrations organised by a specially formed Action Committee. As before, however, the police dealt efficiently with this illegal activity. Another attempt by radical youths to co-ordinate the movement was made early in 1918, when the Freie Jugend Gross-Berlin was formed. This group maintained a rather precarious existence, but is to be recognised as the immediate forerunner of the Freie Sozialistische Jugend Deutschlands (FSJ) which was intimately linked to the Spartacists. This movement, set up in October 1918 with approximately 4000 members, was the first united revolutionary socialist youth movement in Germany and formed the nucleus of what subsequently became the youth organisation of the KPD.[41]

The socialist youth movement came out of the war in a rather bedraggled state. The demands of military service coupled with the secession of oppositional youths resulted in a catastrophic drop in its membership, from 100,000 in 1914 to 36,643 in 1919, as well as in subscriptions to *Die Arbeiter-Jugend*, from 108,000 to 31,000.[42] A good deal of rethinking and reorganisation were clearly necessary if the movement was to re-emerge as a force to be reckoned with in the Weimar era.

Socialist youth was subject to at least as many pressures as other parts of the German youth movement in 1918/19. Quite apart from the political consequences of the war's end, the November Revolution and the creation of the Weimar Republic, which, through the SPD, weighed onerously on socialist youth, there were complex problems to be sorted out within its own ranks. Alongside the traditional notions of class conflict and the abolition of capitalism came the reality of generational clashes which had already appeared in embryonic form before the war. Now, in 1918, even many party members were prepared to admit that the SPD had failed to provide the right kind of leadership and inspiration for its youth movement. There was a grave crisis of confidence in the ability of the party to steer its youth through the storms and tribulations that assuredly lay in store. Like other members of the post-war younger generation, socialist youths were anxious to assert their status and capacities as youths, to add their skills to the construction of a better future for themselves and Germany. Their sense of socialist commitment and idealism was firm and resolute but needed to be channelled into constructive paths. Many of these youths now believed that the best way ahead lay in evolving a synthesis of socialist and Free German Youth ideals, for in the early years after the war the influence of the independent youth movement on sections of proletarian youth was substantial. The expeditions, camping, uniforms, songs and dances which originated with the Wandervogel were taken over by socialist youth on a comparatively large scale.[43] Thus the reconstituted socialist youth movement which appeared in 1919 in the form of the Verband der Arbeiterjugendvereine Deutschlands (VAJV) was not officially tied to the SPD, and, despite being dedicated to socialism its ethos was heavily impregnated with Wandervogel ideas. The party had been an unsuccessful overlord in 1908—18. The youths themselves were now given the chance to help determine their own destiny, within certain limits, for adult (but not SPD) supervision was still important.[44]

The amalgamation of proletarian and bourgeois youth cultures was made explicit at the first national rally of the VAJV, in Weimar in 1920. On this occasion working-class youth formally and publicly assimilated the ideals of the independent youth movement within a socialist framework. Epitomising this development was the formulation by Johannes Schult of socialist youth's own version of the Meissner Formula:

> Within the close community life of both sexes we want to create the aristocracy which will build towards a socialist future where instead of hatred, envy and selfishness the love of humanity among nations will be predominant. We want the renewal of socialism through deed and example from our Youth Movement.[45]

The VAJV was not a politically activist organisation, though it supported the Weimar Republic and its ideals of democracy and humanitarianism. This was made clear by Erich Ollenhauer at the 1920 rally:

> At the birthplace of the German Republic, German working-class youth acknowledges its support for the Republic and its constitution, and swears to educate its members to be citizens who will protect the constitution from any degradation, because it provides the opportunity to achieve socialism through the democratic process.[46]

None the less, the VAJV saw itself primarily as an educational—cultural organisation of a socialist kind, concerned with cultivating in working-class youth an appreciation of socialist, Wandervogel and civic responsibilities.[47] Towards this end it also founded its own publishing house, in 1920.[48]

Socialist youth entered the Weimar era, therefore, with lofty expectations of creating the new socialist paradise.[49] The shackles of the authoritarian and repressive Wilhelmine Reich had been broken for ever, it was thought, and golden opportunities appeared to open up for a decisive and irrevocable advance of socialist ideals. The VAJV sought the amelioration of society on the basis of a 'new man' – a socialist type. The high spirits of socialist youth were quickly illustrated by a memorandum drawn up by the Zentralstelle shortly before being superseded by the VAJV in 1919, and presented to the National Assembly. It called for a generous government programme of educational and protective measures for youth, and the enactment of a National Youth Law.[50] Similar hopes and demands were entertained by those socialist youths too old to be included in the VAJV and who in 1919–20 spontaneously gathered in Young Socialist associations throughout Germany. The Young Socialist movement acted as a kind of intermediary stage between the VAJV and SPD, though in its early history it was also influenced by the Wandervogel.[51] The group was mainly significant as an intellectual forum, especially when the Hofgeismar Circle was formed in 1923.[52] In the mid-1920s some moderate elements of this circle became associated with neo-conservative and revolutionary nationalist groups in the New Front, which was anti-parliamentarian and sought to replace the Republic with a non-party national government dedicated to so-called 'German socialism'. A powerful radical proletarian and Marxist group – the Hanoverian Circle – also arose among the Young Socialists, producing such intense conflict that the 4000-strong movement effectively collapsed. The Hofgeismar group pulled out and disbanded, while a rump of radical leftists staggered on until officially repudiated by the SPD at its 1931 annual conference. At the other end of the age scale, the SPD attempted to extend its totalitarian net by organising very young children and rearing them in the socialist spirit. The resultant Kinderfreude movement, led by Dr Kurt Löwenstein, a Berlin schoolmaster and SPD Reichstag Deputy, had 200,000 children under the age of 14 years under its wing by 1929.[53] From the very beginning of the Weimar period, the SPD was keenly sensitive to the necessity of competing for working-class allegiance against the USPD and KPD, and obviously measures had to be taken if it were to hold on to its grass-roots support.

The socialist youth movement enjoyed a period of vigorous expansion and lively activity from 1919 until the mid-1920s, at which point the hardening of class and political attitudes in Weimar society conspired to divest the movement of much of its early *élan* and fresh idealism. Membership of the VAJV rose from 53,000 in 1920 to 85,000 three years later and then to its pre-war level by 1924/5. The exuberant spirit of these years was effectively captured in a lilting song, 'Mit uns zieht die neue Zeit' (With Us Marches the New Age), written originally for the socialist youth movement in 1920 by Hermann Claudius, but widely adopted throughout the German youth movement. The theme of solidarity among the ranks was also powerfully conveyed by mass annual rallies of socialist youth, such as those in Bielefeld in 1921 and Nuremberg in 1923.[54] While the VAJV's outlook in the early 1920s was informed by both socialism and Wandervogel ideas, its amalgamation at the end of 1922 with parts of the youth group of the USPD, the Sozialistische Proletarierjugend,[55] caused its work to acquire an increasingly political dimension. The new Verband der Sozialistische Arbeiterjugend Deutschlands (SAJ) drew closer and closer to the SPD without actually becoming its official youth group. Involvement in political meetings, demonstrations, parades, and back-up for the party's propaganda campaigns took up more and more of the SAJ's time. This development soon gave rise to quarrelling factions within the group. Otto Schröter, former leader of the Sozialistische Proletarierjugend, and for a short period deputy SAJ leader, was to the fore in demanding a more activist political course. In 1923 the Schröter faction, which was located largely in central Germany, went so far as to argue heatedly that the SAJ unite with the Communist youth movement. The rightists, led by Max Westphal, the SAJ leader, successfully resisted Schröter's pleas, but thenceforth the group did undoubtedly take a more positive interest in everyday politics.[56] Its political commitment was made abundantly clear in the aftermath of the Reichstag elections in September 1930, when the SAJ declared: 'The SAJ is inseparably bound to the socialist working-class movement. The struggle of socialist workers is our struggle, and, just as in the period before the election our units campaigned for the party with their full strength, so we shall stand behind the party in the future, come what may.'[57]

Of all Weimar youth groups, the SAJ was probably the one most dedicated to supporting the Republic and to opposing militarism. Under the slogan 'Never again War', massive anti-war demonstrations were held every August by the socialist youth movement, which as a whole, after 1918, espoused pacifism and internationalism. On the other hand, the political endeavours of the SAJ never matched the sacrificial, reckless standards set by both Communist and National

Socialist youth.[58] Charges of becoming bourgeois were frequently hurled at the SAJ by Communists, with some degree of justification. Like the SPD, the SAJ, though overwhelmingly working-class in social composition,[59] lost something of its character as a class-conscious proletarian youth organisation. In particular, its female members often lacked a definite class awareness and certainly did not possess the stomach for the political fray when it toughened up in the early 1930s.[60]

As it became more involved in politics, the SAJ lost a good deal of its earlier individuality. Partly because of this, and partly also because it often failed to attract the more activist, class-conscious young workers,[61] its membership declined alarmingly from 105,000 in 1925 to 55,000 in 1927 and to 50,000 in 1932.[62] It was strongest in Westphalia, Hamburg, Berlin and central Germany and predictably weakest in southern Germany and rural areas.[63] Poor leadership at the local level may have been a further factor in its decline, though at the national level it had, in Heinrich Schulz (1919–21), Max Westphal (1921–8) and Erich Ollenhauer (1928–33), able personalities directing its operations. Ollenhauer in particular tried to halt the slide by involving the SAJ in schemes for helping the young unemployed, including the setting up of its own voluntary labour-service camps.[64] Despite this, however, the SAJ, like the SPD, spent the last years of Weimar on the defensive, as other, more determined youth organisations stepped up their efforts to attract working-class support. Competition arose in the first instance from a string of usually small, sectarian and non-party affiliated socialist youth groups, such as Freie proletarische Jugend, the Junge Pioniere–Deutscher Arbeiter–Pfadfinderbund, the Jungproletarische Bund, the Ring revolutionärer Jugend, the Sozialistische Jugendverband,[66] the Jungbanner[67] and Leonard Nelson's Internationaler Jugendbund.[68] The most formidable rivalry came, of course, from the Communist youth movement.

The Communist youth movement was born during the turmoil of the November Revolution and the Spartacist rising in Berlin in January 1919, when the FSJ organised in armed 'Young Guards' units and fought on the streets.[69] In Munich, the former left-wing Free German Youth spokesman Alfred Kurella founded a branch of the FSJ which likewise saw active service during the Eisner and Soviet Republic interludes.[70] In 1919 Kurella became the principal linkman between the FSJ and the Russian Communist youth organisation, Komsomol, whose central committee he even joined.[71]

During a lengthy sojourn in Moscow in spring and summer 1919 he discussed the question of revolutionary working-class activity with Lenin himself, and was given the important task of preparing the ground for a Communist Youth International under Soviet control. Kurella, one of the most loyal Soviet supporters among German Communists of the Weimar era, successfully executed his task at the end of 1919 and thereafter worked indefatigably to maintain Komsomol's dominance of the International and to mould the German Communist youth movement into an unquestioning instrument of Moscow.[72]

Following the failure of the radical Left in 1918/19, the FSJ lapsed, like the KPD, into an uneasy period of internal bickering, which led a large proportion of its members to break away to join either the Kommunistische Arbeiterjugend Deutschlands, the youth section of the splinter Kommunistische Arbeiterpartei, or the Sozialistische Proletarierjugend of the USPD.[73] The main body of the FSJ under the leadership of Friedrich Heilmann continued emphatically to support the KPD without being formally tied to it. The FSJ wanted, in the spirit of the times, to remain independent of adult control. As a spokesman expressed it,

> The Freie Sozialistische Jugend recognises that its objectives run parallel with those of the German Communist Party. It extends the heartiest sympathy to this party as the only one representing socialist revolution . . . it refuses, however, in the interests of its independence, to become an organisational part of the German Communist Party.[74]

The FSJ's activities were of a wholly political nature and revealed no traces of Wandervogel influence. Encouraged by the memory of its murdered hero, Karl Liebknecht,[75] the FSJ cultivated an image of being the *avant-garde* of proletarian youth revolution.[76] As such, it was able to grow rapidly for a time, with 12,000 members in early 1919 and 35,000 by October of the same year,[77] before losing support through ideologically motivated secessions. By the time of its fourth national congress, held in Berlin in May 1920, FSJ membership had fallen to 22,000.[78] In an effort to refurbish its revolutionary image and to underline where its loyalties lay amidst the bitter ideological strife within the radical working-class movement at that time, the FSJ changed its name in September 1920 to the Kommunistische Jugend Deutschlands (KJD).[79] However, the youth leaders were still not convinced of the merits of integrating into the KPD, believing that youth had something positive and unique to contribute to the revolutionary struggle on its own account. In any case, the situation in the party was far from stable during 1920 as different factions fought for the upper hand. As a whole, the KPD was anxious to extend its organisational control over the youth group, and at the party's annual rally in December 1920 it sought to move closer to this desired goal by pledging support for its work.[80] By September 1921 the KJD had 27,800 members in 824 local branches,[81] and at its congress in Halle that same month it once again decided to remain an 'organisationally independent mass association . . . under the political leadership of the KPD'.[82] Only during the course of the following year, when the situation quietened down in the KPD, did the KJD come under direct party control as part of the organisation.

The youth sector of the German Communist movement was extended with the foundation in 1919 and 1920 of the first children's groups, noticeably in Berlin, Hamburg, Bremen, Halle-Merseburg and the Ruhr. The inaugural conference of the children's organisation took place in December 1920, and by mid-1922 it comprised 25,000 under 14 year olds in over 300 branches. To provide a united organisation for Communist children, the Jungspartakusbund was set up in 1924. By 1932 it had 65,000 members.[83]

The KJD continued in 1922 and early 1923 with political propaganda work and began seriously canvassing for support in factories. Factory cells were formed, helping to boost membership to 29,000 in early 1923. During the next seven or eight months the group enjoyed the largest expansion in its history. The French occupation of the Ruhr coupled with the consequences of hyper-inflation and Communist uprisings in central and northern Germany served to increase membership to 70,000.[84] Once this revolutionary phase was over, however, and the KJD had been banned, along with the Party by the authorities (this happened in November 1923), support fell away just as dramatically. Although some members joined other youth groups under guise or continued illegally with their work in the KJD, the time had come for a thorough reappraisal of the organisation, its methods, and above all, its relationship to the party.

When made legal again in spring 1924, the KJD chose as chairman Conrad Blenkle, who was resolved unconditionally to integrate the group into the party apparatus. When Ernst Thälmann became KPD leader in autumn 1925, he gave this policy his energetic support now that the emphasis in the German Communist camp was on tight discipline and centralisation. In keeping with his strict subordination of the KPD to the Russian Bolsheviks, the German youth organisation, renamed Kommunistischer Jugendverband Deutschlands (KJVD) in May 1925, strengthened its links with the Komsomol, copying from it many propaganda techniques, including the agitprop innovation.[85] Also in 1925, a number of KJVD members were in the German delegation which visited Russia at the invitation of the Bolsheviks.[86]

A significant appendage to the Communist youth movement came with the establishment of the Rote Jungsturm as the youth section of the Rotfrontkämpferbund (RFB) in 1924.[87] Designed theoretically as a recruiting pool for the RFB, and as a complement to the KJVD's propaganda work by providing a tough body of activists, the Rote Jungsturm, which took in youths aged 16–21 years and from 1928 up to 23 years, really spent most of its time fighting political opponents in the streets as a self-styled defender of the young proletariat against militarist and capitalist exploitation.[88] Members swore to 'remain for ever and always a soldier of the Revolution . . . for ever and always to fight for the Soviet Union and for the victory of the world revolution'.[89] Despite the introduction in 1928 of some political education and defensive sports,[90] the training, discipline, and overall character of the Rote Jungsturm were thoroughly paramilitary in nature. For this reason a certain amount of friction developed between it and the more political KJVD.[91] Double membership of both groups was relatively high: in 1928, when the Rote Jungfront, as it had been renamed two years earlier, had 27,000 members, approximately 25 per cent were also in the KJVD.[92] In 1929, 30 per cent of the Rote Jungfront's 30,000 members were active in the KJVD.[93] The latter went through a difficult and unrewarding period during the late 1920s, which saw its membership drop from 25,000 in 1924 to about 20,000 in 1929/30.[94] This culminated in the events in Berlin on May Day 1929, when a number of KJVD followers were killed during the infamous rioting that then took place. One consolation for it from a narrow sectarian viewpoint was the banning by the authorities of its rival, the Rote Jungfront, shortly afterwards, along with the RFB.[95]

At the beginning of the 1930s the KJVD's lack of progress inevitably invited criticism from many quarters of the party. Its factory-cell movement was near to collapse and it suffered once again from an overspill of the factional in-fighting in the KPD. Moreover, the absence of proper facilities for leaders and ordinary members alike and the chronic shortage of money gravely hindered the KJVD's effectiveness.[96] Once the economic depression began to bite into German working-class society and the National Socialist danger loomed, the group was able to pick up some momentum and attract fresh blood. Membership, which was made up largely of young unemployed, unskilled workers,[97] increased to 50,000 by the end of 1932.[98] None the less, there is no denying the failure of the KJVD to arouse a larger proportion of the young proletariat in a period of profound crisis. A lack of good leadership, crude propaganda methods, a penchant for violence and sheer hooliganism, and the absence of material assistance from the party partly account for the KJVD's uninspiring record. The basic cause, however, was the inability or unwillingness of the KJVD adequately to reflect the needs of young workers. The orientation of its policy to suit Soviet Russia was at the root of the problem. Like the KPD, the KJVD directed too much of its energy against the Social Democrats and thus shares the blame for the tragic splitting of the German working-class movement in the face of the National Socialist upsurge. Even Thälmann, who was more interested in the youth group than most other KPD leaders,[99] was forced to admit in late 1932 that the KJVD lacked teeth and compared it unfavourably with the Hitler Youth.[100] It was an astonishing but frank confession for the Communist leader to make. The KJVD was simply a failure.

The same conclusion is also difficult to avoid in respect of the smallest independent branch of the working-class socialist youth movement in Weimar, the anarchists.[101] The libertarian working-class tradition of the anarchist youth movement, whose most distinguishing feature was anti-authoritarianism, attracted in its best years during the early 1920s no more than 3000–4000 members, approximately one-third of whom were female.[102] The influence of the Wandervogel was not entirely missing from the outlook of the anarchist youths, at least in the early stages, for they too acknowledged the life-reformist impulse behind the Meissner Formula and the concept of youth autonomy. External forms of the Wandervogel were also freely adopted, but it was in the attempt to fuse a bourgeois and a proletarian youth culture that the anarchists lost their way in the later 1920s.[103] Rather than projecting a coherent ideological posture, they merely succeeded in appearing to be one of the most confused parts of the whole Weimar youth movement. However, the two most noteworthy groups, the Freie Jugend Deutschlands (FJ) and the Syndikalistisch-anarchistische Jugend Deutschlands (SAJD), perceived the threat of National Socialism more clearly than most youth organisations, but of course were impotent to do anything about it. Both groups found most of their following in Berlin – Brandenburg, Saxony, Thuringia and Rhineland – Westphalia,[104] but by the early 1930s secessions, personal rivalries involving leaders such as Ernst Friedrich (FJ) and Paul Albrecht (SAJD), and ideological murkiness, had reduced both organisations drastically in size. In 1933 the National Socialists found few problems in disposing of the remnants.

The relative weakness and fragmentation of the working-class youth movement was ultimately of as much political significance as the failure of the German proletarian organisations as a whole to offer sustained resistance to Hitler before 1933, because it permitted the Hitler Youth to develop a substantial following among youths from a working-class background, and thus also to help condition the totalitarian perspectives which were brought to bear on the entire German youth movement in the Third Reich. The reasons, however, for the Hitler Youth's growth from a few hundred members in 1926 to over 55,000 by early 1933 extend beyond the deficiencies of the organised young proletariat.

During the *Kampfzeit* (time of struggle) the NSDAP placed heavy emphasis in its propaganda appeals on the perennial generational conflict between young and old, and Gregor Strasser had poignantly captured the essence of this tactic in his celebrated call, 'Make way, you old ones!' The party liked describing itself as a movement of youth, and the *Machtergreifung* was depicted by it as the victory of young Germany against the gerontocracy of the Weimar Republic. There was considerable truth in the NSDAP's claims, as the sociological and generational composition of its membership and electorate unequivocally demonstrate. Despite the success of its appeal to youth, it was not until 1926 that a reasonably stable youth organisation was set up by the National Socialists. Hitler's decision to create the Hitler Youth (Hitler-Jugend – HJ) under the leadership of Kurt Gruber, a 22-year-old Saxon law student, followed on from his change of political tactics after the failure of the Munich *Putsch*. The *Führer* became reconciled to the notion of winning power through the established legal and constitutional framework of the State, and in practice this meant entering the NSDAP in parliamentary elections and building up its popular support among the electorate. In order to broaden the appeal of National Socialism – in effect, to transform it from a elitist revolutionary to a mass-based evolutionary movement – specialised formations of the NSDAP were set up in the years after 1925, including one for youth.

The focal point of the HJ's activity, which consisted mainly of political and propaganda work, lay in Saxony until the early 1930s. Branches were established throughout Germany, but expansion was unspectacular. In 1929 the HJ had only 13,000 members. Admittedly, the pre-depression years were generally quiet for the National Socialists, as the Republic appeared to have achieved a measure of stability, which depressed the prospects of politically radical groups in the main. But there were also various internal factors militating against the HJ's development: the shortage of able and properly trained leaders, Gruber's inability to conceive of his organisation in truly national terms, a ramshackle administrative apparatus, and pecuniary problems.[105] It was also of critical importance that the HJ was left very much to its own devices by the party and Stormtroopers (*Sturmabteilungen*—SA). The distance from Munich – Gruber having set up head office in his native Plauen – meant that, contrary to regulations laying down measures of tight organisational control over it by both the NSDAP and the Stormtroopers, the HJ in practice enjoyed a good deal of independence.[106] Stormtroopers and members of the NSDAP were generally apathetic towards it, believing that the serious business of politics should be really left to adults. Their indifference was strikingly underlined by their refusal to lend meaningful financial support to the HJ during the period of Gruber's tenure as *Reichsführer* (1926–31). Apart from the political dubiety in which the youth group was held by the party, however, there was also a crucial ideological factor serving to increase its suspicion – namely, the group's unorthodox interpretation of National Socialism.

The HJ's comparative freedom from adult overlordship until 1930/1 allowed it to develop an ideologically distinctive position within Hitler's movement, as well as within the wider German youth movement.[107] The special characteristics of its ideology were a pronounced revolutionary nationalism and a social revolutionary radicalism, and their existence was all the more noticeable because of the passionate sense of commitment, idealism and buoyant activism with which they were propounded by the HJ. Its advocacy of a nationalist socialism was utopian and simplistic and it never intellectualised to any extent about the idea. But the HJ's rejection of class-consciousness, traditionalist conservatism, bourgeois standards and both Marxism and capitalism was honestly held. In their place it offered a national community in which racial criteria and individual merit would be the determinants of position and status. Consequently, the HJ had a decided proletarian character, despite being stridently anti-communist, and directed its message above all to working-class youths, preaching social revolution within a nationalist and egalitarian framework. Gruber, operating from the industrial centres of 'Red' Saxony, was instrumental in infusing the HJ with this socialistic substance. He remarked,

> The Hitler Youth is the new youth movement composed of social revolutionary people of a German kind . . . who are chained to the destiny of the nation . . . in order to emancipate the State and economy from the bonds of capitalist, anti-national forces. Thereafter, the new socialist people's State [*Volksstaat*] of Adolf Hitler will follow.[108]

The HJ gave practical expression of its 'socialism' before 1933 by proposing constructive policies of social, industrial and economic reform aimed at improving the everyday life and living standards of working-class youth. Its concern was particularly apparent in connection with young labourers, factory workers and apprentices – the proletarian groups which made up most of its rank and file membership. The full title of the HJ, 'Hitler Youth, League of German Working-Class Youth' (Hitler-Jugend, Bund deutscher Arbeiterjugend), was therefore wholly consistent with its predominant ideological and sociological character.[109]

The HJ's social revolutionary course was challenged when Baldur von Schirach engineered Gruber's dismissal in October 1931. The event marked an important turning point, for von Schirach was determined to bring the HJ into line with the conservative strategy adopted by Hitler in the NSDAP shortly after the 1928 Reichstag elections.[110] In 1929 von Schirach had unsuccessfully tried to promote a merger of the HJ and the middle-class *völkisch* groups of Bündische Youth.[111] He had more success in eliminating socialist ideas from the Nationalsozialistischer Deutscher Studentenbund (National Socialist German Students' League – NSDStB), of which he had been leader since 1928, and now regarded the HJ's socialist leanings as being in direct defiance of Hitler's strategy. He also argued that the HJ's appeal to proletarian youth had proved extremely limited. At the moment of Gruber's departure, the HJ had 26,198 members, while both the NSDAP and the Stormtroopers had grown proportionately and absolutely much larger. The HJ was strongest in Protestant and non- or lightly industrialised areas, notably in Saxony, Thuringia, Lower Saxony, Schleswig-Holstein and Mecklenburg, and weakest in both predominantly Catholic and heavily industrialised regions, including the Rhineland — Ruhr, Bavaria, Berlin — Brandenburg, and Hamburg.[112]

Von Schirach, as Reich Youth Leader (*Reichsjugendführer der NSDAP*), had supervisory authority over all National Socialist youth and student groups, though Dr Adrian von Renteln, founder and leader of the Nationalsozialistischer Schülerbund (Nazi Secondary Schoolboys' League — NSS), was Gruber's immediate successor as HJ *Reichsführer*. From late 1931 von Schirach took practical steps to give the HJ a more bourgeois image, in keeping with the party. He toned down the social revolutionary content of its propaganda while accentuating nationalist themes; dismissed a number of radical and working-class leaders, replacing them with personnel from the largely middle class NSDStB and NSS;[113] and integrated the HJ more firmly into the party's organisational structure. These measures were partly effective in that the HJ did begin to lose something of its abrasively proletarian personality, and certainly more recruits from a bourgeois background joined it.[114] But its character could not be fundamentally altered within the short period between von Schirach's advent and the *Machtergreifung*. Until 1933 the HJ remained the most conspicuously 'socialist' branch of the National Socialist movement, with a rank-and-file membership that was still mainly working-class.

The role of the HJ in the National Socialist movement before 1933 was clearly subordinate to that of the party and Stormtroopers, but it did succeed in transmitting Hitler's message to an expanding number of youths and lent a good deal of dedication and sacrifice to the cause. After all, no fewer than sixteen of its members lost their lives and many more were injured in the course of the struggle.[115] The HJ, on the other hand, did not reach its full potential before 1933. A series of limiting factors, including organisational weakness, financial shortages, secessions, poor leadership, and hostility from State and school authorities combined to inhibit development. But the HJ did finally convince Hitler after its brilliant rally in Potsdam in autumn 1932 (the *Reichsjugendtag der NSDAP*) that youth had a valuable part to play in his political calculations. The considerable concern for youth displayed by the Third Reich owed much to the HJ's earlier endeavours.

The years before 1933 had also shown that, as regards ideology and organisation, the HJ was a unique phenomenon in the German youth movement. It had no substantive connections with either the pre-1914 Wandervogel or contemporary Weimar groups, but represented a complete break in the youth tradition of Germany, in the same way as the NSDAP was a new kind of political party. As its numerous enemies repeatedly pointed out, the HJ lacked the character of a genuine youth organisation. It was too obviously the youth auxiliary of the NSDAP, and, while the German youth movement generally wanted to eradicate the party system, the HJ through its party sought to do away with the youth movement. In the last analysis, the HJ's totalitarianism demanded that it prove its uniqueness by destroying the youth movement altogether. In 1933 came the opportunity to realise this ambition as a new era dawned for the HJ and for German youth.

Part II
1933 — 1945

5 The Hitler Youth from *Kampfjugend* to *Staatsjugend*

Whoever serves Adolf Hitler, the *Führer*, serves Germany, and whoever serves Germany, serves God.

Baldur von Schirach[1]

The National Socialist take-over of power signalled the beginning of a distinctive era in modern German history in which radical conceptions regarding state and society were introduced. Despite elements of historical continuity between the Weimar Republic and the Third Reich, an intrinsically revolutionary dimension was undoubtedly added in 1933 to the political situation. This animus was specifically provided by the National Socialist insistence on a totalitarian approach to Germany's societal and institutional framework. Every important sphere of activity was to be brought under the control of the State, whose ultimate inspiration was the directive of the *Führer* Adolf Hitler.

Hitler's appointment as Chancellor meant that the NSDAP's years of struggle had been brought to a sudden and victorious end. For the HJ units that marched triumphantly through the Brandenburg Gate on the evening of 30 January 1933 the realisation that their organisation was no longer simply the youth group of a political party must have been rather daunting. The HJ now had a new position and new functions. It was axiomatic that a completely different phase in the history of the German youth movement was about to begin, because, although some practices of the pre-1933 youth movement were carried over into the Third Reich by the HJ, most of the traditional substance of Bündische Youth and other spheres of organised youth activity was destroyed. The year 1933 marks, therefore, a crucial dividing line in the evolution of the youth movement in Germany. Hitler himself soon indicated the essence of what the future role of the HJ should be when he referred to it as 'the architect of the Third Reich',[2] meaning its unique task in leading German youth. The regime immediately let it be known that Hitler's assumption of power signified in a very real sense the victory of youth, which was to be accorded a special status and importance in its future plans.[3] Hitler confirmed this at the party rally in Nuremberg in September 1933, when he announced to the HJ contingent gathered before him, 'You are the Germany of the future . . . on you are now set all our hopes, our people's confidence, and our faith. . . . My youths, you are the living guarantors of Germany, you are the living Germany of the future . . . upon you depends the continued existence of our people . . . .'[4]

The HJ was given the major executive responsibility for realising these sentiments, though its weaknesses, particularly regarding organisation, quality of leadership and size, did not augur well for its active involvement in a vital phase of the National Socialist revolution. If it were to become more than a mere political combat group (*Kampfjugend*), a striking transformation would be demanded of it. The role of the HJ was henceforth to be constructive, in helping to consolidate and popularise the regime, rather than destructive, as it had been in the Weimar Republic. The HJ was now required to expand into every branch of German youth activity, instruct youth in the spirit and ideals of National Socialism, and inculcate the teaching that the State was everything and the individual nothing. Youth work, in other words, was not to be an end in itself: it was to be directed towards service for *Führer, Volk* and *Vaterland*. As one spokesman expressed it, 'The aim of the Hitler Youth is a new youth which, being proud, upright, healthy . . . and glowing with the idea of National Socialism, knows that it is the bearer of Germany's destiny.'[5]

The immediate preoccupation of the HJ in 1933, however, was to bring as many German youths as possible under its organisational control. It fully participated in the co-ordination (*Gleichschaltung*) programme of the regime, which was aimed at the comprehensive Nazification of German society. The NSDAP led the way by quickly dissolving other political parties, and by either destroying or fundamentally reforming a range of important institutions, such as the civil service, police and federal states. This process culminated in the official proclamation of the one-party State in July 1933. If the HJ were to attain a similar position of ascendancy, it would need to deal with its principal adversary, the German youth movement. This task was the most critical one facing it during the first year of Hitler's rule. Compromise was out of the question: the objective was total power. Facilitating the successful implementation of the HJ's plans was the widespread acclaim with which large sections of youth greeted the advent of the Third Reich. Most youth groups of the *völkisch* and nationalist Right disbanded voluntarily as their members streamed into the HJ. But, while declaring their loyalty to Hitler, significant sections of Bündische and confessional youth were resolved to maintain their independence from HJ encroachment, an attitude which compelled the HJ to devise special techniques to break down resistance. These varied according to the particular circumstances of individual groups, but a number of general features soon became apparent. As was to be expected from an organisation that deservedly earned a reputation for violence before 1933, the HJ freely employed tough physical measures on the youth groups' members and property. On occasions the violence reached such heights as to cause alarm in government circles,[6] and even top officials in the HJ itself acknowledged the legitimacy of public concern over this issue.[7] Following the pattern established by the NSDAP, the violence was never co-ordinated from the centre and applied on a national scale, but usually took place with the connivance of von Schirach on the initiative of a local HJ leader. The most blatant example of the use of force occurred when an HJ detachment took over the offices of the Reichsausschuss der deutschen Jugendverbände in Berlin in April 1933. This act was of decisive significance for the HJ's co-ordination programme, because it indicated that legality could be cast aside when it suited its purposes. Moreover, the take-over provided the HJ with detailed information on the groups affiliated to the committee, thus allowing von Schirach to plot their destruction with precision.[8] The German Youth Hostel organisation was brought under HJ domination in similarly rough fashion shortly afterwards.[9]

Just as conspicuous was the HJ's unrelenting use of nationalism in trying to persuade youth that the best interests of Germany would be served by everyone's being united under the one banner. The appeal for a single youth movement had, after all, been long associated with Bündische Youth, and HJ propaganda made it clear that those refusing to join it were un-German and outsiders in the national awakening under National Socialism. The State furnished support in the form of local authority and police intervention where necessary to further the HJ's cause, and then particularly in June 1933, when von Schirach was appointed 'Youth Leader of the German Reich'. While still retaining his title of *Reichsjugendführer*, which was a party rank, von Schirach's new status was equivalent in rank to that of a senior government official below ministerial level. By combining a party and State post, von Schirach's responsibilities in matters pertaining to youth were considerably augmented, and no new youth group of any kind could be formed without his express approval.[10]

A prime target for the HJ was Bündische Youth, for long a bitter enemy. Given the fragmented character of Bündische Youth, a uniform reaction to the political events of 1933 was hardly to be anticipated. Apart from its extreme right-wing component, however, the core of Bündische members remained steadfastly loyal to their groups. Only in rare instances were their ranks noticeably broken, as when in March 1933 the leadership of the Silesian Jungmannschaft, which included some of the most able personalities of the pre-1933 youth movement, publicly declared their allegiance to National Socialism and urged their followers to copy their example in joining the NSDAP and HJ.[11] But there was a good deal of misunderstanding, even naïvety, among Bündische members about the HJ's intentions. They could not bring themselves to believe that it wanted to abolish their groups altogether, but of course this is exactly what the HJ did aim to do. The Bündische outlook was, as before 1933, politically immature, since it failed to perceive what was really happening in Germany. Some of the more realistically minded sought to prepare for the inevitable onslaught by coming together in April 1933 in a new composite association, the Grossdeutsche Bund, under the leadership of Admiral Adolf von Trotha, who was friendly with Reich President von Hindenburg.[12] Von Trotha attempted to ward off the unwelcome attentions of the HJ by issuing numerous patriotic declarations and pledges of support for National Socialism, and by persuading von Hindenburg to intercede personally on his behalf with Hitler.[13] In the end, however, all this frantic activity did the Grossdeutsche Bund little good and it also was compelled to disband and allow its members to join the HJ.[14] Other Bündische elements, despairing of the whole turn of political events, withdrew from youth work altogether, while only scattered remnants, such as Werner Lass's Eidgenossen group, decided to offer illegal resistance.[15] There were, of course, opportunists in the Bündische camp, as there were in every walk of German life in 1933, who climbed on to the National Socialist bandwagon for purely selfish reasons. More importantly, once it became clear that the HJ was determined to destroy Bündische Youth, some of the latter's personnel went over to the HJ and especially its junior branch, the Deutsches Jungvolk, with the intention of continuing the Bündische tradition under the guise of HJ activity. Gerhard Rossbach's Bund Ekkehard came into this category.[16] This strategem did not come to the notice of the HJ until later in 1934, whereupon a wholesale purge of Bündische elements took place.[17] By the end of 1933, however, Bündische Youth had ceased to exist, thus ending the independent youth tradition begun by the Wandervogel some forty years previously.[18]

The various political youth groups, including the socialists and Communists, did not present the HJ with any problems, as they were compelled to dissolve when the political parties were made illegal, but the confessional organisations represented a different challenge. While the Jewish groups constituted a special case and were allowed to remain in existence, the Catholic and Protestant groups were extensions of vested interests which were a problem for the regime as a whole. Having dealt with the political and Bündische groups by the summer of 1933, the HJ turned its attention during the second half of that year to the large confessional youth organisations.

The overwhelming part of Protestant youth openly and rapturously hailed the advent of the Third Reich, but their youth groups were reluctant to surrender their independence to the HJ, particularly when the anti-Christian attitudes of von Schirach became apparent. The Protestant youth leadership initially hoped for a compromise whereby their groups would be permitted to retain some functions on a corporate basis within the HJ.[19] But anxiety about the HJ's aggressiveness and demands for total submission led to the formation in July 1933 of a new umbrella organisation, the Evangelische Jugendwerk Deutschlands, which had 700,000 members under the leadership of Dr Erich Stange, himself an outspoken National Socialist sympathiser. He stressed that this united front of Protestant youth was in no way directed against the National Socialist regime, but it was a nice distinction not readily appreciated in the Germany of 1933. In any event, the resistance of Protestant youth to incorporation into the HJ was effectively broken when Ludwig Müller, leader of the staunchly pro-National Socialist German Christian group within the Protestant Church, was elected Reich Bishop in September 1933. Müller, in his new capacity, controlled the destiny of the Protestant youth groups and lost no time in handing them into the eager clutches of von Schirach. In December 1933 a treaty was signed with the National Socialist Youth Leader which brought the

Protestant groups into the HJ on terms entirely favourable to him. Resistance to the treaty, which came into effect in March 1934, was not really feasible in view of the deep divisions in the Protestant Church in 1934, which included the developing struggle between the Confessing Church and its opponents. Moreover, by early 1934 the independence of the Protestant groups was seen by most of their members to be incompatible with the overall political situation.[20] Consequently, Protestant youth flocked into the HJ with relative smoothness.[21]

Catholic youth proved a tougher obstacle to the HJ, though like the Catholic Church they were willing at first to forget their previous antagonism to National Socialism and seek a rapprochement.[22] The Catholic community had no desire for a second *Kulturkampf* and stepped forward prepared to make its contribution to national rejuvenation, provided its religious and educational interests were respected by the regime. Individual clerics such as Wilhelm Berning, Bishop of Osnabrück, publicly lent support for Hitler and tried to rally Catholic opinion. When the Concordat was concluded between the National Socialists and the Vatican, the basis for a mutually satisfactory bond of co-operation seemed assured, and Catholic youth joined with their elders in proclaiming loyalty to Hitler.[23] Vicar-General Steinmann told a Catholic youth rally in August 1933, 'What we have all longed and striven for has become reality: we have one Reich and one Führer, and we will follow this leader faithfully and conscientiously. . . . We know that he who stands at the head is given to us by God . . . .'[24] Only later, when the regime's hostility towards the Church broke through the veneer of friendliness created by the Concordat did Catholics begin to entertain serious doubts about Hitler. Article 31 of the Concordat had provided certain guarantees for the continued existence of the Catholic youth organisations as long as they remained non-political. But differences of opinion arose over which Catholic groups were covered by Article 31, the Vatican having failed to have them specifically listed before ratifying the agreement. The resultant loophole was cynically exploited by the HJ, with official support.[25] Hitler, for example, asserted in December 1933, a mere five months after the Concordat was signed,

> We claim and declare that all German youth organisations other than ourselves have lost every reason for their continued existence. These organisations must disappear and leave the Hitler Youth a

clear field. That youth leagues should continue to exist on the periphery, protected by I know not what private concern of the churches, is in itself an intolerable situation.[26]

Catholic youth discovered that the fundamental dilemma confronting them was to reconcile their Christianity with their sense of German identity. As time went on, their choice of options was systematically narrowed by the HJ. The Catholic groups remained virtually intact in 1933, but began to lose members during the following year. None the less, von Schirach continued to recognise them as 'an important factor in the life of German youth'.[27] The feeling of solidarity among Catholic youth, their powerful organisation, steadfast leadership, and unstinting support from the ecclesiastical hierarchy allowed them, despite much physical provocation,[28] to hold out against the HJ's totalitarian dynamism far longer than any other sector of the old youth movement. The HJ started to make serious inroads into the Catholic youth membership only in 1935 and 1936, and by a dogged war of attrition gradually wore down the Catholics. A few small groups, however, managed to hang on until the eve of the Second World War, when membership of the HJ became legally compulsory.[29] That they held out for so long against the pressures of a dictatorial State is ample testimony to the inherent strength and wholesomeness of Catholic youth life, which was unmatched by any other sector of the German youth movement.[30] By comparison, the Protestant youth groups were never in the same class.

In the course of late 1933 and 1934 the HJ empire was further extended when youth in trade and industry — apprentices and young factory workers for the most part — were transferred to the HJ from the German Labour Front (Deutsche Arbeitsfront). Also, as a result of an agreement with Walther Darré, von Schirach managed to bring all peasant and agricultural youth groups under his control, and, finally, in November 1934, it was agreed with the Reich Sports Leader, Hans von Tschammer und Osten, that all youths in sports and gymnastics associations should at the same time be members of the HJ. In 1936 the HJ assumed full responsibility for all sports and gymnastic youth training.

By the end of his first year in office, Hitler had emerged as dictator of Germany and the NSDAP was unchallenged as the dominant political force. Whole sections of German society had fallen under National Socialist influence. Those which retained a measure of autonomy, such as the economy, judiciary and Army, were eventually to follow the same path. When radical and oppositional elements were ruthlessly eliminated in the Röhm purge in June 1934 and Hitler took over the office of Reich President on the death of von Hindenburg, the National Socialist revolution, whose salient feature was the acquisition of sheer power, was consummated. By that time too, the HJ had firmly established itself as the dominant force among German youth. By the rapid destruction of its rivals, it had grown from 55,000 members at the beginning of 1933 to over 1 million. The German independent youth movement had been eliminated almost entirely and replaced by an increasingly monolithic structure whose competence reached far and deep into youth life. The HJ had pursued its quarry with cunning, deceit and terror. Von Schirach had proved that his power instincts were as sharp as those of his other colleagues in the Party hierarchy. His task was made easier by the disunited nature of the opposition, which allowed him to concentrate his resources on one adversary at a time and pick off the major segments of the youth movement one by one. The youth movement had many internal weaknesses, but in 1933 it was still a movement of some vitality and its destruction was by no means a foregone conclusion. This should not obscure the fact, however, that at the moment of execution the youth movement's capitulation had an air of undisguised resignation about it. It was almost as if the youth movement sensed that history was against its continued existence, that the time had come for its practices and ideals, which had been found wanting in crisis, to be replaced by something new, untried, but attractively presented within a nationalist framework.

The substantial growth in HJ membership brought considerable organisational problems for von Schirach. The administrative structure which had carried the HJ through the *Kampfzeit* was quite inadequate to cope with newly arisen pressures. Extensive changes were necessary to meet the onerous responsibilities with which the HJ was now charged. A greater amount of centralisation was called for if efficiency were to be achieved in the aspiring totalitarian organisation – a lesson von Schirach had fully recognised after his experience of dealing with the rather ramshackle HJ apparatus of pre-1933 days. In the summer of 1933, therefore, he devised a centralised structure which lasted, with some modification, until the end of the war. Crowning the hierarchical edifice established in July 1933 was the *Reichsjugendführung* (Reich Youth Leadership – RJF), the central co-ordinating administrative unit, which exercised ultimate control over all Hitler Youth affairs. Within the RJF were created a large number of departments (*Abteilungen*), each of which was allocated supervision of a particular sphere of HJ activity: press, propaganda, finance, training, culture and soforth.[31] Playing a crucial role was the Personnel Department, whose task was to integrate the HJ apparatus by controlling the selection of leaders, enforcing discipline and having some influence in determining important promotions (though Hitler had the final word in this respect). The organisational stability of the HJ very much depended on the effectiveness of the Personnel Department. The HJ organised nationally on a vertical basis, in five principal districts (*Obergebiete*), which initially embraced twenty-one districts (*Gebiete*) covering the whole of Germany. Within each *Gebiet* were several sub-divisions, ranging from the smallest unit, the *Kameradschaft*, to the *Oberbann*. The numerical size of each of these units was laid down by regulation, though in practice it could vary a lot. The problem of organisation was most acute in areas – such as Catholic parts of the Rhineland – where before 1933 the HJ had attracted little support, and which were virtually starting from scratch. Later there was also the difficulty of incorporating into this structure regions (such as the Saar and Austria) annexed to the Reich in consequence of Hitler's foreign policy. In the end, however, the HJ organisation was sufficiently elastic to effect these changes without serious disruption. By 1939 the number of *Gebiete* had risen to thirty-eight and by 1943 to forty-three.[32] Within these a whole series of vertical command structures was erected, to correspond with each unit in the HJ's central organisation.

Another serious practical problem facing the HJ as a result of its growth was that of finding an adequate number of able and properly equipped leaders to direct its operations. Shortage of good leaders had been a major handicap for it since its inception, but at least before 1933 the problem was of manageable proportions. In 1933 and 1934, on the other hand, thousands of posts had to be filled in both the central and provincial administrations. One obvious step taken by the HJ was to promote many of the pre-1933 higher leadership appointed by von Schirach after he had taken charge of the party's youth organisations in October 1931. Nearly all top posts were now occupied by those who had been tried and trusted by him.[33] Conversely, this meant that HJ leaders with radical or 'socialist' leanings were further excluded from the centres of power. Only in the lower ranks of the HJ were newcomers given responsibility. This applied in particular to former members of Bündische Youth. A more stringent policy was adopted towards former army personnel, who were expressly forbidden by von Schirach to become leaders in the HJ. The Youth Leader did not consider them suitably qualified for youth work and, besides, he wished to preserve the HJ from militaristic influence.[34]

The HJ did recruit from the professions, provided those involved had a sound National Socialist background. With a large demand for doctors, dentists and lawyers, which obviously could not be met from within its own ranks, the HJ combed other branches of the party for suitable personnel. In this manner a fairly substantial number of appointments were filled, and at a subsequent date teachers and social workers were also employed, usually in lower-ranking positions.[35] The long-term solution, which eventually provided all leaders, was the creation of leadership schools throughout Germany in which specially chosen candidates could be systematically trained according to a detailed programme.[36] Schools of this kind were first opened in 1933 and increased rapidly in number under the supervision of Helmut Stellrecht's Training Department and Georg Usadel's Leadership Schools Department in the RJF. By the end of the first year in operation, twenty-two schools had turned out 7000 leaders, who during an intensive 3-week course received instruction in history, race, physical training, sports and small-calibre marksmanship.[37] The training conformed to the HJ's goal of producing an ideologically reliable and physically sound leadership. Refinements to the scheme were added from time to time, particularly when a Reich Academy for Youth Leadership was set up in Brunswick in 1939.[38] In 1942 an Office for Leadership Training and Instruction was set up with overall responsibility for all leadership matters in the HJ. Thus, the practice of the amateur leadership of the pre-1933 period was eliminated in favour of the highly organised professional functionary, who was in the main better educated and increasingly drawn from the academic middle class.[39] The regime was fully aware of this trend and hence made considerable propaganda play of the fact that several of the movement's top leaders were of working-class origins, including Artur Axmann, head of the important Social Office in the RJF, who has been described as 'the proletarian showpiece of the youth leadership corps'.[40] In 1938 salaried, full-time HJ leaders, of whom there were just over 8000, were accorded the official status of professional careerists, comparable with school-teachers, a move which also helped to enhance the image of bourgeois respectability of these top personnel.[41] Only 20.9 per cent of all HJ leaders in 1939 were working-class.[42]

In filling its leadership posts, the HJ tried hard to adhere to its maxim of 'Youth must be led by youth.' Although there were instances where this was not achieved, it is worth noting that the general age level of the movement's leaders was low; they tended to be much younger, for example, than Bündische Youth leaders, many of whom were decidedly middle-aged. In 1938 the average age of an HJ *Obergebietsführer* was just over 30 years and of a *Bannführer* (middle rank) 25 years.[43] In lower ranks leaders were commonly only a few years older than their charges. There was in the HJ, therefore, no generation gap, which had been the source of so much tension in the early Weimar youth movement. The war, especially from 1942/3 onwards, even accelerated the trend towards youthful leaders, as military call-up took its toll of those already in office.

By the end of 1934 the National Socialist regime had settled down to a period of retrenchment and consolidation at home. The domestic situation had been brought well under control and the process of instilling into Germans the ideals of National Socialism got under way on a large scale. The HJ's development was consistent with this pattern. Membership showed a steady expansion to 3,577,565 by late 1934 and to 5,437,601 by the end of 1936, making the HJ probably the largest youth organisation in the world.[44] None the less, after nearly four years of incessant HJ aggression and propaganda, von Schirach was faced with the disconcerting fact that a substantial percentage of German youth who were eligible for membership still preferred to stay outside the movement. Despite its almost ubiquitous role in the life of youth and despite the fact that it had for some time enjoyed the unofficial status of a *Staatsjugend* – in effect, the exclusive youth organisation of the Third Reich – the HJ had not succeeded in attracting some 4 million young Germans to its ranks. Even the pressure of various State bodies had been enlisted in support of the HJ's totalitarian claims. In August 1935 the Deputy *Führer*, Rudolf Hess, issued a directive underlining the obligation of party members to encourage their children to join the HJ.[45] Civil servants in Catholic areas, where recruitment was weakest, were threatened with blockage of promotion or even dismissal if they did not bring their children into the youth organisation.[46] In November 1935 the Reich Ministry of the Interior decided that future applicants for posts in the civil service would have to produce evidence of successful activity in the HJ as one of their qualifications.[47] The Reichsbund deutscher Beamten (Reich League of German Civil Servants) fully supported the application of these policies of intimidation to its members.[48] Notwithstanding this pressure and even more disconcerting for von Schirach was the noticeable decline in HJ membership in certain parts of Germany, including Berlin, Lower Saxony and areas in the north.[49] Artur Axmann tried to put a brave face on the situation by insisting in a speech in Berlin on 5 November 1935 that the HJ 'must always remain an elite of German youth',[50] but there could be no disguising profund official disquiet over what was regarded as the movement's relative lack of success in propitious conditions.

The reasons why so many youths were staying away were varied but certainly had much to do with the views of parents. Many kept their children from the HJ because of the lax morality there, especially in the Bund deutscher Mädel (League of German Girls – BdM), which enjoyed a dubious reputation in some quarters, and in the HJ proper, concerning which tales of widespread homosexuality were commonplace.[51] Parents were also afraid that HJ duties would disrupt normal schooling, as indeed increasingly happened,[52] or they objected to the aggressively physical approach of the organisation. Furthermore, many Catholic and working-class parents were bound to have political and ideological reservations about allowing their children to become members of a National Socialist formation whose ethos bore few traces of being either Christian or proletarian. In any event, the situation was a direct challenge to von Schirach's policy, which he had repeatedly stressed, of keeping membership of the movement theoretically voluntary. He wrote,

> In the National Socialist State it would be not only practically superfluous but also ideologically false to commandeer the youth by force for service in the Youth Movement. In the State of Adolf Hitler the youth, filled with the memory of its commitment to fight for this State, declares itself gladly prepared to serve it. Only he who voluntarily joins the organisation of the Hitler Youth and voluntarily dedicates his young life for National Socialism strengthens the Movement.[53]

Von Schirach's desire was that his organisation should grow on a mammoth scale because of what he considered to be its intrinsic attractions, thereby demonstrating to the world at large the unrestrained support for Hitler among young Germans. This was indeed a powerful propagandistic motive for maintaining the voluntary principle. There was also a practical motive arising from organisational considerations: incorporation of extra millions of youth into the embryonic structure of the organisation in 1933–5 would have stretched its resources beyond breaking-point. In fact von Schirach instituted a membership ban for a short period in 1934/5, because he saw the need to defer the day of compulsory membership until the HJ was ready to cope. By 1935/6 the HJ had the required capacity, but new members were not as quick to come forward as had been expected. Adding to von Schirach's unease about the state of affairs was his realisation in 1936 that the powerful Catholic youth organisations were not going to wither away into insignificance as quickly as he had hoped. Many of these groups had stood up remarkably well to the HJ's onslaught and remained perfectly viable units with comparatively large memberships. Even when Catholic youths left their groups, it did not automatically follow that they would go over to the HJ, and in 1936 HJ membership in predominantly Catholic regions was well below the national average. For these reasons von Schirach concluded by late 1935 that something drastic would have to be done to bring the recalcitrant millions of German youths into the fold.[54] Terror tactics, intense propaganda, expanding social and recreational amenities and government pressure had all proved insufficiently persuasive. So also had von Schirach himself. His stilted style of public speaking, air of arrogance and adolescent ideas had made him unpopular among his own party comrades as well as among the rank-and-file Hitler youths. There remained nothing for it but to invoke some kind of judicial expedient. This duly came in December 1936 in the shape of the Law for the Hitler Youth (Gesetz über die Hitler-Jugend) which von Schirach, against the bitter opposition of Reich Education Minister Bernhard Rust, finally convinced Hitler was necessary.[55]

A law of this type had been actively discussed by von Schirach and other leading officials since the late autumn of 1935, and a number of drafts had been produced at different times by interested parties.[56] Rust was especially concerned to preserve his spheres of power from HJ encroachment and in April 1936 presented a draft that would ensure precisely that. However, he received no support from Hitler. In fact it was the *Führer's* indecision which was primarily responsible for delaying matters throughout 1936. There was also some discussion about dropping the name 'Hitler-Jugend' in favour of 'Deutsche Reichsjugend' and only at a meeting on 19 October 1936 did von Schirach persuade Hitler to retain the traditional name of the organisation. The youth leader was thoroughly exasperated by the drawn-out negotiations on the law and felt compelled to inform Lammers, chief of the Reich Chancellory, on 12 November 1936 that, 'if a new year begins without the law being promulgated, the disappointment of my colleagues will be great'.[57] As it turned out, the final draft agreed to in November 1936 was almost exactly the same as that proposed by von Schirach a year previously.

The law, which was in a sense complementary to the introduction of universal military service in March 1935 and of Labour Service Duty (*Arbeitsdienstpflicht*) in June of the same year, confirmed in legal terms that the HJ was a State youth organisation. The law formally recognised it as an educational institution alongside the school and parental home for the 'physical, intellectual and moral' instruction of German youth 'in the spirit of National Socialism, serving the people and national community', and upgraded von Schirach's official standing by making him an *Oberste Reichsbehörde* (Supreme Reich Authority) directly answerable to Hitler. Previously he had been subordinate to Rust.[58] Most important of all, the law laid down that the entire youth of Germany aged 10–18 years was to be organised in the HJ.[59] Von Schirach insincerely argued that the law merely completed a trend that was begun by his appointment as Youth Leader of the German Reich in 1933 and the formal recognition of the HJ as a branch of the NSDAP in 1935.[60] In actuality, the law was promulgated because of the failure of von Schirach's voluntary membership policy to achieve a level of recruitment satisfactory to the regime. As such, therefore, the law marked a major turning-point in HJ history by moving the organisation along the path of oppression. But membership of the HJ did not become legally compulsory in 1936, because the executive orders (*Durchführungsverordnungen*) necessary for its enforcement were not issued until March 1939.[61] The delay may have had something to do with the regime's fear of hostile reaction from parents, but more likely it was to hold on to some semblance of voluntarism in a strictly judicial sense, in the knowledge that the law acted as a potent instrument of psychological pressure on youths and their families to join the HJ. The regime's deception of the German public in this manner was brazen but to a large extent efficacious, because during its period of non-statutory application the law did considerably help the HJ to extend its grip on German youth. Despite von Schirach's words of reassurance to parents about the honourable intentions of the law,[62] in practical terms it made it more disadvantageous than ever for youths to remain outside the movement. In seeking work, for instance, youths could discover that not being, or having been, a member of the HJ put off prospective employers, and, even for admission to some further-education centres, this gap in a youth's *curriculum vitae* might raise suspicions about his political or personal reliability. The spirit of voluntarism was further compromised in August 1937 when it was announced that thenceforth the only way to become an NSDAP member was to have served in the HJ for at least four consecutive years. Again, for the better positions and prospects of employment, party membership was at the very least an advantage, at the most a practical necessity. Ambitious youths could easily draw their own conclusions. So also could the mass of Catholic youth in another way. The law meant a tightening of the HJ's drive against their organisations and the offensive was taken a crucial step further when von Schirach reaffirmed in June 1937 the prohibition of dual membership of the HJ and Catholic groups. The pretensions of the HJ had been significantly boosted by the law and encouraged it to think in even more determined fashion of exerting exclusive influence over all German youth. Von Schirach even felt confident enough to ask the Reich Finance Office in April 1937 for more funds to enable the provisions of the law to be fully carried out,[63] but only after calling on Lammers's help did he obtain some degree of satisfaction in this regard.[64] None the less, HJ spirits were running high.

Membership of the entire HJ grew markedly over the next few years to 7,728,259 by the beginning of 1939, an increase of 2½ million on the 1936 figure.[65] This still did not conceal the fact that a notable minority – over 1 million – youths and girls under 18 years of age continued to keep their distance from the HJ.[66] In other words, even after a further extended period of miscellaneous pressures, the spurious voluntary principle had failed to achieve the anticipated conclusive result. This left von Schirach no option but finally to abandon all pretence and have membership of the HJ made legally compulsory. The two executive orders of 25 March 1939 enacted this fundamental change in policy and in April 1940 the whole class of 1929/30 was called up for service in the movement (*Jugenddienstpflicht*).[67] In addition, the HJ gained control of all matters relating to youth welfare, youth hostels and youth in-surance, which had been under the jurisdiction of the Ministry of Education. Rust, having tried hard from the time the orders came in for serious discussion in early 1937 to avoid losing further areas of competence to von Schirach, had to accept this latest rebuff with the same impotent outrage as on previous occasions.[68] The HJ was now established on the same basis as military and labour service, thus ensuring that youths would be under National Socialist control from the age of 10 until at least their early twenties. Hitler had anticipated this situation with considerable pleasure when he informed a youthful gathering in Reichenberg in December 1938 that they would never again be free, for the rest of their lives.[69]

It would be wrong to deduce from the problems encountered by the HJ in bringing the whole of German youth under its domination that there was a serious body of organised resistance to it among youth. An enormous gap existed between an attitude of indifference and sullen withdrawal, on the one hand, and active opposition, on the other. Historiographical evaluation of the German resistance movement to Hitler is a contentious field, and no less is scholarly debate about the scale and importance of youth resistance to the HJ. However, there is to date no substantive or convincing evidence to support the view that the HJ was confronted by grave problems in this respect. Works by Klönne and Ebeling-Hespers leave much to be desired in terms of perspective and objective analysis.[70] A more recent attempt to show there were substantial elements of opposition, particularly among working-class youth after the introduction of the 1936 law, is fundamentally misconceived[71] and not far above the level of doctrinaire Marxist–Leninist historians, who are adept, in this controversy at least, at exaggerating relatively trivial incidents out of all reasonable proportion.[72] On a different level, it has not been demonstrated that there was anything other than marginal disaffection among a small number of HJ personnel.[73]

Before 1939, youth resistance hardly constituted a movement at all, consisting almost entirely of individual acts of sabotage or gestures of futile defiance against the HJ. Clandestine and petty illegal actions were at times perpetrated by small and loosely organised disparate elements drawn from different parts of the pre-1933 youth movement.[74] They arose in local groups for a short period until dispersed by an increasingly efficient Gestapo. Exceptions were the Nerother Wandervogel and d.j.1.11 groups, which offered some cohesive resistance in the early years of National Socialist rule.[75] The extent to which oppositional activity was politically motivated is difficult to assess if we exclude the socialist and Communist youths. In the early years at least, Bündische opposition rarely had a political orientation. More conspicuous was Bündische rejection of the mass character of the HJ. Other elements were more likely to be demonstrating resentment at HJ discipline or regimentation, or even dislike of individual HJ leaders. After all, there were only three political trials involving former youth movement adherents before 1939: the trial of Jungnationalen followers in Essen in 1937, of Father Josef Roussaint and fellow Catholics in the same year, and of the 'Gruppe Sozialistische Nation'.[76] As for the magnitude of oppositional activity, too much should not be made of the Gestapo's establishment of a separate office in December 1936 to track down Bündische dissidents, or of the repeated prohibitions of Bündische groups, latterly in July 1939. The numbers involved were insignificant, as were those who tried to organise resistance from the countries to which they had been forced to emigrate. A German Youth Front, in which former Bündische leaders Hans Ebeling, Karl Paetel and Fritz Borinski were prominent, emerged in Brussels in the late 1930s but failed in its aim to construct a united anti-fascist grouping. It was eventually broken up after the Germans had invaded the Low Countries. In the case of socialist and Communist youth, their illegal work had effectively ceased by the mid-1930s and did not reappear in any co-ordinated form until the war years.[77] In the years immediately after 1933, left-wing youths frequently joined up with Catholic youths, especially in the Rhineland,[78] but, when, after 1935/6, the Catholic groups themselves came under increasing pressure from the HJ, this collaboration dwindled into insignificance. Altogether, 131 former youth movement members lost their lives as a result of resistance involvement between 1933 and 1945, including well-known figures such as Theo Hespers, Adalbert Probst, Max Westphal, Robert Oelbermann, Hermann Maass, Artur Becker and Conrad Blenkle.[79] Despite this sacrifice, the youth resistance was a relatively minor irritant to the HJ before 1939 and did not in any way disrupt either the direction or conduct of its development.

By 1939 the Hitler Youth had undoubtedly achieved the subservience of a substantial majority of German youth to National Socialism. More accurately, a good percentage of this majority was positively attracted to the HJ.[80] After all, youth was the recipient of lavish praise and attention from the regime. It was made to feel an integral part of the system, and its contribution to the creation of the New Germany was highly valued. The colour, pageantry and air of excitement of the pre-war years were bound to attract an eager and idealistic younger generation to the swastika. Just as important, however, were the everyday activities of the HJ, in which the ideological element was paramount.

6 The Hitler Youth and the New Ideology

> . . .we solemnly promise Adolf Hitler to be the most loyal of the loyal.
>
> Baldur von Schirach[1]

The historical evolution of the HJ indicates a number of discernible phases, each of which possesses idiosyncratic features affording it a total composition different in many respects from the others. The *Kampfzeit* had given way in 1933 to the co-ordination interlude, which was followed by a period of organisational expansion lasting until the outbreak of war. During this time the HJ assumed a radically new appearance, developing in its role as a *Staatsjugend* important ideological and broadly educational functions which took it into almost every corner of German youth life. As a pillar of the State, its ideological–educational tasks lay within and outside the established school system, thus requiring it to adopt a double strategy in respect of both fields of activity. Its attitudes and objectives were basically informed, of course, by Hitler's conceptions regarding youth education. Its most vital responsibility was to erect a system which would indoctrinate German youth in National Socialist philosophy and prepare them physically, ideologically, and mentally for the task of upholding and perpetuating the 'Thousand Year Reich'. Von Schirach made clear the character of his organisation when he said, 'The Hitler Youth is an ideological educational community. Whoever marches in the Hitler Youth is not merely a number among millions, but a soldier of an idea. . . . The best Hitler youth is he who, regardless of rank or office, identifies completely with the National Socialist philosophy.'[2]

With most opposition crushed by 1934, the HJ was uniquely placed to fulfil its wide-ranging extra-school task of indoctrination. It brought Hitler's teaching to bear by permeating all its activities with political dialectics, with the purpose of instilling into youth race-consciousness, notions of German supremacy, obedience, loyalty to *Führer* and Fatherland, the virtues of the *Volksgemeinschaft* ethos, and belief in the need for self-sacrifice, under the slogans 'The Flag means more than Death'[3] and 'We are born to die for Germany'[4] — hence producing the desired political soldiers. Racist instruction was the focal point of training courses, rallies and other activities. Complementing this emphasis was the extravagant promotion of the *Führer* cult, for which von Schirach with his profusion of aesthetically poor poems and songs was primarily responsible.[5] The depiction of Hitler as the God-given saviour of Germany was *de rigueur* in HJ publications and propaganda exercises. The conviction that the individual was nothing and the State everything was constantly drummed into the membership, invariably in quasi-mystical language. Von Schirach went to great lengths to stress that the HJ was in the process of developing a national community in miniature in which everyone was treated on an equal basis and where individual merit and capability were the major criteria for advancement (*Leistungsprinzip*). In April 1938 he remarked,

> You stand in this youth next to one another with the same rights and the same duties. There is no special Hitler Youth for the poor or the rich, no Hitler Youth for secondary schoolboys and girls, or for young workers. There is also no special Catholic or Protestant Hitler Youth. In our group belongs everyone who is of German blood. Before the flag of youth everyone is the same.[6]

In this semantic sense, the HJ convinced itself that it was truly a national community based on the ruins of bourgeois, class-ridden society. But, although youths from all social backgrounds were to be found in the HJ, class divisions were never really eradicated, just as they were not either in other spheres of the Third Reich.[7] The *Volksgemeinschaft* concept as understood by the HJ was essentially a mere figment of von Schirach's fertile neo-romantic imagination, devoid of roots in everyday reality.

Party and youth leaders incessantly exhorted German youth to identify with National Socialism, but in the long run the result was that wholesome qualities such as idealism, courage and patriotism, which German youth possessed in abundance, were cultivated not as ends in themselves but in order to strengthen the fidelity of youth to the regime. This misuse of talent only bred intolerance, rigidity and fanaticism. The organisational network set up to ensure this was elaborate and extensive. A sophisticated press and propaganda system was developed: there were HJ newspapers, periodicals, theatre productions, films[8] and radio shows.[9] Every Wednesday evening, beginning on 18 July 1934, the HJ broadcast its own programme, 'Hour of the Young Nation', to coincide with the weekly meeting (*Heimabend*) which HJ units all over Germany held at the same time. It was probably the first time that a youth organisation had manipulated the mass media so adroitly in the service of a totalitarian dictatorship. Backing up and eventually supervising the presentation and content of the indoctrination programme was an Office for Ideological Instruction (Amt für Weltanschauliche Schulung). In time, the HJ transferred its teaching from the political plane to the 'higher' level of a dogmatic, quasi-religious doctrine, a trend accompanying the development of the Hitler cult throughout German society. Symptomatic of this in the HJ was the publication in 1936 of an HJ catechism[10] and the growing emphasis on the mythology of National Socialism. Explanation and reasoning were thus replaced by unquestioning acceptance and emotional response. Significantly, these trends developed at about the same time as the HJ was narrowing down its interpretation of its voluntary-membership principle.[11]

Innocuous pursuits such as camping and hiking, which were staple diet of all youth groups before 1933, were invested with a direct political substance by the HJ.[12] Hiking, which grew in popularity under the auspices of the huge youth-hostel network[13] ceased being merely a pleasurable ramble by a group of friends around the countryside: it became an exercise in physical and ideological development by a drilled formation of HJ youths, a form of service for Germany. The same basic political purpose was extended even to the HJ's vast sports and medical programme, which was a source of particular pride to it.[14] A Reich sports competition was officially inaugurated in 1937, and within two years nearly 7 million were participating.[15] Although it may be true that the youth of Germany came to be among the most well looked after and healthy in Europe, their physical fitness was achieved only at the cost of even more ideological instruction. A similar pattern can be observed in the development of the HJ's Land Service and impressive social-welfare system. A good example is provided by the highly successful National Vocational Competition (*Reichsberufswettkampf*) which Axmann's Social Office in the RJF organised annually from 1934 in conjunction with the German Labour Front.[16] The practical merit of the competition was the encouragement it gave youths to extend their knowledge and expertise in a chosen trade and then to test their technical skills and craftsmanship against others. But participants, and there were no fewer than $3\frac{1}{2}$ million in 1939, had also to display a satisfactory understanding of National Socialism, so that not only the most skilled but also the politically most loyal youths (*Reichssieger*) were presented to Hitler every May Day to receive their prizes. The competition undoubtedly did a good deal to boost the reservoir of apprenticeship talent in German industry, which was badly needed in view of the regime's autarky and rearmament plans,[17] but it was also, like the 'Strength Through Joy' organisation, an ingenious and effective stratagem for engendering interest in and support for the Third Reich among the working class. Any resentments from this source, especially in periods of economic uncertainty, could be channelled by this method into harmless and constructive avenues. At the same time, the competition provided some evidence that the *Volksgemeinschaft* ideal had a populist base, particularly after university students were brought into it in 1935[18] Von Schirach described the competition as 'socialism in action' and claimed it was one way of 'overcoming the false romanticism of the Youth Movement of yesterday:[19] although the HJ lost its previous proletarian character following the large influx of bourgeois youths after 1933, it was anxious to reconcile all social groups within its ranks. The enactment of the 1938 Youth Protection Law (*Gesetz über Kinderarbeit und die Arbeitszeit der Jugendlichen – Jugendschutzgesetz*), which enlarged the physical and legal protection of industrially and commercially employed youth, who were overwhelmingly working-class, as well as the provision of generally better and more plentiful opportunities for apprenticeships and vocational training,[20] bore ample witness to a certain social consciousness in the HJ's make-up. Certainly there is no doubt that working-class youth generally found many attractions in the HJ.[21] It was these and other 'achievements' which caused Hitler to enthuse over the 'success of the Hitler Youth Movement' and to congratulate himself on making, in von Schirach, the perfect choice of youth leader.[22]

From an objective standpoint, however, the results of the HJ's extra-school work were depressing. By the mid 1930s spontaneity in the organisation had been largely eliminated, as the accent fell more and more on uniformity of behaviour, regimentation and repetition among both leaders and ordinary members,[23] with, in some cases, corresponding repercussions on morale and a feeling of boredom.[24]

The responsibilities of leaders, apart from the very highest echelons, became functional and routine. Everyone simply began to perform his duties mechanically, according to meticulously formulated rules and regulations. Curiously, running parallel with this trend was the constant demand for competitive activism, which by the later 1930s was often merely cosmetic.[25] In mitigation, it might be argued that this kind of situation is bound to arise in any organisation, regardless of complexion, once it has attained a certain size, and the HJ was indeed large by 1936. On the other hand, evidence of growing emphasis on paramilitary training in the HJ during the later 1930s was indicative of a widespread heavy-handed and even oppressive attitude in its organisational priorities. This development is clearly consistent with the intentions of the 1936 law. Admittedly, the ebullience of the HJ, its spirit of nationalist *élan*, can perhaps be too readily interpreted as martial ardour, and the stress placed in its propaganda on moulding future 'soldiers of the Reich' was often meant metaphorically. But this cannot disguise the fact that arms practice was established at an early date as part of the HJ's training schedule for leaders, as a result of which twenty-seven of its members were killed in shooting accidents before the war.[26] More telling is the formal co-operation there was between the Army and HJ after 1936 for the purposes of military training, even though this was mainly organised on a local basis and involved a limited number of HJ leaders.[27] A group of officers for liaison with the HJ was created by the Army in 1937, and for a short time Lieutenant-Colonel Erwin Rommel played a leading role in it. Agreements between von Schirach and General Ludwig Beck, Chief of the Army General Staff, in 1938, and Wilhelm Keitel, Chief of the Armed Forces High Command, in 1939, solidified the partnership.[28] The Stormtroopers also entered this area, when in 1939 they were empowered to give pre-military instruction to Hitler youths aged seventeen years and over.[29] The most ominous development, however, was the growth of links between the HJ and the Schutzstaffel (SS). In October 1938 von Schirach agreed that the HJ Patrol Service (*Streifendienst*)[30] should furnish recruits for Himmler's organisation, and in early 1939 a similar arrangement was made in respect of the HJ Land Service (Landdienst) — specifically for the SS *Wehrbauer* (peasant soldier) project.[31] Firm foundations were thus laid for a fuller expansion of the HJ – SS relationship during the war, notably with the Waffen-SS. Finally, on its own account, the HJ had a variety of specialised formations within its structure which provided forms of pre-military training in flying, navigation and other areas of activity useful to the demands of war.[32]

It cannot be said that there was a comprehensive militarisation of the HJ before 1939, as was the case with both the Italian fascist and Soviet youth organisations,[33] because the HJ remained an intrinsically political group. However, its training did acquire a strong military flavour after the mid 1930s, and this facilitated its later involvement in the war effort, including combat duty at the front. Helmut Stellrecht, leader of the Training Department in the RJF, was a vigorous advocate of military instruction for the HJ and expressed his philosophy in these terms: 'Every youth must march, suffer hunger and thirst, be able to sleep on the bare earth, endure all privation cheerfully, be a fighter and a soldier from the moment he first grasps what it is all about.'[34]

Despite the trends towards strict conformism and militarism in the HJ during the later 1930s, it had not reached a state of satiety or been reduced to an outlook of stereotyped doggedness. Its undeniable bureaucratic tendencies had not made it totally unwieldy, even less incompetent, organisationally.[35] In fact its early buoyancy had been replaced with a certain stuffy stability which allowed it to remain reasonably efficient in a cumbersome sort of way. Moreover, a spirit of eager optimism throughout its ranks gave the HJ its own peculiar form of energy which allowed it to overcome the bureaucratic heaviness of the organisation. That this was so was lucidly demonstrated by the HJ's successful adaptation to the exigencies of war in 1939. It then had sufficient organisational flexibility and capacity for improvisation to effect a fundamental reorientation in function.

By 1939 the HJ had overcome various limiting factors – such as the inherent negativism of its ideological teaching, the relative shortage of time at its disposal, and the continuing though somewhat diminished influence of school, church and parental authorities – and was successfully performing its task of making the majority of youth think and act as one in the extra-school sphere. The degree of manipulation involved in this process was extensive, of course, though youth's captivation by some features of the HJ's activity, especially in sports and other outdoor pursuits, should not be underestimated. However, it was not good enough, as far as the HJ was concerned, to have access to German youth only outside school hours. The school system which had to be confronted posed complex problems, not least because it had established roots which were deeply embedded in German society. The HJ's involvement in schools ran parallel to its role outside them, although the ultimate aims it pursued were exactly the same. The battle had to be waged if the HJ were to dominate the hearts and minds of German youth as decisively as it wanted.

From the outset, the Third Reich regarded education, particularly of youth, as one of the most crucial areas in its struggle to legitimise the National Socialist revolution. It was widely accepted in official circles that 'with a correct or false education of youth stands or falls the National Socialist State',[36] a view fully endorsed by Hitler.[37] The proposed intrusion of the regime into the schools was not a novel idea, for politics had already entered this sphere, particularly at secondary-school level, during the Weimar era. National Socialism presented a unique challenge, however, because it constituted a crusade against the rational, humanist and intellectual traditions of Western civilisation. The regime was determined to abolish what it considered to be the liberal and humanitarian educational system of the Weimar Republic, with its alleged emphasis on individualism, and to replace it by a system which would be dedicated to developing the collective *Volk* personality within rigidly defined racial and ideological limits.[38] Reich Interior Minister Wilhelm Frick under-lined this point in May 1933: 'The time when the cultivation of the self-centred individual personality was seen as the most essential task of school is over. The new school is based fundamentally on community ideals . . . schools are to serve the national interest.'[39]

Hitler's conviction of 'the criminal follies committed under the Weimar Republic in the field of education' and his contempt for academic education, teachers and intellectuals were at the heart of the National Socialist view of what had to be done in the schools.[40] His personal failure at school and subsequent rebuffs by centres of further education in pre-1914 Austria inevitably coloured his outlook, as did the experience of the trenches during the First World War (*Fronterlebnisse*) and the demand for action which characterised right-wing, nationalist thinking in Germany after 1918. He believed the war had shown 'the inadequacy of intellectualism as a primary aim of education'.[41] The ideal was to produce youths who were 'slim and strong, swift as greyhounds, tough as leather, and hard as Krupp steel'.[42] A shift away from an academic to a physical emphasis was Hitler's aim in school for only in this way would the future *völkisch* State be created.[43] Formal teaching, the acquisition of scientific and objective knowledge, the cultivation of critical faculties, were all relegated to a lowly position in the National Socialist scale of educational priorities. Instead, the stress was to be on ideological indoctrination, including a 'proper' understanding of history,[44] character-building, and of course race-consciousness. Hitler was adamant about the last element:

> The crown of the *völkisch* State's entire work of education and training must be to burn the racial sense and racial feeling into the instinct and intellect, the heart and brain of the youth entrusted to it. No boy and no girl must leave school without having been led to an ultimate realisation of the necessity and essence of blood purity.
>
> The *völkisch* State will have to make certain that by a suitable education of youth it will some day obtain a race ripe for the last and greatest decisions on this earth. And the nation which first sets out on this path will be victorious.[45]

Anti-intellectual trends were evident in German education before 1933, with concomitant demands for a return to intuition and anti-rationalism as the basis for instruction. In a sense, therefore, the National Socialists were merely intensifying certain attitudes already fashionable in some, mainly conservative, educational circles.[46] Nevertheless, the Third Reich did not produce a clear programme of educational reform until 1937/8, when new plans for primary and secondary schooling were announced.[47] Until then periodic directives from Hitler (*Führerbefehle*) constituted in the absence of any real pedagogical theory the main source of guidance in National Socialist school practice. The political demands of the State were uppermost in a policy that was pragmatic, empirical and administratively confusing. It is within the broad context of such imperatives that the HJ's role in schools is to be analysed.

The indiscriminate anti-intellectualism of the HJ in the *Kampfzeit* made it an unlikely contender for constructive leadership in the schools, and von Schirach's remarks did not inspire much confidence:

> For us feeling is more important than understanding. A working youth whose heart beats passionately for our *Führer* is more essential for Germany than a highly educated aesthete who dampens every stirring of his weak feelings with rational considerations.[48]

Views of this type were hardly likely to lead to a continuation of the independent youth movement's noteworthy contribution to the development of educational theory and practice in Germany.[49] On the contrary, they caused an immediate and enduring conflict with the school authorities, even though they were also for the most part National Socialists.[50] Rival competencies and personal power struggles were of course the very stuff of which the administration of the Third Reich was made, and education was no exception to Hitler's reluctance to rationalise the way public affairs were conducted. The failure clearly to delimit the powers of State and party institutions resulted in bureaucratic in-fighting of a particularly vicious kind. Not only did the Ministry of Education have to contend with the importunity of the HJ, but the Stormtroopers, Propaganda Ministry, German Labour Front and even the Army sought at one time or another to create their own spheres of influence in the school system. Leading figures such as Wilhelm Frick, Alfred Rosenberg, Phillip Bouhler, Goebbels and above all, Martin Bormann, were all involved. The challenge from the HJ, however, was the most persistent and ultimately the most deleterious, for it simply extended the pattern of disruption and intimidation in schools established before 1933 by its companion organisation, the NSS.[51]

Von Schirach's belief that youth had to be led by youth and that the fundamentals of National Socialist education could be properly imparted only by the HJ was bound to engender conflict with the more intellectually slanted approach of the schools. Early attempts to promote mutual compatibility, as in the School Law (Reichsschulgesetz) of December 1933, were abortive.[52] The heady atmosphere of revolutionism prevalent at large in Germany during 1933 was not conducive to accommodating attitudes, especially among the young. The demand for action at all costs in the service of the *Führer's* will caused a serious backlash against the schools and their notions of academic standards. Non-National Socialist teachers were denounced or even dismissed, textbooks were carefully scrutinised so that only those reflecting a nationalist bias were permitted to circulate,[53] and the 'Heil Hitler' salutation was introduced in the classroom at the end of the year.

In accordance with its semantic attachment to the *Volksgemeinschaft* ethos, the HJ wanted to impregnate the school system with its own brand of egalitarianism. It was instrumental in having the exclusive students' corporations abolished and in having school caps, a badge of social (middle-class) as well as of academic (Gymnasium -grammar school) status, banned altogether.[54] The *Gymnasia*, which were widely regarded as bastions of a conservative, bourgeois scholastic tradition, were favourite targets for HJ abuse. Such initiatives were defended by it as practical examples of its socialism and condoned by the regime because they fitted in with its own general anti-intellectual predilections, as expressed, for example, in the campaigns to reduce the status of universities and student enrolment in them. Hence the number of matriculated students fell from 88,823 in the summer term 1933 to 40,645 in the corresponding term of 1939.[55] Von Schirach, a man of considerable intellectual pretensions, had the ambition to head a Ministry of Youth,[56] and his resolve to have the HJ achieve parity with, and ultimately to supersede, the schools, added a further dimension to the developing unstable relationship between the two institutions.

One particular expedient cynically employed by von Schirach to further HJ interests at the expense of the school authorities was the generational conflict. Although he tried hard to play down this problem in German society as a whole after 1933, for the sake of national unity, he assiduously worked for its continuation in schools, specifically in the teacher–pupil relationship. Pupils who were also leaders in the HJ were encouraged to reject the authority of teachers as well as traditional curricular and teaching methods. Such vestiges of 'bourgeois' education were denounced as irrelevant in a National Socialist State. Often to the fore in this campaign were those elements in the HJ who came either from a working-class background or who had been associated before 1933 with the organised proletarian youth movement. These youths frequently carried over into their activity in the HJ's educational sphere a distinctively anti-secondary school mentality, which lent a particularly sharp edge to their confrontation with schools.[57] Their feelings of intellectual inferiority and class resentment, augmented in most cases by their actual physical exclusion from secondary education, which was of course a preserve of the middle and upper classes, account for this pronounced antipathy. Teachers who tried to resist such trends were invariably told by the HJ that they were too old to understand what was happening in Germany. The HJ mounted several campaigns during 1933–5 to have older teachers replaced by younger and more actively pro-National Socialist ones, with von Schirach taking the lead. He exacerbated the situation by deliberately excluding teachers from holding important leadership posts in the HJ during the early phase of the regime, and by publicly affirming that academically qualified personnel were unsuitable for the task of harnessing youth's energies in the school for National Socialism.[58] He called for a new type of National Socialist teacher who was more in keeping with the HJ's non-academic approach to education, because only then, he contended, would the school system be fully permeated by National Socialism. In the meantime, he advised existing teachers that, 'the more the teacher strives to gain a sympathetic understanding of the spirit and law of the Hitler Youth, the more success he will have'.[59] The immediate consequences of the HJ's attitude were unmistakable.

During 1933 and 1934, reports of incidents ranging from petty acts of disobedience to outright use of physical force by Hitler youths against teachers during school hours reached such serious proportions that even high party officials became concerned. In November 1933 a Committee for Education was set up under NSDAP auspices to discuss the threat to school discipline posed by the HJ's obstreperous behaviour. The HJ was subsequently warned to respect the authority of the school and to impress upon its members that they were to fulfil the schools' requirements for work and discipline.[60] The HJ's insistence on making service demands of its members during school hours resulted in pupils' being too tired to apply themselves to their studies. Extensive disruption of one important cornerstone of German school life – namely, homework – also became widespread. Confronted with the HJ's assault tactics and with evidence of an unprecedented degree of disorder and falling academic standards in schools of all levels, the educational authorities sought a compromise with the HJ. That they should have been compelled to come to terms with a determinedly anti-intellectual body was itself appropriate comment on the standing of education in the Third Reich as a whole, and also on the quality of Education Minister Rust, who was one of the weakest and least influential members of the National Socialist administrative hierarchy.[61] A schoolteacher (*Studienrat*) by profession until entering parliament in 1930, he was usually no match for his more aggressive power-hungry colleagues and, more damagingly, was unable to enlist Hitler's support in his struggle to counteract the HJ.

Rust's policy of conciliation resulted most notably during the early years in an agreement concerning the institution of the so called State Youth Day (*Staatsjugendtag*)in July 1934, whereby Saturdays were to be kept free of routine schoolwork for HJ members. Non-members were to attend school as usual and, in addition, take a course in political instruction.[62] Rust had made an important concession, for the HJ was now legally recognised as having a firm place in the school system, and he made a number of public statements extolling the benefits of co-operation between the two.[63] Any thoughts, however, that the HJ would be placated by the agreement were dispelled before very long. Following a brief respite in its antagonism towards the schools, during which von Schirach tried to be reassuring about further relations,[64] the HJ returned to its old ways, particularly as it was seen to be unprepared organisationally and intellectually for its responsibilities within the State Youth Day concord.[65] It redoubled its efforts to have its leaders appointed to parent–teacher councils, in order to safeguard its interests in schools, and became even more solicitous about securing the confidence of parents, a point on which von Schirach laid heavy emphasis, especially after the introduction of the 1936 HJ Law. Right up to the war he stressed the importance of the family unit and the vital role of parents in education in what was probably an attempt to mobilise even greater pressure on the third element of the educational trinity, the schools.[66] A further important advance was made by the HJ in 1934, when schools were obliged to appoint an HJ *Schuljugendwalter* (School Youth Warden),[67] whose function was to adjudicate disagreements between teachers and those pupils who belonged to the Hitler Youth. This new position inevitably strengthened the youth organisation's authority in schools, especially as the *Schuljugendwalter* was usually biased in favour of pupils. The long term aim of Dr Kurt Petter, who was in charge of school affairs in the RJF, was to use the *Schuljugendwalter* as a means of obtaining a major voice for the HJ in academic decisions within the school.[68]

The promulgation of the HJ Law in 1936 made it clear that von Schirach envisaged no long-term compromise with anyone. Henceforth, the HJ, as a reflection of its enhanced educational standing in law, began to make more and more of the running in schools, and its determination to reduce their status was poignantly illustrated by von Schirach's enthusiastic collaboration with Robert Ley, the prime mover, in establishing the innovative Adolf-Hitler-Schulen (AHS) in 1937. These schools were erected outside the conventional school sector and put under the jurisdiction of the party and HJ. Rust was infuriated by these developments and pointedly asked Ley to abandon the whole project.[69] When this failed and once again he received no sympathy from Hitler,[70] Rust unsuccessfully tried to thwart the scheme by encouraging his officials in the Education Ministry to interfere directly in the administration of the

AHS when they in fact had no legal right to do so,[71] and by trying to prevent teachers from transferring to these schools from the State system.[72] Once under way, the AHS, of which there were twelve by the end of the war, catering for 2027 pupils,[73] were meant to produce the future political and administrative elite of the Third Reich, who would, in von Schirach's words, 'believe in the impossible'.[74] The AHS were not, however, part of an elaborate National Socialist plan for a new form of education but were rather designed to develop as a party-controlled school system alongside the State schools,[75] and were an independent part of the string of educational establishments — including also the National Political Institutes of Education (Napola)[76] and the National Socialist Order Castles (*Ordensburgen*) — [77] set up by the regime. The administration of the six-year programme in ideological, physical and intellectual training in the AHS clearly reflected the HJ's unconventional educational outlook. There were no traditional examinations, grades or report cards and the teacher—pupil relationship was open and informal. Emphasis in the curriculum was on the development of intuition rather than intellect.[78] Because of this, these schools never attained any noteworthy academic stature, as even the party acknowledged, and generally failed to fulfil expectations.[79] Despite this, Rust was forced to accept a further undermining of his authority and of the school system.

The HJ was able to use the 1936 law in its fight to abolish both State and private Catholic schools, which had been specifically protected by the 1933 Concordat (Articles 21—5). Bormann was the mastermind behind this attack, which succeeded in closing all Catholic schools by 1939.[80] Catholic and Protestant children thereafter attended the so called German Community Schools (*Gemeinschaftsschulen*), which National Socialist educational theorists regarded as a decisive step forward towards the realisation of a true national community.[81] The fact that a good many of the Catholic schools were of a high academic standing did not seem to enter into the argument. The ultimate aim of the HJ was to eliminate religious instruction altogether from schools, though tentative moves in this direction, such as removing crucifixes from classroom walls, often were effected against considerable popular opposition.[82]

Another major casualty of the HJ's relentless encroachment on school life was the teaching profession. Teachers, particularly the more academically oriented, found their scope for enterprise and initiative drastically curtailed to a point where they became mere cogs in an over-regimented system. Even fully committed National Socialist teachers despaired of what was happening to professionally accepted notions of schooling in the face of the HJ's onslaught.[83] Indeed, the teachers' own organisation, the Nationalsozialistischer Lehrerbund (National Socialist Teachers League – NSLB), connived at this deterioration by frequently supporting the Hitler Youth's actions.[84] The NSLB vigorously advocated the involvement of teachers in National Socialist activities as part of their normal school duties, but the final objective was naturally a comprehensively politicised and pliable teaching profession.[85] The wider consequences of the decline in teachers' authority and social status were soon manifested in, among other things, an acute teacher shortage at all levels of schooling with the exception of the *Gymnasia*, which still retained sufficient prestige to attract the most highly qualified personnel. Many students who in ordinary times would have become teachers on leaving university or some form of further education were now attracted to the professional career structure created in the HJ in 1938, or to better-paid positions in industry and commerce. The Ministry of Education heavily criticised the HJ for causing the shortage, while von Schirach in typical fashion blamed the teachers themselves.[86] His solution to the problem and to the more general crisis in the schools was to reiterate his previous demands for the training of a new type of teacher according to precepts enunciated by the HJ. Von Schirach's new 'leader – teacher' was to be 'a physically and spiritually hardened comrade who will not be a schoolmaster but a master of life'.[87] He set up the HJ's own teacher-training institutes, but their lack of adequate financing, low intellectual standards and over-emphasis on sports and paramilitary training underlined their incapacity to solve the problem of teacher shortage.[88]

The last peacetime years of the regime did not see any improvement in the overall situation of the schools. HJ leaders continued to impose their demands for less homework, more leisure time and more sports on school authorities throughout Germany. The types of secondary schools were cut down in number from 40 to 3, and the HJ also helped to have the period of study at the secondary level reduced in 1938 from 9 years to 8, and at the middle level from 6 years to 4.[89] In many schools HJ leaders succeeded in winning a measure of control which equalled that of head teachers, and normal functioning of the daily routine of schools was often made impossible unless HJ requirements of one kind or another were met. In 1939, after Rust had made an official protest to Lammers at the Reich Chancellory,

Deputy Reich Youth Leader Hartman Lauterbacher defended the time taken off school by HJ members engaged in harvest work. Needless to say, Lauterbacher carried the day.[90] The whole system of examinations and pupils' progress became hopelessly distorted, owing to illegitimate interference by HJ personnel. Thus, academically poor pupils who also happened to be in the HJ were permitted, at the discretion of their HJ leader, to proceed to the next class, when in usual circumstances they would have been compelled to repeat a year, or even to withdraw from school entirely. Teachers who protested at such action were either ignored or reprimanded, or even threatened with dismissal.[91] Complaints about declining academic standards in schools had little or no impact on the HJ or its political masters. By the late 1930s it was patently obvious that, as far as the regime was concerned, academic attainment was not a principal criterion in ascertaining the success or failure of the school system. What mattered was the training of ideologically sound adherents of National Socialism.

While a thorough-going revolution had not taken place in German school education by 1939, there can be little doubt that substantial destructive inroads into the traditional school sector had been made, and that the organisation largely responsible was the HJ. Throughout six years of unremitting and aggressive anti-intellectual behaviour, it had managed to reduce academic standards in schools to an unparalleled degree. Discipline had been severely disrupted, truancy was on the increase, teachers' authority and status had been fundamentally undermined, teacher shortages were seriously hampering the system, and an ever-expanding ideological and political content had been imposed on curricula. The once universally prestigious German school system had been rendered virtually unrecognisable, without there being a coherent alternative to replace it. It is little wonder that in 1939 the schools and the educational aurhorities were thoroughly demoralised. The HJ had shown itself to be both a revolutionary force for destroying established sources of authority and a counter-revolutionary force for securing the totalitarian control of a reactionary regime. As an educational factor it signally epitomised the intellectual vacuity of National Socialism, for its contribution to the school sector by 1939 was irredeemably negative.[92]

The onset of the war altered the terrain on which the HJ–school struggle was fought out. As the war dragged on, normal conditions of life in Germany became more and more disturbed, and the younger generation suffered from the absence of fathers at the front, mothers out working in factories, and from their own involvement in various kinds of war work (*Kriegseinsatz*). The school routine was upset even further, of course, especially as the HJ made increasingly heavy demands on members' time. In the atmosphere of war the anti-learning attitude encouraged by the HJ in schools since 1933 was strengthened. It no longer seemed to matter to many youths about abstract concepts of mathematics or irregular English verbs when there was a battle for the nation's existence going on.[93] The HJ was accordingly able to intensify its pressure on the schools for an ever-greater say in the running of their affairs. It received solid support from the NSDAP, which sought to capitalise on the military victories of 1939–42 in order to extend National Socialist control over the entire educational system.

The tilting of the balance of power in schools towards the HJ was strikingly underlined in a series of measures during the early war years. In 1940 it became possible for boys and girls who were required for war service to take their school-leaving certificate (*Abitur*) without having to sit the customary final examinations. In 1940 of 61,000 holders of this certificate no fewer than 31,000 received it by the new regulation. A similar scheme, where war service was allowed to compensate for academic failings, was also introduced into the universities.[94] These moves were indicative of the lower standards of examination which the HJ had been promoting for some time, regardless of the alarm felt by other Reich authorities at the low calibre of school graduates. In 1940, for example, the *Oberpräsident* of Saxony had seen fit to issue a devastating critique of the schools, but laying the blame firmly on the shoulders of the HJ.[95] The SS Security Service (*Sicherheitsdienst*) reported also in 1940 an all-round decline in pupils' performance, especially at the primary and vocational levels.[96] Universities joined in the wave of protest and often felt it necessary to put on refresher courses for first-year undergraduates.[97] In 1942 some university authorities seriously debated the possibility of no longer recognising the *Abitur* as proof of an applicant's suitable academic quality.[98]

The continued hostility of Rust towards von Schirach was justified in the sense that the latter was more determined than ever to achieve his aim of a united youth educational system under his control as a Minister of Youth. In a secret memorandum of 11 September 1939 to his top officials, he hinted at the possibility of his taking over responsibility during the war for all educational matters,[99] and at the same time let it be known that Hitler had promised him the education portfolio and that only the intervention of the war had prevented this plan from being put into effect.[100] Later the same year, however, he tried hard to secure a share at least in the law-making work of the Education Ministry.[101] When in 1940 Hitler promoted him NSDAP *Gauleiter* and *Reichsstatthalter* in Vienna, von Schirach's base for launching his ambitions in the school sector was widened, because at the time of his new appointment he was also designated 'Reich Leader· for Youth Education of the NSDAP' (*Reichsleiter für die Jugenderziehung der NSDAP*).[102] In effect, he had now been given authority to concern himself directly with educational affairs affecting not only the HJ but also the schools and NSLB. Practical results soon became apparent. In January 1941 a new agreement was signed between Rust and von Schirach defining the educational areas of competence of the school and HJ and the extent of their co-operation.[103] The basic structure of the agreement was similar to that of the ill-fated State Youth Day scheme of 1934, but, significantly, the HJ was now allotted a good deal more time and influence in school matters, including the power to determine school holidays. Rust was being forced to yield more and more ground and was unable to secure support for his viewpoint from any important source within the party. Decisive for his weak position was Bormann's hatred for him and Hitler's contempt. In 1942 the *Führer* denounced Rust as a pedant and blamed him for holding up fundamental reforms in schools.[104] From 1940 there was talk in party circles that Rust would be dismissed, and Bormann for one made a considerable effort to achieve this, but, von Schirach's claims notwithstanding, there was no obvious replacement, and, in any case, Hitler was reluctant to drop one of his 'Old Fighters'.

The HJ's enhanced position *vis-à-vis* the Ministry of Education was again underscored in early autumn 1941, when a new plan for teacher-training was approved for primary schools.[105] In practice, the agreement for the teacher-training institutes soon gave the HJ authority to determine who should be admitted to them. This was formally confirmed in a further accord between Rust and the new HJ leader, Axmann, in November 1942. It was also expected that in future the teaching staff at the institutes would be HJ leaders.[106] The implications for who controlled what in the school sector were very clear. If Rust had any lingering doubts about his diminishing status they were surely dispelled by Hitler's decision in 1942 to allow the AHS leaving certificate, which was of poor academic quality, to be recognised as a full qualification for entry to higher centres of education, including the universities. This meant that the AHS certificate did not require the official stamp of approval from the Ministry of Education.[107] To add insult to injury, Rust was not officially informed of this development until the decision was on the point of practical implementation, but his bitter complaints once more fell on deaf ears.[108]

Despite the fact that at a conference in Munich in December 1941 von Schirach confessed to regret at having encouraged the HJ to denigrate teachers — what an admission! — and calling for a new era of co-operation with school authorities,[109] the decline in educational standards in schools became worse as the military situation deteriorated for Germany, and as more and more of the nation's resources and energies were directed towards the war effort. The call-up deprived schools of even more male teachers, while children were summoned more often for war fatigue, which from 1943 also included service as anti-aircraft auxiliaries (*Luftwaffenhelfer*).[110] School timetables became liable to extensive disruption, and school buildings were frequently requisitioned. Reports of the gloomy picture in schools flooded in from many official quarters. Even Himmler expressed alarm and Hitler continued to voice his dissatisfaction.[111] The most crushing indictment of the schools came, however, in a lengthy report written in 1942 by Gauleiter Paul Wegener, a protégé of Bormann's, on the condition of the party and its ancillary organsations.[112] He deplored the effects of the HJ's incursions into the school system, blaming it for many of the problems that had arisen. Wegener's mentor, Bormann, was certainly no friend of von Schirach's, whose standing with Hitler he successfully undermined in the early 1940s. Moreover, Bormann, who was probably the most influential single individual in the formulation of educational policy during the war, bitterly resented the ambitions of other party leaders in this sphere. He had warned Ley in 1941 to stop meddling in school affairs and was equally hostile to von Schirach's unyielding ambitions.[113] In 1942, for example, the former HJ leader had unsuccessfully tried to obtain from Hitler a special commission as head of a war aid scheme (*Kriegshilfswerk der deutschen Jugend*) with wide-ranging responsibilities relating to the educational sphere, including schools,[114] and the following year, when once again Rust's dismissal was being eagerly debated in party circles, he had pushed forward his claims, with support from his old ally Ley, for the Ministry of Education.[115] Bormann quashed von Schirach's in-

itiative with ease, because by that time the Youth Leader had fallen
foul of Hitler, mainly on account of his cultural policy in Vienna and
attitude towards the Jewish question.[116] In any event, by 1943 the
worsening war situation effectively precluded any further thoughts
within the party about fundamental change in schools. Major
disorders in the home front were to be avoided at all costs. However,
the National Socialist spirit had thoroughly permeated the schools by
then, and for this the HJ bore much responsibility. During its long
battle with the educational bodies, it had asserted its dominance of the
partnership in the schools and the ascendancy of its anti-academic
ethos.

The area of conflict between the schools and Hitler Youth during
the war also encompassed the enlarged *Kinderlandverschickung* (Child
Evacuation Scheme – KLV), which came into operation in 1941.
Originally conceived in 1934 as a means of giving urban children in
poor health an opportunity to convalesce or have a holiday in the
countryside, the KLV was transformed during the war into a scheme
for evacuating children aged 10–16 years from bomb-threatened
areas to safe areas of the Reich. HJ theorists saw in the KLV a chance
for effecting a total educational process in which the influence of
parents and teachers would be gradually eliminated to the advantage
of the HJ's educational claims.[117] In other words, the scheme became
in wartime another battle-ground for the competing interests of the
three principal institutions in child education. The camps in which the
evacuated children were housed fell under the joint control of an
NSLB teacher and an HJ leader. Teaching was supposed to be closely
patterned on the conventional school model, but in actuality much
more emphasis was laid on physical pursuits such as sports and
hiking – an unmistakable reflection of HJ influence. Classes were also
conducted less formally and were subject to more improvisation than
in ordinary schools. The prevailing atmosphere was likewise less
scholastic than usual. But, although in general terms the HJ came to
exercise the greatest influence in these camps and eliminated to a large
extent the voice of parents, it lacked the resources to realise its
grandiose concept of an education under its exclusive control.[118] Its
ideological indoctrination programme in the camps had modest
results and the presence of teachers was not reduced nearly as much as
it desired.[119] By 1944, when 800,000 children had passed through
the KLV scheme, administration of the 3500 camps still lay by and
large under joint teacher–HJ control.[120] The camps were too poorly
run to produce the sort of educational revolution wanted by the

HJ,[121] and, despite the optimistic reports concerning the quality of teaching,[122] parents continued to harbour profound misgivings.[123] During the closing stages of the war, all theoretical presuppositions about the role of the KLV had to be renounced amidst the accelerating chaos in Germany.

The most obvious manifestation of the HJ's direct intervention in the schools was the havoc it wrought. The tactics pursued by von Schirach from the beginning of the Third Reich onwards produced a fundamental decline in the substance and status of academic school education. War conditions merely furnished an even more favourable background for the HJ's destructive anti-intellectualism. Its educational role can also be assessed in terms of its capacity to open up secondary education to less privileged sections of the younger generation. The HJ's much proclaimed egalitarianism might have been expected to produce something of a social revolution in the school sector. Did this happen? This is an extremely complex issue which has attracted considerable scholarly interest, but it is not our purpose here to delve into the intricacies of the debate. Instead, the following observations are simply designed to intimate in outline form some of the more important points which have been so far advanced. In broad terms, it might be argued that the HJ helped promote a break with traditionalism by giving a strong impetus towards modernity in education, specifically by encouraging public rather than private values. Furthermore, by de-emphasising academic achievement in the criteria selected for determining success at school, the HJ may have opened up to a very limited extent better opportunities for a small number of working-class children. The AHS is the most obvious example of this trend. Although a majority of pupils in these schools were from comfortable middle-class homes,[124] most of them would not normally have progressed beyond the primary-school level because of their academic deficiencies.[125] This would certainly have been the case with working-class AHS pupils. As we have seen, the AHS did open up higher education to less academically qualified youths in 1942. The avenues of upward mobility were also created more extensively for youths who would normally have had no prospect of advancement under traditional academic standards of selection when the *Hauptschule* was introduced into Germany in 1942, although the HJ was not involved in this development. Enrolment and instruction in the *Hauptschulen* were free of charge, thus allowing poorer children to get on.[126] In the ordinary schools before 1942 it is extremely doubtful whether the HJ made any real advances in helping children from less privileged homes to progress up the ladder. All things considered, the extent to which the HJ created better educational prospects for the lower-class youth was insignificant. Certainly, there was no social revolution accomplished by the HJ or indeed the party. In 1945 there were still more elements of continuity and traditional practice than of revolutionary change in the school system. As in so many other spheres of German society, the National Socialist impact was made through the medium of unconstructive power politics aimed at total control and subjection.

The new ideology had been ruthlessly stamped on German youth by the HJ through its activities inside and outside school. The Second World War provided the severest possible test for the efficacy of the National Socialist youth movement's indoctrination programme. The opportunity to put into practice what had been constantly preached had at last come.

7 Götterdämmerung

There is only victory or annihilation. Know no bounds in your love for your people; equally, know no bounds in your hatred of the enemy!

Artur Axmann

The Second World War fundamentally changed the character of the HJ. It became in addition to a *Staatsjugend* also a *Kriegsjugend*, a youth movement which was increasingly drawn into activities directly related to Germany's war effort (*Kriegseinsatz*). Von Schirach called on the HJ in September 1939 to make its own special contribution to achieving victory,[2] and very quickly the emphasis in its work was switched from the likes of ideological instruction and sport to a range of assorted duties which had nothing to do with any genuine concept of youth education. HJ members now helped gather in the harvest, plant crops, collect old materials such as iron, paper, wood and clothing, distribute ration cards, act as temporary firemen, road workers, road-sweepers, railway porters, postmen, general handymen, and also as messengers for the party and military authorities. BdM girls became stand-in nurses, clerks, typists, telephonists and so on.[3] Axmann, who in 1940 took over from von Schirach, as HJ leader, defined the situation in this way:

> Every job must be directed towards the necessities of war. Each duty that we fulfil serves victory! This struggle encompasses all aspects of German life. The struggle is not only conducted with front line soldiers, but also with the moral and economic strength of the homeland. Youth can also help bring victory.[4]

The National Socialist leadership wanted to make youth feel that they too were crucial to the drive for victory, and without doubt the HJ's role on the home front was valuable in this respect. The ensuing release of manpower for the armed forces was one result of its contribution. Another was its equally important role in helping to boost morale at home, with the Propaganda Ministry taking care that photographs of Hitler youths engaged in various forms of war work were given liberal space in the press. During the period of German victories, the war duties of the HJ were performed in a certain romantic spirit, for the fighting did not yet impinge too much on their daily lives. Many youths saw their new role as significant, but also as good fun, especially when all seemed well and final victory just ahead.

On another level, the HJ revealed during these early war years that its quest for leadership was not confined to Germany alone. Since 1933 it had established contact with youth groups outside the Reich, above all in those parts of Europe where there were ethnic German minorities. Before the war, consequently, National Socialist youth organisations or even HJ units had emerged in the Sudetenland, Austria, Poland, Memel and elsewhere. When the German forces overran these areas, co-operation among the youth of countries under Axis influence considerably increased. The HJ was a prime instigator in this direction, and its efforts were crowned in September 1942 when it organised a conference in Vienna attended by European fascist and National Socialist youth movements, including the Falange youth of Spain, the Walloon Rex youth, the Brannik youth of Bulgaria, the Lavante youth of Hungary, the Hlinka youth of Slovakia and others from Italy, Norway and Croatia. A European Youth Association bound together by an anti-Communist and anti-semitic outlook was set up, with Axmann and the Italian Fascist Party official Aldo Vidussoni, appointed acting joint presidents.[5] However, although officially described by the NSDAP as 'a new weapon in the struggles of this war',[6] little was heard of the new grouping after 1943.

The mood in the HJ, as elsewhere in Germany, changed drastically once military successes were no longer forthcoming. The defeat at Stalingrad in early 1943 was, of course, the crucial turning-point not only for the German Army but also for the nature and extent of the HJ's commitment to the war. In December 1943 a decree was promulgated for the intensification of HJ war service on the home front which for the first time gave the youth organisation an official status in the war effort,[7] thus underlining the serious situation in which the Third Reich found itself at this comparatively early date. In a way this decree complemented the 1936 HJ Law and the *Jugenddienstpflicht* of 1939, for it emphasised the legal duty of service to the State on the part of German youth and hence of their statutory responsibility to serve the interests of National Socialism.[8] From this time on, there was also a conscious re-creation by the HJ leadership of the militant spirit of the pre-1933 era as it strove to encourage youth to expend greater effort on the sagging military situation. An official HJ report put it clearly:

> There is no fundamental difference between the youth of that time (pre-1933) and today. The spirit which then inspired a fearless minority today stands as the motivating force behind the entire younger generation of the Reich . . . there exists between the Hitler youths who once gave their lives for Germany in the *Kampfzeit* and those who sacrifice their lives in bomb attacks or on the military fronts a holy bond of brotherhood![9]

As the war further deteriorated from Germany's standpoint and frantic efforts were being made by the regime to unearth new sources of manpower, the HJ was put on a total-war footing.[10] At the same time the augmentation of its war role only increased its problems with recalcitrant elements among youth.

The HJ's transformation into a *Kriegsjugend* was not accomplished without considerable organisational and disciplinary difficulties. As its leaders volunteered or were called up for military service, posts of responsibility in the movement had to be filled by inexperienced younger members or by war-wounded veterans of the armed forces, who were drafted into the HJ even though in most cases they had little or no conception of youth leadership. To some extent, therefore, von Schirach's dictum of youth being led only by youth was negated, and from an organisational point of view the HJ accordingly suffered. By 1942/3, its administration in many areas was in a chaotic state and there were loud demands from party circles for a full-scale restructuring of the HJ.[11] Of more immediate concern to it, however, was the alarming increase in juvenile delinquency which accompanied the onset of the war, and the rising incidence of illegal youth activities.

In January 1940 Education Minister Rust indicated his disquiet at the rise in juvenile delinquency since the beginning of the war, but argued that the problem should be combated by educational rather than police measures.[12] As usual, his advice went unheeded, but there was no denying the seriousness with which more influential officials regarded the situation, including the SS and the HJ itself. A secret report compiled by the RJF noted that during the first six months of 1940 Hitler youths committed no fewer than twenty murders and were additionally implicated in 6522 cases of theft, 900 cases of homosexuality, and 568 cases of petty fraud and embezzlement.[13] The HJ's own internal policing procedures were ill equipped effectively to deal with this challenge, and so the police had to intervene. A number of police orders restricting the movement and activity of youth had already been issued in 1939, but in March 1940 a more significant and far-reaching measure came into force, the Reich Police Order for the Protection of Youth (Polizeiverordnung zum Schutz dee Jugend).[14] This established a national curfew for youth under eighteen years of age, beginning at dusk. Young people were now barred from restaurants and pubs after 9 p.m. unless in the company of an adult. Youths under sixteen years were entirely barred from these places unless under adult supervision; the same rules applied to cinema visits. In addition, there were strict regulations governing the consumption of alcohol and smoking in public for under-sixteen-year-olds. Contraventions of the order were liable to attract fines or even in more serious cases could mean a three-week term of imprisonment. Similar restrictions had been placed on youth during the First World War, but in 1940 the measure was supplemented six months later by a new form of detention for youthful offenders – *Jugenddienstarrest* – which was introduced by the HJ.[15] The specific aim of the measure was to counteract the increase in the number of Hitler youths opting out of war service or who were generally considered not to be fulfilling their duties as their superiors thought fit. Serious culprits were liable to brief periods of detention in specially created Youth Education Camps (*Jugenderziehungslager*) where some form of corrective treatment would be administered. Less serious offences carried a penalty of regular reporting to local police offices. Perhaps the most ominous aspect of the decree was the power given to the Gestapo to enforce parts of it.[16] The progressively coercive character of the HJ (*Zwangjugend*) was thus accentuated.

Apart from the spiralling juvenile-crime figures, another manifestation of the younger generation's unrest during the war was the appearance in somewhat greater number than before the war of illegal groups of boys and girls at a local level, particularly in larger towns and cities. These groups adopted exotic names and a rather flamboyant sartorial style, as well as unorthodox habits, such as listening to jazz, lounging in cafés or even attacking HJ units. The large majority of groups were non-political in outlook but, on the other hand, were not simply composed of hooligans or misfits. Their principal *raison d'être* appears to have been resentment at the harsh regimentation and rigours of war service, to which youth was being more and more subjected in the HJ. Clearly, for a small minority of German youth the demands of war did not stimulate the self-sacrificial spirit asked of them by HJ leaders. The activities of the groups at times engendered grave concern in official circles. The SS Reich Security Office frequently reported incidents involving the groups from 1941/2 onwards, and Axmann was so infuriated by the antics of the so called 'Swing Youth' in Hamburg that in January 1942 he demanded that the SS take drastic action against those involved.[17] By 1943 the HJ, under pressure from its various wartime operations, lacked the resources to move against these oppositional elements and hence handed over responsibility for supervisory and disciplinary duties within its organisation to the police. Even so, the problem continued to cause some apprehension in the regime right up until the German home front disintegrated in 1944/5.[18] By that time it no longer mattered.

The degree of youthful opposition, in wartime, to the HJ and the regime as a whole should not, however, be exaggerated, even when the youth movement's understandable efforts to play down the problem are taken into consideration.[19] The disaffected and dissident elements were undoubtedly small in number and there is no question of their having constituted a properly co-ordinated resistance movement among German youth. The HJ had carried out its work too thoroughly for this to be a real possibility. The only important act of organised resistance was that concerning the White Rose Circle in Munich: here Hans Scholl, a medical student at the university and a former HJ member, distributed anti-Hitler literature with the assistance of his sister Sophie and friends until his capture and execution in 1943.[20] Such acts of bravery were very much the exception among youth, the overwhelming majority of whom remained steadfastly loyal to the Third Reich until at least near the end. Indeed, the most noteworthy contribution of youth to the German resistance movement lay not in the activity of illegal groups but in the endeavours of individual former members of the pre-1933 youth movement. The number of one-time Bündische personnel in the Resistance has been described as 'astonishingly high'.[21] They were conspicuous in the Kreisau Circle, for example,[22] and the elitist concepts of Bündische Youth significantly influenced the constitutional views of the conservative–nationalist part of the Resistance.[23]

One of the most distasteful features of the HJ's work in war as far as opposing youths were concerned was its progressive militarisation, a trend already in evidence before 1939. When war broke out, the HJ's active military engagement was at once shown by the induction of its leaders into the armed services. HJ personnel normally enlisted in elite regiments of the Army, such as the 'Grossdeutschland', in which von Schirach himself served for a short period in 1940, or in crack Waffen-SS formations.[24] By 1944 some 30,000 youth leaders had been killed at the front,[25] and many more had been wounded, including Axmann, who lost an arm in Russia. Another sign of the times was the HJ's decision in January 1941 to change its Office for Physical Education into one for Military Training, which then assumed responsibility for pre-military training given to Hitler youths.[26] Before long, however, the HJ's military role was formally defined in a series of agreements involving both the Army and the SS.[27] A proposal in 1940 for National Training Camps (*Reichsausbildungslager*)[28] was the prelude to Hitler's decree of March 1942 setting up HJ Military Instruction Camps (*Wehrertüchtigungslager*). These camps provided intensive pre-military training for youths aged sixteen and a half years or over in short courses under the direction of Army and Waffen-SS personnel.[29] The HJ retained control over camp organisation, discipline and ideological education. By the end of 1943 there were 226 of these camps, while a small number of the National Training Camps were kept on for the purposes of specialised training and leadership preparation. By early 1944, no fewer than 1½ million youths had passed through one or other of these two types of camp, most of them going on to join the Army.[30] The crushing losses sustained by the armed forces, especially on the Eastern Front, impressed the regime with the need to intensify the preparation of HJ members for field service.

For fear of arousing parental hostility, the regime avoided as far as possible publicity about the activist military role of the HJ. It also wanted to avoid the embarrassment of Allied propaganda claims that Germany was running so short of manpower that mere youths had to be called up to do the fighting. The reality of the matter was, however, that in 1943 Hitler youths were directed to anti-aircraft batteries as auxiliaries (*Luftwaffenhelfer*),[31] and later the same year, in the aftermath of Stalingrad, volunteers were sought from its ranks for service in the newly established 12th SS Panzerdivision 'Hitler-Jugend'. In the Battle of Normandy in summer 1944 this division displayed against discouraging odds a fanatical courage which was acknowledged by even its bitterest adversaries.[32] None the less, in 1944 a feeling of hopelessness about the outcome of the war began to percolate through the ranks of the HJ leadership, and more and more HJ publications preferred to avoid references to military themes, concentrating instead on matters of a cultural and historical kind.[33] This did not prevent Axmann from shamelessly exhorting his youths to further sacrifices in the closing stages of the war, when they, whether organised in individual units or in the Volkssturm, usually distinguished themselves in the fighting (above all, in Breslau, the Ruhr, Frankfurt an der Oder, and finally, Berlin). Obituary notices for HJ members were a regular feature of the daily press in 1944/5. The heroism of these youths as the Third Reich collapsed around them was warmly acknowledged by Hitler in his Political Testament – 'a contribution unique in history' – but this was small consolation when they had to face up to the post-war reckoning. This was a younger generation cruelly misled and finally shattered by an unscrupulous political creed.

Conclusion

The evidence presented in this study indicates that the emergence of the German youth movement had as much to do with a notion of youthful emancipation as with the problems of generational conflict and sociocultural malaise in bourgeois life at the turn of the century. Beginning with the Wandervogel, but rapidly spreading to other spheres of organised youth, was a modernistic quest which impugned long-established views and assumptions about the role of youth in society. The approach was emotional rather than intellectual, but none the less serious and purposeful. By the end of the First World War the younger generation had been fully accepted as an entity in itself, and worthy of due consideration by adults. The concepts of youth autonomy and self-education became widely accepted, and lending invaluable support was the Hohe Meissner spirit, which shone down like a fluorescent beacon on the subsequent development of the entire youth movement. Complementing this recognition of youth's new social status was the youth movement's, and particularly its independent sector's, demonstration that the younger generation had many positive and constructive reformist suggestions to make and actually implement for the benefit of the nation as a whole.

The achievements of the Wandervogel and its successors in the social, cultural, and above all, educational fields are clear, substantial and indisputable. Sections of confessional and even political youth took up and sometimes extended these accomplishments. Groups such as the Catholic Quickborn and the early post-war socialist youth movement left an indelible and distinctive mark on youth culture on this account. Assessed according to their own criteria, the Jewish organisations also enjoyed considerable success, especially once their work assumed a greater sense of urgency and a definite practical objective as Hitler's menacing shadow loomed. Unfortunately, the Protestant youth movement was too hidebound by the social and political background whence it came to be able to register a similarly wholesome impact. Much the same conclusion must be reached concerning the endeavours of political youth groups during the late

Weimar period. The leftist groups in particular were invariably ineffective by any standard. Generally, however, the activity of the German youth movement in the broadly non-political sphere was inspired by a conspicuous idealism and genuine commitment. In this respect, the driving force behind this contribution, the Wandervogel and Bündische Youth, distinguished themselves as lively constituents of that neo-conservative utopian–reformative impulse which was such an important feature of Germany's social and political character in the first quarter of the twentieth century.

The fundamental question mark against the youth movement relates to its political role. While neither Bündische Youth nor its predecessors can be legitimately regarded as direct forerunners of National Socialism, they were part of the Protestant, bourgeois milieu which created the attitudes conducive to the rise of the NSDAP. The political immaturity and negligence of the youth movement is beyond doubt, but, then, these deficiencies of what was after all a non-political movement must not be exaggerated. The context of its full range of activity is to be underlined. Besides, other, more experienced sections and institutions of Weimar society, from which a lead might have been reasonably expected, were at the end of the day at least as much to blame for the catastrophe of National Socialism. By 1933, therefore, the German youth movement had displayed both fundamental strengths and equally fundamental weaknesses. Its overall record of performance is somewhat mixed: it was neither a complete success nor a total failure, though on balance positive characteristics probably outweighed negative ones.

The year 1933 signifies a decisive dividing line in the history of the youth movement, for as the Hitler Youth evolved as the exclusive youth organisation of the Third Reich it released a counter-revolutionary dynamic which finally destroyed the inherent fabric of the pre-Hitler youth movement. The Hitler Youth did adopt certain ideas and practices from the latter, it is true, but these were distorted out of all recognition within the nefarious political ambience of National Socialism. The Hitler Youth was not interested in developing an innate youth culture. Its purpose was overtly political and ideological, to encompass and discipline a whole generation of youth in the spirit of the *Führer's* teaching. Its involvement in extending its totalitarian control over the organisation of youth and in challenging the traditional prerogatives of schools and parents in education amply emphasise its destructive capacity. The Hitler Youth changed the directions along the historical path tramped by German youth.

Instead of being led to the 'new man' in a new paradise based on humanitarian principles, German youth was led to untold misery and humiliation. This was hardly the aim set by the early Wandervogel leaders, such as Hoffmann-Fölkersamb or Fischer. The von Schirachs and Axmanns were the types who latterly seized the initiative, imposed their repugnant doctrines, and inevitably invoked *Götterdämmerung.* Consequently, in 1945 the German youth movement was well and truly at an end.

Documentary Appendix

1. From the proclamation announcing the youth meeting at the Hohe Meissner, 1913:

   German youth stands before a historic turning-point in its development. Youth, until now only an appendage of the older generation, excluded from the public affairs of the nation and forced into a passive role of learning – into a frivolous, negative role in society – is beginning to assert itself. It is attempting, independently of the dull customs of adults and of the constraints of hateful convention, to shape its own life. It is striving for a way of life which corresponds to youthful forms, which at the same time also enables it to take itself and its actions seriously, thus allowing youth to become a special factor in the general world of culture. Youth wants its capacity for pure enthusiasm about the highest tasks of humanity and its capacity for unbroken faith and belief in a noble existence to be developed into a refreshing, rejuvenating element in the spiritual life of the nation. And youth believes that our nation needs nothing more today than such a spiritual rejuvenation. Youth, which is prepared in an emergency at any time to give its life for the rights of the nation, wants also . . . to dedicate its innocent blood for the Fatherland. But youth distances itself from all forms of cheap patriotism. . . . We are all united in the endeavour to create a new, noble German youth culture.

   Source: 'Die Freideutsche Jugendbewegung, Pädagogisches Magazin' no. 597 (1915) p. 9.

2. Free German Youth's reaction to the November Revolution is conveyed in the following statement by one of its leaders, Otto Haase:

   We are standing at a turning-point of history. The old German

State apparatus has collapsed in a heap of ruins. . . . The authoritarian State has fallen, the foundations for the People's State have been created. Overnight, the proletariat has seized power in order to place it in the service of law, a great act of humanity. . . . The Revolution has shown us that the German bourgeoisie no longer possesses a philosophy or a reliable organisation. . . . What must we Free German Youth now do? Above all, away with reserved and delaying tactics which only give rise to political indifference; join the front ranks of those fighting for the idea. . . . It is no longer good enough for Free German Youth to hide behind questions of secondary importance, it is no longer good enough to hand over responsibility for the most vital questions of State to a minority of the working proletariat. The achievements of the Revolution are in danger of being wiped out by reaction and radicalism. . . . The revolutionary bourgeoisie must defend the results of the Revolution side by side with the proletariat against all comers. We Free German Youth salute the Revolution because we see in it the empirical basis for a rational order of society.

Source: 'Im deutschen Volksstaat', *Rundbrief für Freideutsche in Niedersachsen*, 1918, no. 8.

3.   A definition of German Boy Scout philosophy:

The founders of Boy Scoutism desired to give an impetus to a youth culture whose aim was the harmonious training of the body, mind and soul. A certain predilection for things military for a time overshadowed the original Boy Scout ideals, which are directed towards seeking out and locating the correct path through life, until it once again met up with the youth movement . . . thus the way was clear for our cultivation of a German youth culture. We Boy Scouts want to eagerly cooperate in the creation of this culture and bring our views strongly to bear. We have something to give it. We have cultivated values in the past which will be worthwhile and useful in youth work. Our principle of constant preparedness to help others allows us to recognise that unbridled licence for freedom leads to selfishness and therefore fully contradicts social ideals. The Boy Scouts, who have always cherished social ideals in a fundamental way, want responsibility with freedom and neighbourly love, while sharply rejecting egoism and boundless licence.

We also reject, therefore, unrestrained romanticism and effeminate sentimentality. . . .

Otherwise, we cherish . . . love of homeland and local customs, the experience of nature, folk-songs and festivals, flute and mandolin playing, German poetry . . . friendship with Boy Scouts of all nations, thus serving the cause of international reconciliation without renouncing our perceptions of German pride and German honour. . . . We look after our body through serious, not playful, but competitive participation in sports and games, gymnastics and swimming . . . .

Source: *Der Feldmeister, Führerzeitung und Bundesblatt der Deutschen Pfadfinderbundes*, 1920, no. 5/6.

4. A definition of the Deutsche Freischar group:

The Deutsche Freischar is a group of people that wants, on the basis of its experience in the youth movement, to lead its life towards itself and the nation in unconditional personal freedom together with a strong sense of responsibility. . . . The Deutsche Freischar takes over on the basis of its fundamental strength certain tasks of a political, cultural and educational type, with the aim of creating a new nation and Reich. These tasks include the creation of new, sensible social reforms, new educational communities in every kind of school . . . co-operation with all social classes, training in political awareness. . . . The Deutsche Freischar demands of its branches participation with all strength in those spheres which are part of everyday civic and national life, particularly at work, in the family . . . and education. . . . The basis for communal work is inner truthfulness, respect for other views, and readiness for mutual service.

Source: *Deutsche Freischar*, 1928, no. 1, pp. 2 ff.

5. A leader in the Adler und Falken, Hans-Joachim Lemme, describes the group's views thus:

We are through our blood nationalist: we want a Greater Germany which serves the German ethnic minorities in central Europe as an identity and life form. We are socialist in the real sense, that we always place the common good before individual interests, and fight capitalism, that is, the concentration of economic power in impersonal companies or in the hands of irresponsible individuals . . . and strive for the emancipation of the workers from economic, intellectual and spiritual slavery. Hence, National Socialism is essentially related to our fundamental outlook. We can never as a group become involved in daily politics, not do we wish to. We none the less hope to be, in a higher sense, politically effective.

Source: *Der Führer*, 1929, no. 4, p. 5.

6.   The Quickborn offers a description of itself:

Quickborn is an essentially Catholic youth movement. It stands as a group on the basis of the real Church, acknowledges its authority and lives according to its truth, community and strength. Our whole time is spent in struggle with the subjective spiritual outlook, particularly in the religious sphere. We see and affirm the importance and right of powerful, personal individuality. We trust we shall mould in the Catholic youth movement responsible, creative, devout personalities. This can only be possible, however, if we integrate spiritedly into the Church . . . .

Source: *Quickborn*, 1924, no. 1 (Mai).

7.   Udo Smidt, leader of the BK, in 1931:

The thing which at the moment is most closely associated with National Socialism, which at a modest estimate is looked upon with glowing but often ill-informed sympathy by 70 per cent of our youths, must be seen in our ranks less as a political and more as an ethical matter. . . . It appears to me almost hopeless to try and refute in detail the policies of National Socialism through petty schoolmasterly tactics and fault-finding, and all well-intentioned efforts of our leaders. We must take care of our above-party attitude.

Source: Udo Smidt, *In den Tag hinein. Botschaft und Bericht aus dem Bund deutscher Bibelkreise* (Wuppertal-Barmen, 1931).

8. The crucial paragraph in the *Prunner Gesetz* of Blau-Weiss in August 1922:

> We are the Jewish youth of Germany who want to go to Palestine, a part of the whole nation, yet a special entity within it . . . because of our origin and essence. . . . We shall build a Blau-Weiss colony which will realise Zionism, Zionism in a form which can be understood by youth.

Source: *Führerzeitung des Blau-Weiss*, 1922, no. 2.

9. The resolution on the 1905 Russian Revolution adopted by the general meeting of the Verband junger Arbeiter on 30 September 1906 in Mannheim:

> The first general meeting of the Verband . . . regards as one of its most important tasks the directing the attention and hearts of German proletarian youth to the heroic struggle of our brothers and sisters in Russia. We workers' sons gathered here take particular pride in being alive to class-consciousness in the world-historical epoch of the Russian Revolution. . . . We send our enthusiastic greetings to the Russian freedom fighters, among whom youth is conspicuously represented. We admire in the war of extermination against blood-dripping Czarism the enormous energy and the inexhaustible sacrificial courage of the Russian working class. We mourn with you at the bier of our . . . wickedly murdered Russian comrades and hope with you for victory shortly . . . .

Source: *Die Junge Garde*, 1906, no. 8 (Nov).

10. A declaration of the SAJ at its National Conference in Görlitz, December 1922:

> At the grave of Walter Rathenau we renew our unreserved support for the German democratic Republic. We shall be prepared at every hour and in all places to defend its well-being and existence. . . . With this solemn declaration, however, we must once again attach the demand that the Reichstag and Reich government give a living substance to the articles of the Weimar

constitution which relate to reform of the educational system, reform of apprentice-training, and protection of working youth. . . . The improvement of the living conditions of working youth is the most important prerequisite for the creation of the new generation through which . . . every new spirit of the Weimar constitution will be expressed. . . . We want the ideals of the youth movement to be permitted to flourish in the enduring and devoted work for the democratic and social Republic, which opens up the prospect of a happy future to our nation and the road to socialism to the working class.

Source: Werner Kindt (ed), *Die deutsche Jugendbewegung, 1920 bis 1933. Die Bündische Zeit. Quellenschriften* (Düsseldorf, 1974) p. 1021.

11. From the Guiding Principles adopted by the FSJ in February 1919:

The German Revolution places new tasks before the proletarian youth movement. . . .
    Proletarian youth is convinced that only through the removal of the capitalist social order, only through the final elimination of all hired labour can its ultimate aim be realised: the classless, socialist Republic of the working masses. It declares itself, therefore, against every domination and co-partnership of capitalist elements (coalition government, National Assembly) and demands that total power be invested exclusively in the hands of the revolutionary Workers' and Soldiers' Councils.
    Proletarian youth has from its origins fought with all its strength against war and militarism. It has recognised that the slogans about national defence are made up merely in order to protect property, to ensure more profit for capitalists, and especially, to divert the proletariat from the necessary class struggle. Proletarian youth once again affirms in friendly fashion its belief in the international brotherhood of all workers and in the struggle against international capitalism. . . . Proletarian youth refuses to allow itself to be coerced into any militia or other military systems. But it is happily prepared to help the proletarian revolution through the establishment of Red Guards . . . .

Source: *Die Junge Garde*, 1919, no. 3.

12. The KJVD affirms the Soviet connection:

Each of our districts is linked with a district of the Russian Komsomol, and almost all of our cells and local branches have connections with their Komsomol counterparts . . . through this connection we are able to be informed very precisely about conditions in the Soviet Union and receive much material and useful hints for our own work. It is therefore necessary that we continue to build up the link. . . .

Source: Der Junge Bolschewik, 1927, no. 9, pp. 13−14.

13. From Ernst Thälmann's speech to the KJVD national conference in Leipzig, April 1930:

Eleven years of the bourgeois Republic have opened the eyes of proletarian youth. Twelve years of socialist construction in the Soviet Union have awakened your enthusiasm for the cause of proletarian revolution. We salute the millions-strong organisation of the Russian Komsomol, we salute the Red Army and the Red Navy. . . . We require new methods in order to attract youth into our ranks in all areas of struggle. From this day forth, the KJVD carries out the decisive switch to the masses of young workers and closes up the united fighting front against the fascist terror organisations and against social fascism.

Three principal tasks lie before the young proletariat:

(1) the fight against the danger of imperialist war and for the defence of our socialist Fatherland, the Soviet Union;
(2) the fight against the exploitation of young male and female workers and for their political rights, for equal rights for youths with adults;
(3) the fight against national fascism and its terror organisations, the fight against social fascism, and for the winning over of young workers, also the social democratic and Christian young workers in the factories and offices, for the brotherly fighting association of proletarian youth with adult workers, for the overthrow of capitalist domination, for the dictatorship of the proletariat. . . .

. . . mobilise the masses of the young proletariat for the struggle against their exploiters. . . . Be helpers and leaders of proletarian youth in all struggles. Despite terror and prohibitions, forward to struggle and victory.

Source: *Rote Fahne*, 23 Apr 1930.

14. Ernst Thälmann to a KJVD meeting in November 1932:

We must not allow this young generation to fall under the demagogy of National Socialism! We must recognise, however, that National Socialism has succeeded in catching a certain part of this youth. We Communists must manage to win these young masses for ourselves, for Communism. . . . One of the most serious and important problems facing the KJVD is . . . to develop a broad ideological mass offensive to attract the young masses who are now going over to this red fascism. . . . Not only by proletarian military preparedness must we break the influence of the Nazis over young workers, but in this situation by the broadest ideological mass struggle. . . .

The false solution which Comrade Neumann defended for so long, the solution 'Strike the fascists wherever you meet them', particularly prevented our KJVD from developing an effective and successful mass policy for winning over the young Nazi followers. . . . We must investigate what binds many youths to the Nazi movement. We must draw serious lessons from the work methods of our enemies. Why are we so dry and insipid in our work? More vivacity, more enthusiasm, more verve, more movement, more passion must be brought into our work methods! We must create magnets in order to pull in proletarian youth to the KJVD! . . . mainly through the fault of its leadership has the KJVD hitherto turned its back on the masses.

Source: *Zur Geschichte der Arbeiterjugendbewegung in Deutschland. Eine Auswahl von Materialien und Dokumenten aus den Jahren 1904– 1946* (East Berlin, 1956) pp. 268–70.

15. The position of the SAJD *vis-à-vis* fascism is outlined:

The Eighth National Congress of the SAJD recognises in fascism the gathering of all reactionary powers whose objective is the ultimate spiritual and social enslavement and the destruction of working class organisations. Just as in Italy, so also in Germany does fascism attempt to evoke a response among the working masses through socialist-sounding demands in its public propaganda . . . the task of fascism in Germany is to mislead the *déclassé* social groups and the unknowing working masses about the real causes of their social and civil misery. Only if one perceives this can the theory of unproductive and creative capital be properly assessed. Through this mystical slogan the attempt is being made to impede the way of the masses to socialist understanding. . . . National Socialism, the religion of the modern State, is a necessary prerequisite for inciting the masses to a new slaughter of nations. With the ascent of fascism, the danger of war comes nearer and nearer. . . .

Thus, it is clear to us which role in capitalism the Nazis fulfil: to thwart the class-conscious development of the proletariat in the interests of a regulated exploitation. . . . The Eighth National Congress directs the call to the entire young proletariat: join the SAJD, come into the syndicalist economic Industrial Federations, in order to organise as an economic class front the battle against capitalism, fascism and State tyranny.

Long Live the Social Revolution!

Long Live the struggle for a free, socialist councillor society!

Source: Junge Anarchisten, VIII (1931) no. 1.

16. The reaction of the Deutsche Freischar leadership to the National Socialist advent to power:

To the National Socialist German Workers' Party, Berlin,
Berlin, 8 March 1933.

We declare our entry into the NSDAP.

Convinced of the importance of the National Socialist movement for the construction of the German People's State [*Volksstaat*], we consider it our duty now to integrate ourselves into your party organisation. Until now, we have, as leaders of the Deutsche Freischar and the Silesian Jungmannschaft, rejected any party political connections. Along with the National Socialist movement, our Border Defence Unit East – as the Wandervogel Formation [*Hundertschaft*] – our trips to frontiers and foreign countries, and since 1922, our trips to German settlements in South East Europe, and our early start in 1925 with a German Labour Service, made up of a well-known *advant-garde* of the Bündische youth movement, were attempts to set an example for the rest of young Germany. We have debated and realised new forms of youth education with young peasants, workers and students. Now the decision of our nation for a National Socialist-led government gives us the assurance that the time has come for the realisation of a united organisation of youth with a strongly led German people. With this, we hope that German Bündische Youth will follow our example in not failing to hear the commandment of the hour!

Signed Dehmel, Bargel, Dr Kügler, Dr Raupach, Wolff.

Source: Quoted in Karl O. Paetel, 'Die deutsche Jügendbewegung als politisches Phänomen', *Politische Studien*, VIII (1957) p. 9.

17. Statement by the leadership of the Protestant Jugendbund für entschiedenes Christentum, April 1933:

We have always valued and esteemed our Fatherland and our State in their German uniqueness. . . . Our members felt themselves to be, on the one hand, true Christians, and on the other, true Germans. There is no need, therefore, for us to change our attitude as the new national uprising and reawakening floods over the German Fatherland and sweeps away the petty States as well as the Marxist–materialistic spirit. For this reason we can in an unreserved and joyful fashion say yes. . . . We thank God for this wonderful turning-point in German history, which he has carried out through the Reich Chancellor Adolf Hitler and his party. . . .

We readily declare our joy in public at the national reawakening of our people . . . by participating in nationalist demonstrations . . . .

Source: *Führerhilfe*, Apr 1933.

18. The leadership of the KJMV in April 1933:

We stand at a decisive hour in the political development of Germany. The change-over in the State leadership and the national revolution among our people present the Jungmännerverband as a whole, but also the leaders of all our associations, with new and responsible questions and tasks. . . . We are resolved to co-operate in the great aim of bringing about a greater, united Germany on the basis of social well-being and Christian culture, so that the movement currently running through our people will result in a real renewal and unity of the nation. . . . Our special task remains, however, as before: readiness to work for the education of German youth and the shaping of the German State according to the spirit and principles of a lively and undiluted Christianity.

Source: Heinrich Roth (ed.), *Katholische Jugend in der NS-Zeit. Unter besonderer Berücksichtigung des Katholischen Jungmännerverbandes. Daten und Dokumente* (Düsseldorf, 1959) p. 57.

19. Extract from an open letter sent by Wilhelm Pieck to 'all former members of the Social Democratic working class youth organisation' on 4 August 1934:

Young Friends and Comrades!
. . . the urgent task stands before you more than ever before of creating along with Communist youth a united front of working youth for the struggle against the Hitler dictatorship and its anti-youth measures. Your youth, your existence, your future, your life is in serious danger! . . . You must seize the initiative in your ranks! Clasp the brotherly hand which we extend to you!. . . Let us create together the brotherly, unified fighting front against our enemy, fascism, the Hitler dictatorship! Let us join together again just like before the First World War in one common fighting organisation, in one youth association, in one party, in one trade union! We have the strength to bring down the Hitler dictatorship if we can once again create unity in battle and unity in organisation. . . . In this struggle the unity of youth and of the working class must be created, the elements needed to bring down fascism must be developed. . . . Young comrades, boys and girls of the former Social Democratic youth movement! Do not ignore

this letter! . . . Create once again with Communists the unity and revolutionary *élan* of working youth! Each and every one of you bears a responsibility for this! Each and every one of you is an agitator and organiser of this great work of proletarian unity and of the victory of the working class.

Source: Wolfgang Arlt (ed.), *Deutschlands Junge Garde. 50 Jahre Arbeiterjugendbewegung* (East Berlin, 1954) pp. 235 ff.

20. The Law for the Hitler Youth, 1 December 1936:

The future of the German nation depends on its youth. The whole of German youth must therefore be prepared for its future duties. The Reich Government has accordingly decided on the following law, which is published herewith:

1. The whole of German youth within the frontiers of the Reich is organised in the Hitler Youth.
2. The whole of German youth is to be educated, outside the parental home and school, in the Hitler Youth physically, intellectually and morally in the spirit of National Socialism for service to the nation and community.
3. The task of educating the whole of German youth in the Hitler Youth is being entrusted to the Reich Youth Leader of the NSDAP. He is therefore 'Youth Leader of the German Reich'. He has the status of a Supreme Reich Authority with headquarters in Berlin and he is directly responsible to the *Führer* and Reich Chancellor.
4. The requisite legal decrees and general administrative orders for the carrying out and supplementation of this Law will be issued by the *Führer* and Reich Chancellor.

Berlin, 1 December 1936   The *Führer* and Reich Chancellor
Adolf Hitler

Source: *Reichsgesetzblatt Teil I* no. 113 (3 December 1936). p. 993.

21. Hitler's letter to von Schirach intimating his new appointment, 1940:

Berlin, 10 August 1940

Dear Party Comrade Schirach!

Reichsstatthalter and *Gauleiter* Bürckel is taking over new, important duties for the Reich and must therefore leave his present sphere of work. I have appointed you, Party Comrade Schirach, to the post of *Reichsstatthalter* and *Gauleiter* in Vienna. Since it was your wish to leave your regiment at the end of the Western campaign, you will today assume your new office.

My confidence in your ability to carry out the new social and cultural—political tasks springs from an appreciation of your past achievement in creating and heading the youth movement of the German Reich. Your name will be forever associated with this work. You are, therefore, also in the future exclusively responsible to me in your capacity as *Reichsleiter* for the German youth movement.

Accept once more my sincere thanks.

In heartfelt association,
    Your,
    Adolf Hitler.

Source: Bundesarchiv NS 26/358.

22. *Reichsführer*-SS Himmler to Heydrich on the subject of Hamburg's 'Swing Youth', 26 January 1942:

I know that the Secret State Police has already taken action once. But it is now my opinion that the whole evil must be energetically eradicated. I am against taking half measures.

All ringleaders, male and female, as well as teachers who are dissident-minded and support the Swing Youth, are to be sent to concentration camps. There these youngsters must first of all be thrashed and then exercised and compelled to do hard labour. Any kind of work camp or youth detention camp is too mild for these fellows and useless girls. The girls are to be employed as weavers and agricultural workers during the summer.

They are to be kept in concentration camps for two to three years. It must be made clear that they can never again engage in study. The parents must be investigated to ascertain whether they supported their children. If they did, then they must also be confined in concentration camps and their property confiscated.

Only if we attack this problem in a brutal fashion can we avoid
this dangerous anglophile tendency from spreading during a time
when Germany is fighting for its existence.

Source: National Archives (Washington), T-175/20/2525.

23. From a pamphlet distributed by the White Rose Circle in
Munich, February 1943:

Fellow students,
   Our people, our nation stands appalled. The men of Stalingrad
have surrendered. 330,000 German men have been thrust into
death and destruction by the strategy of a genius, the irresponsible,
senseless corporal of the First World War. *Führer*, we thank
you. . . . Do we want to sacrifice the remnants of Germany's
youth to the debased instincts of a power-hungry party clique?
Never again! The day of reckoning has come, the day when
German youth will settle accounts with the most despicable
tyranny ever suffered by our nation. In the name of German youth,
we demand from Adolf Hitler's State the restoration of personal
freedom. . . .
   We grew up in a State where every free expression of opinion
has been ruthlessly suppressed. Hitler Youth, Stormtroopers and
SS have attempted during the most receptive years of our lives to
drill, revolutionise, and drug us. 'Ideological education' was the
description for this horrible method of stifling incipient independent thought in a maze of empty phrases. . . .
   There can only be one word of action for us: Fight the Party!
Leave the Party organisations. . . . What is at stake is true science
and genuine intellectual freedom. . . . Each of us must join in the
struggle for our future, for a life in freedom and honour in a State
which is aware of its moral obligations.
   Freedom and honour! For ten long years, Hitler and his
followers have worn out, abused and corrupted these words to the
point of disgust. . . . What freedom and honour mean to them
they have shown in ten years of destroying all physical and spiritual
freedom, of destroying the moral substance of the German
nation. . . . The German name will be forever disgraced unless
Germany's youth finally arises, avenges and atones at the same
time, crushes its tormentors, and builds a new concept of Europe.

Students! The eyes of the German people are upon us. Germany expects us to break the National Socialist terror in the year 1943 by the power of the spirit. . . .

Source: Inge Scholl, *Die weisse Rose* (Frankfurt, 1955) pp. 151 ff.

24. Hitler's proclamation to the Hitler Youth, 7 October 1944:

My Hitler Youth!
I have received with pride and joy the news of the registration as war volunteers of the class of 1928. In this hour of danger to the Reich ... . you have provided a shining example of fighting spirit and fanatical commitment to battle, no matter what sacrifices may be required. The youth of our National Socialist movement, both at home and at the front, have fulfilled the expectations of the nation. Your volunteers have given exemplary evidence of their loyalty and unshakable will to victory by service in the 'Hitler Youth', 'Greater Germany', and *Volksgrenadier* divisions, and as individual fighters in all branches of the armed forces. . . . We are aware of the merciless extermination plans of our enemies. For this reason we will fight on even more fanatically for a Reich in which you will be able to work and live in honour. You, however, as young National Socialist fighters, must do even more than the rest of the nation in terms of steadfastness, perseverance and unbreakable toughness. The sacrifices made by our heroic younger generation will produce a victory which will guarantee the proud, free development of our people and of the National Socialist Reich.

Adolf Hitler

Source: Max Domarus (ed.), *Hitler: Reden und Proklamationen 1932– 1945. Kommentiert von einem deutschen Zeitgenosse* (Munich, 1965) pp. 2153–4.

25. Baldur von Schirach at his trial in Nuremberg:

I educated this generation in faith and loyalty to Hitler. The youth movement which I built up bore his name. I believed that I was serving a leader who would make our people and the youth of our country great and happy and free. Millions of young people believed this, together with me, and saw their ultimate ideal in National Socialism. Many died for it. Before God, before the German nation, and before my German people, I alone bear the guilt of having trained our young people for a man whom I for many long years had considered unimpeachable, both as a leader and as Head of the State. . . . The guilt is mine that I educated the Youth of Germany for a man who murdered millions. . . . The younger generation is guiltless.

Source: *The Trial of the Major War Criminals before the International Military Tribunal* (Nuremberg, 1947—9) XIV, pp. 369—70.

Notes

INTRODUCTION

1. Anthony Esler (ed.), *The Youth Revolution: The Conflict of Generations in Modern History* (Lexington Mass., 1974) p. 155.
2. The concept of continuity is regarded as axiomatic in the special issue of the *Journal of Contemporary History* entitled 'Generations in Conflict' – V (1970). An interesting overview of this theme is provided by Herbert Butterfield in *The Discontinuities between the Generations in History: Their Effect on the Transmission of Political Experience* (Cambridge, 1972).
3. Alan B. Spitzer, 'The Historical Problem of Generations', *American Historical Review*, LXXVIII (1973) p. 1354. Mannheim's important study *The Problem of Generations* was published in 1928. See also his *Essays on the Sociology of Knowledge* (London, 1959), especially pp. 276–322.
4. Herbert Moller, 'Youth as a Force in the Modern World', *Comparative Studies in Society and History*, X (1968) p. 237 ff.
5. Friedrich Heer, *Revolutions of Our Time: Challenge of Youth* (London, 1974).
6. Anthony Esler, *Bombs, Beards, and Barricades: 150 Years of Youth in Revolt* (New York, 1971) pp. 35 ff.,115–16.
7. Oscar Wilde, *The Picture of Dorian Gray* (London, 1907) p. 48.
8. Joseph Held, 'Embattled Youth: The Independent German Youth Movements in the 20th Century' (Doctoral dissertation, Rutgers State University, NJ, 1968) p. 280.
9. Walter Z. Laqueur, *Young Germany: A History of the German Youth Movement* (London, 1962) p. xi. He was a member of the Werkleute group (see Ch. 3).
10. Winfried Mogge, '"Dämme wider die Vergesslichkeit". Neue Aufgaben des Archivs der deutschen Jugendbewegung', *Ludwigsteiner Blätter*, 116 (Sept 1977) p. 6.
11. See in particular, Hans Blüher, *Die deutsche Wandervogelbewegung als erotisches Phänomen* (Berlin, 1912), and his *Die Rolle der Erotik in der männlichen Gesellschaft*, 2 vols (Jena, 1912).
12. Cf. George L. Mosse, *The Crisis of German Ideology: Intellectual Origins of the Third Reich* (New York, 1971); Armin Mohler, *Die konservative Revolution in Deutschland 1918–1932. Ein Handbuch* (Stuttgart, 1950); Klemens von Klemperer, *Germany's New Conservatism: Its History and Dilemma in the Twentieth Century*, 2nd edn (Princeton, NJ, 1968).
13. Jakob Müller, *Die Jugendbewegung als deutsche Hauptrichtung neukonservativer Reform* (Zurich, 1971).
14. Harry E. Pross, *Jugend, Eros, Politik. Die Geschichte der deutschen Jugendverbände* (Berne, 1964), and *Die Zerstörung der deutschen Politik. Dokumente 1870–1933*

(Frankfurt a. M., 1959); Howard Becker, *German Youth. Bond or Free?* (London, 1946).

15. Theodor Wilhelm, 'Der geschichtliche Ort der deutschen Jugendbewegung', in Werner Kindt (ed.), *Grundschriften der deutschen Jugendbewegung* (Düsseldorf, 1963) p. 8.

16. Otto Stählin, 'Der Begriff "deutsche Jugendbewegung"', *Jahrbuch des Archivs der deutschen Jugendbewegung (JADJB)*, IX (1977) pp. 163, 170, 175 f., 180—4.

17. Adam Wandruszka, 'Die deutsche Jugendbewegung als historisches Phänomen', *Quellen und Forschungen aus italienischen Archiven und Bibliotheken*, LI (1972) p. 518.

18. Mention must be made here of the ongoing efforts to assemble all kinds of historical matter relating to the youth movement by the Archive of the German Youth Movement at Burg Ludwigstein/Werra. See also the remarks of the Archive's late director, Hans Wolf, in his article 'Zur Geschichte des Archivs der deutschen Jugendbewegung auf Burg Ludwigstein 1920—1968', *JADJB*, II (1970) pp. 115—21.

19. Helmut Grau, *d. j. l. ll.* [Deutsche Jungenschaft].—*Struktur und Wandel eines subkulturellen jugendlichen Milieus in vier Jahrzehnten* (Frankfurt a M., 1976); Barbara Schellenberger, *Katholische Jugend und Drittes Reich. Eine Geschichte des Katholischen Jungmännerverbandes 1933—1939 unter besonderer Berücksichtigung der Rheinprovinz* (Mainz, 1975); Antje Vollmer, 'Die Neuwerkbewegung 1919—1935' (Doctoral dissertation, Free University Berlin, 1973).

20. The best studies are Heinrich Kupffer, *Gustav Wyneken* (Stuttgart, 1970); Richard W. Dougherty, 'Eros, Youth Culture and Geist: The Ideology of Gustav Wyneken and Its Influence upon the German Youth Movement' (Doctoral dissertation, University of Wisconsin, 1977); Hans Urs von Balthasar, *Romano Guardini. Reform aus dem Ursprung* (Munich, 1970); and Gerhard Mahr, *Romano Guardini* (Berlin, 1976).

21. Werner Kindt (ed.), *Die Wandervogelzeit. Quellenschriften zur deutschen Jugendbewegung, 1896—1919* (Düsseldorf, 1968), and *Die deutsche Jugendbewegung, 1920 bis 1933. Die Bündische Zeit. Quellenschriften* (Düsseldorf, 1974). See also Rudolf Kneip (ed.), *Jugend der Weimarer Zeit. Handbuch der Jugendverbände 1919—1938* (Frankfurt a M., 1974); and B. Schneider, *Daten zur Geschichte der Jugendbewegung* (Bad Godesberg, 1965).

22. For example, Elizabeth Korn *et al.* (eds), *Die Jugendbewegung: Welt und Wirkung. Zur 50. Wiederkehr der Freideutschen Jugendtages auf den Hohen Meissner* (Düsseldorf, 1963); and Peter Nasarski (ed.), *Deutsche Jugendbewegung in Europa. Versuch einer Bilanz* (Cologne, 1967).

23. Alfred Kurella, *Unterwegs zu Lenin. Erinnerungen* (East Berlin, 1967).

24. Laqueur, *Young Germany*; Felix Raabe, *Die Bündische Jugend. Ein Beitrag zur Geschichte der Weimarer Republik* (Stuttgart, 1961); Karl Seidelmann, *Die Pfadfinder in der deutschen Jugendgeschichte, Teil I. Darstellung* (Hanover, 1977); Müller, *Die Jugendbewegung als deutsche Hauptrichtung.*

25. Karl Seidelmann, *Bund und Gruppe als Lebensformen deutscher Jugend* (Munich, 1955); Karl O. Paetel, *Das Bild vom Menschen in der deutschen Jugendführung* (Bad Godesberg, 1954).

26. L. Fick, *Die deutsche Jugendbewegung* (Jena, 1939).

27. As far as I know, there is no detailed history of the Hitler Youth 1933—45 in preparation.

28. A. Klönne, *Hitlerjugend. Die Jugend und ihre Organisation im Dritten Reich* (Hanover 1956); W. Klose, *Generation im Gleichschritt. Ein Dokumentation* (Oldenburg, 1964); H.-C. Brandenburg, *Die Geschichte der HJ. Wege und Irrwege einer Generation* (Cologne, 1968).

29. E. Blohm, *Hitler-Jugend. Soziale Tatgemeinschaft* (Witten, 1977). Into the same category comes Gottfried Griesmayr and Otto Würschinger: *Idee und Gestalt der Hitlerjugend* (Munich, 1979).

30. H.-J. Koch, *The Hitler Youth: Origins and Development 1922–45* (London, 1975). A shrewd assessment of this book which draws attention to its dubious use and quotation of sources is included in Michael H. Kater's review article 'Die unbewältige Jugendbewegung. Zu neuen Büchern', *Archiv für Sozialgeschichte*, XVII (1977) pp. 559–64.

CHAPTER 1

1. The best analytical survey of this whole problem in English is Volker R. Berghahn, *Germany and the Approach of War in 1914* (London, 1973). The thesis he and others propound has recently come in for critical scrutiny by a number of German and British scholars, who have sought to make some modifications. See, for example, Geoff Eley, 'Defining Social Imperialism: Use and Abuse of an Idea', *Social History*, III (1976) pp. 265–90.

2. Paul de Lagarde, 'Über die Klage, dass der deutschen Jugend der Idealismus fehle', in *Deutsche Schriften* (Göttingen, 1892) p. 381.

3. Fritz Stern, *The Politics of Cultural Despair: A Study in the Rise of the Germanic Ideology* (New York, 1965) pp. 125, 197–223.

4. Hans Bohnenkamp, 'Jugendbewegung als Kulturkritik', in Walter Rüegg (ed.), *Kulturkritik und Jugendkult* (Frankfurt a. M., 1974) pp. 23–4.

5. Gilbert Krebs, 'Expressionismus und Jugendbewegung', *JADJB*, I (1969) p. 34.

6. Walter Z. Laqueur, *Weimar: A Cultural History 1918–33* (London, 1974) pp. 114–15.

7. Walter Rüegg, 'Jugend und Gesellschaft um 1900', in Rüegg, *Kulturkritik*, pp. 50–1.

8. Karol Szemkus, 'Gesellschaftliche Bedingungen zur Entstehung der deutschen Jugendbewegung', in Rüegg, *Kulturkritik*, pp. 44–5.

9. F. H. Tenbruck, *Jugend und Gesellschaft* (Freiburg, 1962) pp. 77–8.

10. Erik Homburger Erikson, 'Hitler's Imagery and German Youth', *Psychiatry*, V (1942) p. 475 ff.

11. Heinz S. Rosenbusch, *Die deutsche Jugendbewegung in ihren pädagogischen Formen und Wirkungen* (Frankfurt a. M., 1973) p. 15.

12. Wilhelm, in Kindt, *Grundschriften*, p. 9.

13. Ferdinand Tönnies, *Gemeinschaft und Gesellschaft* (Leipzig, 1887).

14. Charlotte Luetkens, *Die deutsche Jugendbewegung* (Frankfurt a. M., 1925) p. 45.

15. J. Burchhardt, *Briefe an seinen Freund Friedrich von Preen (1840–93)*, ed. Emil Strauss (Stuttgart, 1922) p. 18.

16. Fick, *Die deutsche Jugendbewegung*, p. 68.

17. George Thomson, 'The Influence of the Youth Movement on German Education' (Doctoral thesis, University of Glasgow, 1934) p. 194.

18. Rosenbusch, *Die deutsche Jugendbewegung*, pp. 19–21.

19. Gerhard Ziemer and Hans Wolf, *Wandervogel und Freideutsche Jugend* (Bad Godesberg, 1961) p. 7.

20. There has been considerable debate among historians about who should be regarded as the authentic founder of the Wandervogel, Hoffmann or Karl Fischer. Recent opinion favours Hoffmann. See Hans Wolf, 'Gedenkworte. Zum 100. Geburtstag von Hermann Hoffmann-Fölkersamb', *JADJB*, VII (1975) pp. 151—3. The fullest account of Hoffmann's role is given by Walther Gerber in his *Zur Entstehungsgeschichte der deutschen Wandervogelbewegung. Ein kritischer Beitrag* (Bielefeld, 1957).

21. Kindt, *Die Wandervogelzeit*, p. 20.

22. A personal recollection of this expedition is provided by Heinrich Becker in his *Zwischen Wahn und Wahrheit. Autobiographie* (East Berlin, 1974) p. 42 ff.

23. Hoffmann returned to Germany in 1913 and during the First World War served as Consul-General in Haifa. He died in 1955 in Kiel.

24. Kindt, *Die Wandervogelzeit*, p. 39.

25. See Helmut Wangelin, 'Zum Wort Wandervogel', *JADJB*, VII (1975) pp. 149—50.

26. A title used by wandering minstrels in the Middle Ages.

27. See Ziemer and Wolf, *Wandervogel und Freideutsche Jugend*, pp. 49—90; and Georg Korth, *Der Wandervogel, 1896/1906* (Frankfurt a. M., 1967).

28. Gerhard Ziemer, 'Nordhessen und die deutsche Jugendbewegung', *Hessisches Jahrbuch für Landesgeschichte*, XIX (1969) p. 348.

29. Willibald Karl, *Jugend, Gesellschaft und Politik im Zeitraum des Ersten Weltkriegs* (Munich, 1973) p. 62.

30. John R. Gillis, *Youth and History: Tradition and Change in European Age Relations 1770—Present* (New York, 1974) p. 154.

31. For example, Ernst Bloch, *Freiheit und Ordnung* (East Berlin, 1947) p. 163.

32. Walter Jantzen, 'Die soziologische Herkunft der Führerschicht in der deutschen Jugendbewegung, 1900 bis 1933', in *Führungsschicht und Eliteproblem: Konferenz der Ranke-Gesellschaft* (Frankfurt a. M., 1957) p. 130. The best and most detailed work on this aspect is Ulrich Aufmuth, *Die deutsche Wandervogelbewegung unter soziologischem Aspekt* (Göttingen, 1979), especially pp. 86ff, 236.

33. Müller, *Die Jugendbewegung als deutsche Hauptrichtung*, p. 19.

34. Janos Frecot, 'Die Lebensreformbewegung', in Klaus Vondung (ed.), *Das Wilhelminische Bildungsbürgertum. Zur Sozialgeschichte seiner Ideen* (Göttingen, 1976) p. 140 ff.

35. Karl O. Paetel, *Jugend in der Entscheidung 1913—1933—1945* (Bad Godesberg, 1963) p. 19.

36. Hans Lissner, 'Wie der Zupfgeigenhansl entstanden ist', in Kindt, *Grundschriften*, pp. 68—70. See also Hilmar Höckner, *Die Musik in der deutschen Jugendbewegung* (Wolfenbüttel, 1957); and Fritz Jöde, *Vom Wesen und Werden der Jugendmusik* (Mainz, 1954).

37. H. Breuer, 'Wandervogel und Volkslied', in *Wandervogel, deutscher Bund*, IV (July 1910) p. 81 f.

38. Hermann Bach, 'Wesen und Form der Leibesübung in der Jugendbewegung vor dem Ersten Weltkrieg', in *JADJB*, III (1971) pp. 12—23.

39. Wilhelm Geissler, *Kunst und Künstler in der Jugendbewegung*, I (Burg Ludwigstein, 1975) pp. 7, 62.

40. Becker, *German Youth*, pp. 91—2.

41. Mario Domandi, 'The German Youth Movement' (Doctoral dissertation, Columbia University, New York, 1960) p. 42.
42. Daniel Gasman, *The Scientific Origins of National Socialism: Social Darwinism in Ernst Haeckel and the German Monist League* (London, 1971) p. 155.
43. Such councils were required by Prussian law to overlook the activities of any youth associations in schools.
44. Pross, *Jugend, Eros, Politik*, p. 72.
45. Hans Bohnenkamp, 'Jugendbewegung und Schulreform', in E. Korn *et al.* (eds), *Die Jugendbewegung*, pp. 39–43.
46. Karl Seidelmann, 'Wyneken und Geheeb: historische Prominenz aus der Frühzeit der Landerziehungsheime', *JADJB*, III (1971) p. 75. See also a useful discussion of Lietz in Sterling Fishman's otherwise disappointing study, *The Struggle for German Youth. The Search for Educational Reform in Imperial Germany* (New York, 1976) pp. 56–68.
47. Heinrich Kupffer, 'Gustav Wyneken – Leben und Werk', ibid., II (1970) p. 25.
48. Achim Gercke, 'Gustav Wyneken und die Jugendpädagogik', ibid., I (1969) pp. 41–3.
49. Dougherty, 'Eros, Youth Culture and Geist', pp. 1–2, 63–93, 266–307.
50. Alfred Ehrentreich, 'Freie Schulgemeinde Wickersdorf', *Zeitschrift für Pädagogik*, XXI (1975) p. 87 ff.
51. Laqueur, *Young Germany*, p. 13.
52. Kupffer, *Gustav Wyneken*, p. 275.
53. Dougherty, 'Eros, Youth Culture and Geist', pp. 403–90.
54. See later in text.
55. Ziemer and Wolf, *Wandervogel und Freideutsche Jugend*, pp. 21–2.
56. Hans Wolf, 'Der Alt-Wandervogel als Traditionsbund der Jugendbewegung', *JADJB*, V (1973) p. 32.
57. Blüher, *Die deutsche Wandervogelbewegung als erotisches Phänomen*. The background to the publication of this book is interestingly discussed by Gerhard Ziemer in his 'Hans Blühers Geschichte des Wandervogels. Die erste Deutung der deutschen Jugendbewegung', *JADJB*, IX (1977) p. 186 ff.
58. Gerhard Ziemer, 'Hans Blühers "Achse der Natur"', ibid., II (1970) p. 7.
59. Hans Blüher, *Wandervogel, Geschichte einer Bewegung* (Jena, 1912) p. 112.
60. Kindt (ed.), *Die Wandervogelzeit*, p. 183.
61. Becker, *German Youth*, p. 66.
62. Laqueur, *Young Germany*, pp. 51–2, 57 ff.
63. Heinrich Ahrens, *Die deutsche Wandervogelbewegung von den Anfängen bis zum Weltkrieg* (Hamburg, 1939) p. 18.
64. See, for example, Will Hoheisel, 'Der Wandervogel in baltischen Landen', *JADJB*, IX (1977) pp. 103–46.
65. For an expression of the opposite view, see Mosse, *The Crisis of German Ideology*, pp. 172 ff., 180 ff. A sharp critique of Mosse's argument is given by Helmut Wangelin in his 'Der Wandervogel und das Völkische', *JADJB*, II (1970) pp. 49 ff., 69–70.
66. Siegfried Copalle and Heinrich Ahrens, *Chronik der deutschen Jugendbewegung*, I (Bad Godesberg, 1954) pp. 152 ff.
67. Laqueur, *Young Germany*, pp. 76–8.
68. Held, 'Embattled Youth', p. 49 ff. The Austrian and Sudeten German Wandervogel movements officially adopted the 'Aryan paragraph' in 1913.

69. Laqueur, *Young Germany*, p. 80, puts the number at 'a few hundred'.
70. Rudolf Kneip, 'Die Sachsen und die Einigungsbestrebungen im Wandervogel', *JADJB*, VIII (1973) pp. 156–9.
71. Schneider, *Daten zur Geschichte der Jugendbewegung*, p. 30.
72. Kindt, *Die Wandervogelzeit*, p. 18.
73. Ibid., pp. 231–4.
74. The Wandervogel groups were the Bund deutscher Wanderer, Deutsche Akademischer Freischar, Akademische Vereinigung Marburg and Jena, Jungwandervogel, the Austrian Wandervogel, and the United Wandervogel. The last group did not actually take part in official discussions at the meeting, but it did attach its name to the Meissner Formula (Ziemer and Wolf, *Wandervogel und Freideutsche Jugend*, p. 439).
75. Karl Seidelmann, *Die deutsche Jugendbewegung* (Bad Heilbrunn, 1966) p. 49.
76. Fritz Borinski and Werner Milch, *Jugendbewegung: The Story of German Youth 1896–1933* (London, 1945) p. 13.
77. The last sentence in the Formula was inserted at the insistence of the racist Deutsche Vortruppbund, led by Hermann Popert. It was this group which originally conceived the idea of staging a large youth gathering in 1913.
78. Schneider, *Daten zur Geschichte der Jugendbewegung*, p. 32.
79. Adolf Grabowsky and Walter Koch, *Die Freideutsche Jugendbewegung* (Gotha, 1920) p. 13.
80. Karl, *Jugend, Gesellschaft und Politik*, pp. 123–5.
81. Peter R. Hofstätter, 'Fieber und Heil in der Jugendbewegung', in *Jugend in der Gesellschaft, Ein Symposium* (Munich, 1975) p. 142.
82. Held, 'Embattled Youth', pp. 91–4.
83. Fritz Jungmann, 'Autorität und Sexualmoral in der freien bürgerlichen Jugendbewegung', in Max Horkheimer (ed.), *Autorität und Familie* (Paris, 1936) p. 673.
84. For a rather too sanguine picture of the youth movement at this stage, see Gilbert Krebs, 'Was bleibt Heute von der Jugendbewegung – von Aussen Gesehen?', *JADJB*, VI (1974) p. 66.
85. Hertha Siemering, *Die deutschen Jugendpflegeverbände* (Berlin, 1918) *passim*.
86. Seidelmann, *Die Pfadfinder in der deutschen Jugendgeschichte*, ch. 1.
87. Klaus Saul, 'Der Kampf um die Jugend zwischen Volksschule und Kaserne. Ein Beitrag zur "Jugendpflege" im Wilhelminischen Reich 1890–1914', *Militärgeschichtliche Mitteilungen*, X (1971) p. 97 ff. See also Hermann Giesecke, *Die Jugendarbeit* (Munich, 1971) p. 17.
88. Hans Wolf, 'Von Wandervögeln, Scouts und Pfadfindern', *JADJB*, III (1971) p. 34.
89. Gillis, *Youth and History*, p. 161.
90. See Dr Edmund Neuendorff's patriotic declaration on behalf of the autonomous youth movement in *Wandervogelmonatsschrift*, IX (1914) 1. Kriegsheft, p. 257.
91. See H. Scheil, *Langemarck. Der Opfergang einer heldischen Jugend* (Breslau, 1934); and H. Thimmermann, *Der Sturm auf Langemarck. Von einem, der dabei war* (Munich, 1940).
92. Laqueur, *Young Germany*, p. 82.
93. Kindt, *Die Wandervogelzeit*, pp. 800–1.

CHAPTER 2

1. Katherine Larson Roper, 'Images of German Youth in Weimar Novels', *Journal of Contemporary History*, XIII (1978) p. 499.
2. Wolf, in *JADJB*, III, p. 38.
3. Hermann Siefert, *Die Bündische Aufbruch 1919–1923* (Bad Godesberg, 1963) p. 10.
4. Ernst Kantorowicz in *Freideutsche Jugend*, Aug–Sep 1919 (special issue).
5. *Leitsätze der demokratisch-sozialistischen Gruppe der Freideutschen Jugend* (Berlin, 10 Nov 1918).
6. Knud Ahlborn, *Kurze Chronik der Freideutschen Jugendbewegung 1913 bis 1953* (Bad Godesberg, 1953) p. 11.
7. Gerhard Ziemer, 'Begriff und Grenzen der Jugendbewegung', *JADJB*, I (1969) p. 8.
8. Jungdeutsches Wollen (Hamburg, 1920) p. 9.
9. Wilhelm Ehmer, 'Die Hofgeismarer Tagung', in Kindt, *Grundschriften*, pp. 230–43.
10. Wilhelm Ehmer, 'Die Bedeutung Hofgeismar', ibid., pp. 251–6.
11. Hans Pluta, 'Muck Lamberty und die "Neue Schar"' im Jahre 1920 in Thüringen. Erinnerungen eines Teilnehmers', *JADJB*, II (1970) p. 103.
12. Adam Ritzhaupt, *Die Neue Schar in Thüringen* (Jena, 1921). Lamberty was allowed to deliver an address in Erfurt Cathedral – the first layman to have been accorded this privilege since the Reformation.
13. Borinski and Milch, *Jugendbewegung*, pp. 21–2.
14. Held, 'Embattled Youth', pp. 176–7.
15. Rudolf Kneip et al., *Jugend zwischen den Kriegen. Eine Sammlung von Aussagen und Dokumenten über den Sachsenkreis im Freideutschen Konvent* (Heidenheim, 1967) p. 16.
16. Gerhard Ziemer, 'Die Übergangszeit zwischen Wandervogel und Bündischer Jugend', *JADJB*, IV (1972) p. 55.
17. Ziemer and Wolf, *Wandervogel und Freideutsche Jugend*, p. 27. The influence of the Wandervogel as a whole on the Freikorps is fleetingly discussed by Robert G. L. Waite in his *Vanguard of Nazism: The Free Corps Movement in Postwar Germany 1918–1923* (New York 1969 edn.) pp. 17–21.
18. The 'settlement movement' of the 1920s is discussed in more detail later in this chapter.
19. Hermann Mau, 'Die deutsche Jugendbewegung. Rückblick und Ausblick', *Zeitschrift für religiöse Geistesgeschichte*, I (1948) p. 135 ff.
20. There were no mixed groups in Bündische Youth. Girls' sections existed in a majority of groups but enjoyed only a subordinate status.
21. Kindt, *Die Bündische Zeit*, p. 1746.
22. Paetel, *Bild vom Menschen in der deutschen Jugendführung*, p. 29.
23. Karl Seidelmann, 'Das Bündische in Unserer Existenz – Vom Jugendbund zum Lebensbund', *JADJB* V (1973) pp. 52 f., 61–2; and Seidelmann, *Bund und Gruppe als Lebensformen*, passim.
24. For a puzzling and quite unconvincing interpretation of Bündische Youth as a religious movement in basic inspiration, see Ludwig Liebs, *Glauben an Gott und die Götter. Jugendbewegung und Bündische Jugend als religiöses Phänomen* (Heidenheim, 1976).

25. A counter-hypothesis is provided by Richard Löwenthal, *Romantischer Rückfall* (Cologne, 1970).

26. A good description of Bündische contacts with German youth outside the Reich is given by Hans Richter and Helmut Neumann in 'Leben über die Grenze', in Korn *et al.*, *Die Jugendbewegung*, pp. 159–84. The strong impetus given by the Deutsche Freischar to Bündische work among German minorities is described by Alice Gräfin Wallwitz in her 'Zur Bedeutung des Volkstumsprinzips in der bündischen Auslandsbegegnung', *JADJB*, VIII (1976) pp. 40–1. More comprehensive coverage of Bündische work in general in the East is provided by Dorota Jablonska, 'Der Einfluss der deutschen Jugendbewegung auf die Jugend der europäischen Länder', ibid., VI (1974) pp. 22–30; and ibid., IX (1977) p. 7 ff. Bündische activity in Poland is outlined by Erich Scholz: 'Die deutsche Jugendbewegung in Polen zwischen den Weltkriegen', ibid., pp. 31–40. Also of substantial use is Nasarski, *Deutsche Jugendbewegung in Europa*, esp. pp. 77–184, 213–20, 226–37.

27. Claus Dietrich in *Die Junge Front*, 1 Aug 1929. See also Hans J. Schoeps's remark in *Rückblicke. Die letzten dreissig Jahre (1925–1955), und danach* (Berlin, 1963) p. 51: 'the physically and intellectually most well developed youths, who were also the nicest looking, were to be found in the Bündische Youth'.

28. Helmut Grau, 'Bündische Jugend – Spielweise der "Bourgeoisie"? Aspekte des Wandels der Sozialstruktur bündischer Gruppen vor und nach dem II. Weltkrieg', *JADJB*, IV (1972) p. 65. A breakdown of the social status of Artamanen members is given in Raabe, *Die Bündische Jugend*, p. 77. See also W. Jantzen in *Führungsschicht und Eliteproblem*, pp. 127–37.

29. Gerhard Ziemer, 'Karl Oelbermann und der Nerother Wandervogel', *JADJB*, VII (1975) p. 142.

30. Raabe, *Die Bündische Jugend*, p. 66, quotes a figure of 56,350 for 1927.

31. Ibid., p. 69.

32. George L. Mosse, *Germans and Jews: The Right, the Left, and the Search for a 'Third Force' in pre-Nazi Germany* (New York, 1970) pp. 122, 126–7.

33. Gerhard Ziemer, 'Zum Verhältnis Jugendbewegung und Stefan George', *JADJB*, III (1971) p. 9. See also Siefert, *Bündische Aufbruch*, pp. 15–16, and Laqueur, *Young Germany*, pp. 135–6.

34. Normann Körber, 'Das Bild von Menschen in der Jugendbewegung und unsere Zeit' in Kindt, *Grundschriften*, p. 472; and Karl Seidelmann, Der "neue Mensch", in Korn *et al.*, *Die Jugendbewegung*, p. 15 ff.

35. E. Jünger, *Der Kampf als inneres Erlebnis* (Berlin, 1933) pp. 76–7.

36. Paetel, *Bild vom Menschen*, p. 27.

37. Burkhart Schomburg, 'Lebensführung und Umweltgestaltung', in Korn *et al.*, *Die Jugendbewegung*, p. 129.

38. Cf. Werner Kindt (ed.), *Hermann Schafft. Ein Lebenswerk* (Kassel, 1960).

39. Cf. Ulrich Linse, *Die Kommune der deutschen Jugendbewegung. Ein Versuch des Überwindung des Klassenkampfes aus dem Geiste der bürgerlichen Utopie. Die 'kommunistische Siedlung Blankenburg' bei Donauwörth 1919/1920* (Munich, 1973). Established during the Kurt Eisner regime in Bavaria by members of the Free German and socialist youth movements, the settlement was conducted along non-political utopian–communist lines (p. 10). Koch was a devoted pupil of Gustav Wyneken (p. 56), but saw Communism as the hope for the future (pp. 147–8).

40. Emil Blum, *Die Neuwerk-Bewegung 1922–1933. Kirche zwischen Planen und Hoffen* (Kassel, 1973) p. 35.

41. Ibid., pp. 15–18, 20–1, 26–8; and Vollmer, 'Die Neuwerkbewegung 1919–1935', pp. 52 ff., 76 ff.

42. Ibid., pp. 32–7.

43. Vollmer, 'Die Neuwerkbewegung', pp. 52 ff., 125 ff., 169 ff., 197 ff. See also E. Blum, *Der Habertshof. Werden und Gestalt einer Heimvolkshochschule* (Kassel, 1930).

44. Helmuth Croon, 'Jugendbewegung und Arbeitsdienst', *JADJB*, V (1973) p. 66 ff.

45. Karl Bühler, 'Arbeitsdienst als Erziehungsaufgabe in frühen Theorien der zwanziger Jahre', *JADJB*, VII (1975) pp. 43–6.

46. Michael H. Kater, 'Die Artamanen – völkische Jugend in der Weimarer Republik', *Historische Zeitschrift*, CCXIII (1971) p. 595 ff., Bühler, in *JADJB*, VII, p. 50.

47. Helmuth Croon, 'Arbeitslager und Arbeitsdienst', in Korn *et al.*, *Die Jugendbewegung*, pp. 221–4; Bühler, *JADJB*, VII, pp. 57–8. For the account of a participant, see Eugen Rosenstock, 'Das Arbeitslager für Jungarbeiter, Jungbauern und Jungakademiker in Löwenberg vom 14. bis 31. März 1928', in *Freie Volksbildung*, III (1929) p. 217 ff.

48. Thomson, 'Influence of the Youth Movement on German Education', p. 223.

49. Kupffer, in *JADJB*, II, p. 26.

50. Gerhard Schmolze, 'Gustav Wyneken and die bayerische Revolution 1918/19', *JADJB*, VIII (1976) p. 125 ff.

51. Rosenbusch, *Die deutsche Jugendbewegung*, p. 43.

52. Theodor Wilhelm, *Pädagogik der Gegenwart* (Stuttgart, 1960) p. 84.

53. Wilhelm Roessler, *Jugend im Erziehungsfeld* (Düsseldorf, 1957) p. 195.

54. Kindt, *Grundschriften*, p. 25.

55. Rosenbusch, *Die deutsche Jugendbewegung*, pp. 143–4.

56. Cf. Erich Bitterhof (ed.), *Georg Götsch, Lebenszeichen. Zeugnisse eines Weges* (Wolfenbüttel, 1969).

57. Cf. James L. Henderson, *Adolf Reichwein. Eine politisch-pädagogische Biographie* (Stuttgart, 1958); and Ursula Schulz (ed.), *Adolf Reichwein. Ein Lebensbild aus Briefen und Dokumenten* (Munich, 1974).

58. Karl Vogt, 'Was bleibt an geistiger Wirkung – von einem Deutschen gesehen', *JADJB*, VI (1974) pp. 76–8.

59. Thomson, 'Influence of the Youth Movement on German Education', p. 338.

60. Bohnenkamp, 'Jugendbewegung und Schulreform', in Korn *et al.*, *Die Jugendbewegung*, pp. 39–42.

61. Kindt, *Die Bündische Zeit*, pp. 1409, 1444–7.

62. Wilhelm Flitner, 'Reformpädagogik' in Rüegg, *Kulturkritik*, pp. 137–46; and Jürgen Henningsen, *Der Hohenrodter Bund* (Heidelberg, 1958).

63. Rosenbusch, *Die deutsche Jugendbewegung*, pp. 142–3; and Werner S. Nicklis, 'Tendenzen zeitgenössischer Pädagogik und die Ideale der Jugendbewegung', *JADJB*, VII (1975) pp. 16–28.

64. Hans-Michael Elzer, 'Reformpädagogik und Jugendbewegung', *JADJB*, VII (1975) p. 6.

65. Rosenbusch, *Die deutsche Jugendbewegung*, p. 142.

66. Kindt, *Die Bündische Zeit*, p. 1477.

67. Ibid., pp. 1478—80.
68. Elizabeth Korn, 'Das neue Lebensgefühl in der Gymnastik', in Korn *et al, Die Jugendbewegung*, pp. 101—5.
69. Schomburg, ibid., p. 122.
70. Ahlborn, *KurzeChronik*, p. 15.
71. Franz Hargasser, 'Der Einfluss der Jugendbewegung auf die Erwachsenenbildung', *JADJB*, VII (1975) p. 31.
72. Karl Vötterle, 'Fünfzig Jahre Finkenstein', ibid., p. 105.
73. Helmut ·Neumann, 'Vom Grenzschulheim Boberhaus der Schlesischen Jungmannschaft', ibid., IX (1977) pp. 253—5.
74. Alwin Müller, 'Laienspiel — Spiel der Gemeinschaft?', in Korn *et al. Die Jugendbewegung*, p. 70 ff.
75. Borinski and Milch, *Jugendbewegung*, p. 33.
76. Kindt, *Die Bündische Zeit*, p. 1722.
77. Hans Bohnenkamp, 'Das Erbe der Jugendbewegung', *Frankfurter Hefte*, XVI (1961) pp. 834—6.
78. Karl Seidelmann, 'Die Pfadfinder in der deutschen Jugend-Geschichte der zwanziger Jahre', *JADJB*, VI (1974) p. 110.
79. Kindt, *Die Bündische Zeit*, pp. 389—90.
80. Karl Seidelmann, 'Weltpfadfinderbewegung und deutsche Pfadfinderei zwischen 1919 und 1933', *JADJB*, III (1971) p. 43. See also the interesting memoirs of a former Boy Scout leader: Karl Wappen, *Unter dem Lilienbanner. Erlebnisse und Betrachtungen eines alten Pfadfinders* (Frankfurt a. M., 1969).
81. Seidelmann, *Die Pfadfinder in der deutschen Jugendgeschichte*, pp. 42—91. A number of Boy Scout groups continued to exist independently of the Deutsche Freischar. Amalgamations of several groups took place in 1929 (Deutscher Pfadfinderverband) and 1932 (Reichsschaft deutscher Pfadfinder), and they remained part of the Bündische movement until 1933.
82. Kneip (ed.), *Jugend der Weimarer Zeit*, pp. 30—1.
83. Developments in Saxony are discussed in detail in Kneip *et al., Jugend zwischen den Kriegen*, p. 16 ff; and Rudolf Kneip, *Wandervogel — Bündische Jugend. 1905—1943. Der Weg der sächsischen Jungenschaft zum grossen Bund* (Frankfurt a. M., 1976) *passim*.
84. Kneip, *Jugend der Weimarer Zeit*, pp. 76—7.
85. Erich Scholz, 'Russlandfahrten und Russlandromantik der deutschen Jugendbünde', in Nasarski, *Deutsche Jugendbewegung in Europa*, pp. 316—24.
86. Grau, *d. j. l. ll.*, chs 1 and 2.
87. Cf. Werner Helwig (ed.), *Tusk — Gesammelte Schriften und Dichtungen* (Heidenheim, 1962); and Erich Meier (ed.), Eberhard Köbel (Tusk), '. . . seh ich Schwäne nordwärts fliegen' (Heidenheim, 1977).
88. Kneip, *Jugend der Weimarer Zeit*, pp. 85—7; and Kindt, *Die Bündische Zeit*, pp. 1197—9.
89. Grau, *d. j. l. ll.*, p. 43 ff., and 'Eberhard Köbel-tusk in Gestapo-Haft und auf dem Wege in die Emigration', *JADJB*, VII (1975) pp. 145—8.
90. The name was derived from the Indian sun-god, Artam. It was suggested as a sign of the group's pure Aryanism by the *völkisch* writer Willibald Hentschel, who became the intellectual mentor of the Artamanen.
91. Alwiss Rosenberg, 'Bäuerliche Siedlungsarbeit des Bundes Artam. Ein agrarpolitischer Versuch bündischer Jugend', *JADJB*, IX (1977) pp. 202 f., 212 ff.

92. Alwiss Rosenberg, 'Die Artamanen und der Arbeitsdienst', *JADJB*, IX (1977) pp. 231–4.
93. Walter Palesch, 'Artamanen – die ideologische Konzeption einer grossstadtfeindlichen Bewegung in Theorie und Praxis' (Diploma thesis, University of Mannheim, 1977) pp. 57, 107 ff; and Kater: 'Die Artamanen', pp. 609 ff., 622 ff.
94. Kater, in *Historische Zeitschrift*, CCXIII, pp. 624 ff.
95. Bundesarchiv Koblenz (BA), Hauptarchiv der NSDAP, NS26/1285.
96. Wolfgang Schlicker, 'Die Artamanen-bewegung. Eine Frühform des Arbeitsdienstes und Kaderzelle des Faschismus auf dem Lande', *Zeitschrift für Geschichtswissenschaft*, XVIII (1970) p. 73.
97. Georg Anton, *Die Geusen* (Hannover, 1963) pp. 34 ff.
98. In 1930 Adler und Falken had 3390; Freischar Schill, 1000; Die Geusen, 1800; Schilljugend (renamed Bund Ekkehard in 1929), 250.
99. Cf. Karl O. Paetel, *Versuchung oder Chance? Zur Geschichte des deutschen Nationalbolshevismus* (Göttingen, 1965); and Otto-Ernst Schüddekopf, *National-bolshevismus in Deutschland 1918–1933* (Berlin, 1973) p. 224 ff.
100. Kneip, *Jugend der Weimarer Zeit*, pp. 204–5.
101. Fritz Borinski, *et al.*, *Jugend im politischen Protest. Der Leuchtenburgkreis 1923–1933–1977* (Frankfurt a. M., 1977) p. 9 ff.
102. Pross, *Die Zerstörung der deutschen Politik*, p. 155; Becker, *German Youth*, Conclusion; Mosse, *Crisis of German Ideology*, pp. 188–9; Roessler, *Jugend im Erziehungsfeld*, pp. 230–1; Michael H. Kater, 'Bürgerliche Jugendbewegung und Hitlerjugend in Deutschland von 1926 bis 1939', *Archiv für Sozialgeschichte*, XVII (1977) p. 174. For a scathing description of the youth movement, see Joachim C. Fest, *The Face of the Third Reich* (London, 1970) pp. 220–6.
103. Will Vesper (ed.), *Deutsche Jugend. 30 Jahre Geschichte einer Bewegung* (Berlin, 1934) p. ix f.
104. Baldur von Schirach, *Die Hitler-Jugend. Idee und Gestalt* (Leipzig, 1934) pp. 13–15, 22.
105. Laqueur, *Young Germany*, pp. 197–8, 217; Raabe, *Die Bündische Jugend*, pp. 152–78, 200–1; Borinski and Milch, *Jugendbewegung*, p. 43; Wandruszka, in *Quellen und Forschungen aus italienischen Archiven*, p. 514 ff; and Karl Seidelmann, 'War die Jugendbewegung präfaschistisch?', *JADJB*, VII (1975) pp. 66–74.
106. Joseph Held, 'Die Volksgemeinschaftsidee in der Deutschen Jugendbewegung: Tätigkeit und Weltanschauung einiger Jugendvereine zur Zeit der Weimarer Republik', *Jahrbuch des Instituts für deutsche Geschichte*, VI (1977) pp. 460–1.
107. Willi Walter Puls, 'Auf dem Wege zur Politik', in Korn *et al.*, *Die Jugendbewegung*, pp. 149–50.
108. Müller, *Die Jugendbewegung als deutsche Hauptrichtung*, p. 290.
109. Timothy W. Mason, *Sozialpolitik im Dritten Reich. Arbeiterklasse und Volksgemeinschaft* (Opladen, 1977) p. 76 ff.
110. Cf. Thomas Nipperdey, '1933 und Kontinuität der Deutschen Geschichte', *Historische Zeitschrift*, (1978) pp. 86–111.
111. Kater, in *Archiv für Sozialgeschichte*, XVII, pp. 165, 174.
112. One example should suffice: Hans Ebeling's *The German Youth Movement* (London, 1945) pp. 7 f, 20 ff.
113. Paetel, *Bild vom Menschen*, p. 44.

114. Michael E. Jovy, 'Deutsche Jugendbewegung und Nationalsozialismus. Versuch einer Klärung ihrer Zusammenhänge und Gegensätze' (Doctoral dissertation, University of Cologne, 1952) pp. 122, 170, 180, 225; also Raabe, *Die Bündische Jugend*, p. 137.

115. Walter Z. Laqueur, 'The German Youth Movement and the "Jewish Question". A Preliminary Survey', *Yearbook of the Leo Baeck Institute*, VI (1961) pp. 200–1; Jovy, 'Deutsche Jugendbewegung und Nationalsozialismus', p. 224.

116. Gerhard Ziemer, 'Die Deutsche Jugendbewegung und der Staat', *JADJB*, v (1973) p. 47.

117. Peter D. Stachura, *Nazi Youth in the Weimar Republic* (Santa Barbara and Oxford, 1975) pp. 15–16, 97 ff.

118. The Protestant youth leader Udo Smidt admitted in 1931 that 70 per cent of Bibelkreise members were pro-National Socialist – U. Smidt, *In den Tag hinein. Botschaft und Bericht aus dem Bund deutscher Bibelkreise* (Wuppertal-Barmen 1931). See p. 172, document no. 7.

119. A grossly exaggerated estimate of the extent of Bündische sympathy for the NSDAP in the early 1930s is given by the later well-known historian of the youth movement, Werner Kindt, in his article '"Bund oder Partei?" in der Jugendbewegung', *Das Junge Deutschland*, XXVI (1932) no. 12, p. 397.

120. A partial assessment of the Bündische-Hitler Youth relationship is provided by Ulrike Schmidt: 'Über das Verhältnis von Jugendbewegung und Hitlerjugend', *Geschichte in Wissenschaft und Unterricht*, XVI (1965) pp. 19–37.

121. Heinz Däubler in *Die Kommenden*, July–Aug 1929.

122. A detailed account of the Hitler Youth's recruitment from Bündische Youth is given in Stachura, *Nazi Youth*, pp. 108–10.

123. Karl O. Paetel, 'Die deutsche Jugendbewegung als politisches Phänomen', *Politische Studien*, VIII (1957) p. 6.

124. For a broader discussion of the whole theme see my 'Deutsche Jugendbewegung und Nationalsozialismus: Interpretationen und Perspektiven', *JADJB*, XII, 1980.

CHAPTER 3

1. Smaller religious groups also established youth auxiliaries; for example, the Seventh Day Adventists had the Reichsverband der deutschen Adventjugend, which had 9000 members in 1931, and the Mormons set up the Mormon Boy Scouts (Mormonenpfadfinder) in 1920. See Kneip, *Jugend der Weimarer Zeit*, pp. 187, 210.

2. Paul Hastenteufel, *Jugendbewegung und Jugendseelsorge. Geschichte und Probleme der katholischen Jugendarbeit im 20. Jahrhundert* (Munich, 1962) p. 12.

3. Ibid., p. 20.

4. Schellenberger, *Katholische Jugend*, p. 2 f.

5. Walter Dirks, 'Anfänge und Folgen katholischer Jugendbewegung', in Korn *et al.*, *Die Jugendbewegung*, p. 243.

6. Held, 'Embattled Youth', p. 249.

7. Felix Messerschmid, 'Bilanz einer Jugendbewegung. Quickborn und Rothenfels von den Anfängen bis 1939', *Frankfurter Hefte*, XXIV (1969) p. 789.

8. *Süddeutsche Monatshefte*, XXIII, no. 7 (Apr 1926) p. 163.

9. Romano Guardini, 'Quickborn – Tatsachen und Grundsätze' (1920), in Seidelmann, *Die deutsche Jugendbewegung*, p. 81.

10. Josef Pieper, *Noch wusste es niemand. Autobiographische Aufzeichnungen 1904–1945* (Munich, 1976) p. 42, tells of his joining Quickborn in 1919 and of his happy times spent at the Burg.

11. Domandi, 'The German Youth Movement', p. 241.

12. Dirks, in Korn *et al.*, *Die Jugendbewegung*, p. 244.

13. Guardini's ideas and personality are best analysed in Mahr, *Romano Guardini*; Balthasar: *Romano Guardini*; W. Ferber: 'Romano Guardini 1885–1968', in Rudolf Morsey (ed.), *Zeitgeschichte in Lebensbildern* (Mainz, 1973); and Felix Messerschmid, 'Romano Guardini. Aufsätze', *Geschichte in Wissenschaft und Unterricht*, XII (1970) pp. 709–58

14. He laid down the intellectual basis for this communion in a short but significant work, *Neue Jugend und katholischer Geist* (Mainz, 1921).

15. Guardini in Korn *et al.*, *Die Jugendbewegung*, p. 82 ff.

16. Kindt, *Die Bündische Zeit*, p. 680.

17. Felix Hargasser, 'Der Einfluss der Jugendbewegung auf die Erwachsenenbildung', *JADJB*, VII (1975) p. 39.

18. Kindt, *Die Bündische Zeit*, p. 684.

19. Renamed Kreuzfahrer-Jungenschaft in 1927.

20. Renamed Jungkreuzbund in 1926.

21. Franz Henrich, *Die Bünde katholischer Jugendbewegung. Ihre Bedeutung für die liturgische und eucharistische Erneuerung* (Munich, 1968) pp. 32 f., 37.

22. The Jesuit Ludwig Esch was the first General Secretary and real driving force behind Neudeutschland in the early stages. See Helmut Holzapfel, *Pater Ludwig Esch. Ein Leben für die Jugend* (Würzburg, 1963).

23. Kindt, *Die Bündische Zeit*, pp. 697–8; Johannes Zender, *Neudeutschland. Erinnerungen* (Freiburg, 1949) p. 16 f.; see also for background Henrich Jansen Cron (ed.), *Dreissig Jahre Bund Neudeutschland* (Cologne, 1949); and Ronald A. Warlowski, 'Neudeutschland. German Catholic Youth 1919–1939' (Doctoral dissertation, University of Pittsburgh, 1964).

24. Seidelmann, *Die Pfadfinder in der deutschen Jugendgeschichte*, pp. 121–4; Kneip, *Jugend der Weimarer Zeit*, p. 90.

25. Schellenberger, *Katholische Jugend*, p. 5.

26. Pross, *Jugend, Eros, Politik*, p. 471.

27. Schellenberger, *Katholische Jugend*, p. 19.

28. Ibid., p. 13.

29. Hans Müller (ed.), *Katholische Kirche und Nationalsozialismus: Dokumente 1930–1935* (Munich, 1965) p. 5.

30. Waltraud Köchel, 'Geschichte und Staatsauffassung im Bildungsprozess der katholischen Jugendbewegung in der Weimarer Republik' (Diploma thesis, Pädagogische Hochschule Rheinland, Abteilung Köln, 1976) pp. 84 ff. 145 ff.

31. Schellenberger, *Katholische Jugend*, p. 6.

32. Karl Kupisch, *Der Deutsche CVJM. Aus der Geschichte der Christlichen Vereine jünger Männer Deutschlands* (Kassel, 1958) p. 23 ff.

33. Kindt, *Die Bündische Zeit*, pp. 518, 596.

34. Seidelmann, *Die Pfadfinder in der deutschen Jugendgeschichte*, pp. 115–6.

35. Manfred Priepke, *Die evangelische Jugend im Dritten Reich 1933–1936* (Hanover, 1960) p. 12.

36. Pross, *Jugend, Eros, Politik*, p. 469.

37. Dieter-Horst Toboll, 'Evangelische Jugendbewegung 1919—1933, dargestellt an dem Bund deutscher Jugendvereine und dem Christdeutschen Bund' (Doctoral dissertation, University of Bonn, 1971) p. 10.

38. Hans-Christian Brandenburg, 'Neue Jugend im Protestantismus', in Korn *et al.* (eds), *Die Jugendbewegung*, pp. 238—40.

39. Else Frobenius, *Mit uns zieht die neue Zeit* (Berlin, 1927) p. 288.

40. Kindt, *Die Bündische Zeit*, pp. 519—25.

41. Köngen is the name of a village lying at the foot of the Swabian Alps, and there a bridge crosses the Neckar river. The name was adopted to symbolise the bridging of the two philosophies, Christianity and youth movement, by the group.

42. Hans-Christian Brandenburg and Rudolf Daur, *Die Brücke zu Köngen. Fünfzig Jahre Bund der Köngener 1919—1969* (Stuttgart, 1969) pp. 34—5.

43. Kneip, *Jugend der Weimarer Zeit*, p. 50.

44. Brandenburg and Daur, *Die Brücke*, pp. 113, 117 ff.

45. Toboll, 'Evangelische Jugendbewegung', pp. 27—8, 37, 111.

46. Priepke, *Evangelische Jugend*, pp. 19—20.

47. Ibid., pp. 22—3.

48. Ibid., pp. 23—4.

49. Leopold Cordier, *Evangelische Jugendkunde*, II (Schwerin, 1925) p. 680.

50. Priepke, *Evangelische Jugend*, pp. 13, 27.

51. Ibid., pp. 17—18.

52. Toboll, *Evangelische Jugendbewegung*, pp. 123—4, 130, 255—6, 274.

53. Karl-Wilhelm Dahm, 'German Protestantism and Politics 1918—39', *Journal of Contemporary History*, III (1968) p. 44.

54. Heer, *Revolutions of Our Time*, p. 60.

55. Rafael W. Merlin, 'Wandervogel und Blau-Weiss. Über die jüdische Jugendbewegung in vor-Hitler Deutschland' (MS., Hessischer Rundfunk, Frankfurt, 1968) *passim*.

56. Hermann Meier-Cronemeyer, 'Jüdische Jugendbewegung', *Germania Judaica*, VIII (1969) p. 8 f.

57. Ibid., pp. 16—17.

58. Herbert Strauss, 'The Jugendverband. A Social and Intellectual History', *Yearbook of the Leo Baeck Institute*, VI (1961) pp. 206, 212—14.

59. Meier-Cronemeyer, in *Germania Judaica*, VIII pp. 18, 25; Kindt, *Die Wandervogelzeit*, p. 731.

60. Hans Tramer, 'Blau-Weiss, Wegbereiter für Zion', in Korn *et al.*, *Die Jugendbewegung*, p. 204.

61. Chanoch Rinott, 'Major Trends in Jewish Youth Movements in Germany', *Yearbook of the Leo Baeck Institute*, XIX (1974) pp. 80—2. A more detailed analysis of Buber's influence on the Jewish Youth Movement as a whole is provided by Chaim Schatzker, 'Martin Buber's Influence on the Jewish Youth Movement in Germany', *Yearbook of the Leo Baeck Institute*, XXIII (1978) pp. 151—71, esp. pp. 163 ff.

62. Tramer, in Korn *et al.*, *Die Jugendbewegung*, p. 204.

63. Kindt, *Die Bündische Zeit*, p. 773 f.

64. Chaim Schatzker, 'The Jewish Youth Movement in Germany between the Years 1900—1933' (Doctoral dissertation, Hebrew University, Tel Aviv, 1969) pp. 53 ff., 61 ff.

65. Tramer, in Korn et al., *Die Jugendbewegung*, p. 206.
66. Schatzker, 'The Jewish Youth Movement', pp. 162–90.
67. Tramer, in Korn et al., *Die Jugendbewegung*, p. 203; Schatzker, 'The Jewish Youth Movement', pp. 191 ff.
68. Kneip, *Jugend der Weimarer Zeit*, p. 40.
69. Hermann Meier-Cronemeyer, *Kibbuzim. Geschichte, Geist und Gestalt* (Hanover, 1969) p. 74.
70. Tramer, in Korn et al., *Die Jugendbewegung*, p. 219; Meier-Cronemeyer, in *Germania Judaica*, VIII, p. 70.
71. In 1925 Brith Haolim merged with the *Jung-Jüdischer Wanderbund*. Details in Richard Markel, 'Brith Haolim. Der Weg der Alija des Jung-Jüdischen Wanderbundes (JJWB)', *Bulletin des Leo Baeck Instituts*, IX (1966) pp. 119–89.
72. Meier-Cronemeyer, in *Germania Judaica*, VIII, pp. 65–6.
73. Ibid., pp. 64–5.
74. Ibid., 51–2, 75 ff.
75. Werner Rosenstock, 'The Jewish Youth Movement', *Yearbook of the Leo Baeck Institute*, XIX (1974) p. 97.
76. Strauss, ibid., VI, pp. 207, 217 ff, 234 ff.
77. Rinott, ibid., XIX, p. 77.
78. Kindt, *Die Bündische Zeit*, p. 771.
79. Kneip, *Jugend der Weimarer Zeit*, pp. 140, 206.
80. *Jugendführung, Zeitschrift für Pädagogik der reifenden männlichen Jugend*, 1929, pp. 57–9.
81. Carl J. Rheins, 'The Schwarzes Fähnlein, Jungenschaft 1932–1934', *Yearbook of the Leo Baeck Institute*, XXIII (1978) pp. 173–97.
82. Eliyahu Maoz, 'The Werkleute', *Year Book of the Leo Baeck Institute*, IV (1959) pp. 166–72, 175 ff.: Meier-Cronemeyer, in *Germania Judaica*, VIII, pp. 85, 109. In 1933 the name was changed, significantly, to Werkleute, Bund jüdischer Jugend.
83. Jizchak Schwersenz and Edith Wolff, 'Jüdische Jugend im Untergrund. Eine zionistische Gruppe in Deutschland während des zweiten Weltkrieges', *Bulletin des Leo Baeck Instituts*, XII (1969) p. 8.
84. Kneip, *Jugend der Weimarer Zeit*, p. 56.
85. Cf. Hans-Joachim Schoeps, *Bereit für Deutschland, Der Patriotismus deutscher Juden und der Nationalsozialismus* (Berlin, 1970).
86. Mosse, *Germans and Jews*, p. 107 ff. See also Carl Jeffrey Rheins, 'German Jewish Patriotism 1918–1935' (Doctoral dissertation, State University of New York, 1978), for discussion of Vortrupp and similar-minded organisations.
87. Meier-Cronemeyer, *Germania Judaica*, VIII, pp. 101–3.
88. Schwersenz and Wolff, in *Bulletin des Leo Baeck Instituts*, pp. 11–13; for details of the youth resistance group Chug Chaluzi, see p. 23 ff.
89. Hermann Meier-Cronemeyer, 'Wirkungen der Jugendbewegung im Staatsaufbau Israels', *JADJB*, VI (1974) pp. 54–7.

CHAPTER 4

1. Named after the prominent Centre Party politician Ludwig Windthorst (1812–91).

2. Pross, *Jugend, Eros, Politik*, p. 473.
3. Stählin, in *JADJB*, IX, pp. 170–1.
4. Paetel, *Jugend in der Entscheidung*, p. 86. The DDP's successor in 1930, the German State Party, had the Reichsgruppe Bündische Jugend in der Deutschen Staatspartei as its youth organisation.
5. Paetel, *Jugend in der Entscheidung*, p. 87.
6. Kneip, *Jugend der Weimarer Zeit*, pp. 39, 135–6.
7. For details of pre-1926 youth developments in the NSDAP, see Stachura, *Nazi Youth*, pp. 5–16.
8. Erich Eberts's book, *Arbeiterjugend 1904–1945. Sozialistische Erziehungsgemeinschaft-Politische Organisation* (Dipa-Verlag, Frankfurt a. M.) had still not appeared when the manuscript of this book was completed in summer 1979.
9. Heinrich Eppe and Wolfgang Uellenberg, *70 Jahre Sozialistische Jugendinternationale. Zur Geschichte der internationalen sozialistischen Kinder- und Jugendorganisationen* (Bonn, 1976) p. 11.
10. Some useful details are given by Gotthold Krapp, *Die Kämpfe um proletarischen Jugendunterricht und proletarische Jugendweihen am Ende des 19. Jahrhunderts* (East Berlin, 1977).
11. By the 1869 Commercial Code (*Gewerbeordnung*), employers had paternal educational jurisdiction (*väterliche Erziehungsgewalt*) over apprentices, most of whom lived with them.
12. Helmut Lehmann, 'Wie die Arbeiterjugendbewegung entstand', in Wolfgang Arlt (ed.) *Deutschlands Junge Garde. 50 Jahre Arbeiterjugendbewegung* (East Berlin, 1954) p. 21 ff.
13. Something of the flavour of young working-class life during the last quarter of the nineteenth century is conveyed by Günter Bers (ed.), *Arbeiterjugend im Rheinland – Erinnerungen von Wilhelm Reimes und Peter Trimborn* (Wentorf, 1978) pp. 23–47, 48–76.
14. Johannes Schult, *Aufbruch einer Jugend. Der Weg der deutschen Arbeiterjugendbewegung* (Bonn, 1956) p. 32.
15. Max Peters, *Der Weg zum Licht* (Berlin, 1907) p. 11 ff, and *50 Jahre Arbeiterjugendbewegung 1904–54* (Bonn, 1954) p. 21 ff.
16. Erich Schumann, *Wir gingen mit Karl Liebknecht – Erlebnisse aus der Arbeiterjugendbewegung 1908–1918* (East Berlin, 1960) pp. 54–63.
17. Alex Hall, 'Youth in Rebellion: The Beginnings of the Socialist Youth Movement 1904–1914', in Richard J. Evans (ed.), *Society and Politics in Wilhelmine Germany* (London, 1978) pp. 248–9.
18. Karl Korn, 'Die Arbeiterjugendbewegung, Einführung in ihre Geschichte', in Seidelmann (ed.), *Die deutsche Jugendbewegung*, pp. 69–70.
19. Paul Schiller, 'Die Jugend entlarvt Polizeispitzel', in Arlt, *Deutschlands Junge Garde*, pp. 49–51.
20. Karl-Heinz Jahnke *et al.*, *Geschichte der deutschen Arbeiterjugendbewegung* (Dortmund, 1973) p. 46; Schult, *Aufbruch einer Jugend*, p. 35 ff.
21. Jahnke *et al.*, *Geschichte der deutschen Arbeiterjugendbewegung*, pp. 48, 55–6.
22. Ibid., p. 37.
23. Karl Korn, 'Die Arbeiterjugendbewegung', in Kindt (ed.), *Grundschriften*, pp. 257–8; Schult, *Aufbruch einer Jugend*, pp. 24–5.
24. The whole issue is surveyed by Bernhard Krabiell in his 'Die selbständigen

Arbeiterjugendorganisationen Deutschlands 1904 – 1908 und ihr Verhältnis in Partei und Gewerkschaften' (Diploma thesis, University of Frankfurt a. M., 1976).

25. Erich Lindstaedt, *Mit uns zieht die neue Zeit. Fünfzig Jahre Arbeiterjugendbewegung* (Bonn, 1954) p. 26.
26. Schult, *Aufbruch einer Jugend*, pp. 96 f., 100 ff.
27. Saul, in *Militärgeschichtliche Mitteilungen*, X, pp. 97 ff., 103 – 4, 112 ff.
28. Carl E. Schorske, *German Social Democracy, 1905 – 1917. The Development of the Great Schism* (New York 1972 edn) pp. 103 – 5.
29. Schult, *Aufbruch einer Jugend*, pp. 59 – 63.
30. Jahnke *et al.*, *Geschichte der deutschen Arbeiterjugendbewegung*, p. 70; Schult, *Aufbruch einer Jugend*, pp. 66, 73.
31. The paper is fondly recalled by Willy Dehnkamp in his 'Zum Bildungshunger der Arbeiterjugend', *JADJB*, x (1978) p. 66.
32. Karl Korn, *Die Arbeiterjugendbewegung* (Berlin, 1922) pp. 176, 249.
33. Jahnke *et al.*, *Geschichte der deutschen Arbeiterjugendbewegung*, pp. 65, 73. Included among this radical section of the youth committees were later Communist Party stalwarts such as Walter Ulbricht, Otto Grotewohl, Willi Münzenberg, Georg Schumann, Hermann Remmele and Hermann Matern.
34. Saul, in *Militärgeschichtliche Mitteilungen*, x, p. 111.
35. Ibid., pp. 123 – 5.
36. Gillis, *Youth and History*, pp. 162 – 3.
37. Jahnke *et al.*, *Geschichte der deutschen Arbeiterjugendbewegung*, p. 124.
38. Ottokar Luban, 'Die Auswirkungen der Jenaer Jugendkonferenz 1916 und die Beziehungen der Zentrale der revolutionären Arbeiterjugend zur Führung der Spartakusgruppe', *Archiv für Sozialgeschichte*, XI (1971) p. 191 ff.
39. Erich Wiesner, 'Vom Kampf der revolutionären Jugend in den Kriegsjahren 1916 bis 1918', in Arlt, *Deutschlands Junge Garde*, pp. 123 – 30.
40. Luban, in *Archiv für Sozialgeschichte*, XI, pp. 205 – 9, 202 f.
41. Harry Kuhn, 'Die Gründung der Freien Sozialistischen Jugend Deutschlands' in Arlt, *Deutschlands Junge Garde*, pp. 144 – 6.
42. Schorske, *German Social Democracy*, pp. 107 – 8.
43. Heinrich Steinbrinker, 'Der Geist der Gemeinschaft. Wechselwirkungen zwischen Arbeiterjugendbewegung und "bürgerlicher" Jugendbewegung bis 1933', *JADJB*, X (1978) p. 13 ff.
44. Helmuth Hägel, 'Die Stellung der sozialdemokratischen Jugendorganisationen zu Staat und Partei in den Anfangsjahren der Weimarer Republik', *Internationale Wissenschaftliche Korrespondenz zur Geschichte der deutschen Arbeiterbewegung*, XII (1976) pp. 169 – 70.
45. E. R. Müller, *Das Weimarbuch der arbeitenden Jugend* (Berlin, 1920) p. 55.
46. In *Arbeiter-Jugend*, XII(1920) no. 15, p. 161. See also Ollenhauer's brochure *Arbeiterjugend und Republik* (Berlin, 1922).
47. Hägel, in *Internationale Wissenschaftliche Korrespondenz zur Geschichte der deutschen Arbeiterbewegung*, XII, p. 174.
48. Cf. Max Schwarz, *Der Arbeiterjugend – Verlag Berlin 1920 – 1933. Eine Bibliographie* (Bonn, 1977), which provides a list of the house's publications.
49. Erich Lüth, 'Jugendbewegung vor den Forderungen der Politik', *JADJB*, x (1978) p. 100.
50. Schult, *Aufbruch einer Jugend*, p. 127.

51. Frank Lepinski, 'Die jungsozialistische Bewegung, ihre Geschichte und ihre Aufgabe', in Kindt, *Grundschriften*, p. 468.

52. The best analysis of the Hofgeismar circle is provided by one of its leaders, Franz Osterroth: 'Der Hofgeismarkreis der Jungsozialisten', *Archiv für Sozialgeschichte*, IV (1964) pp. 525–69.

53. Ferdinand Brandecker, 'Erziehung durch die Klasse für die Klasse. Zur Pädagogik der Kinderfreudebewegung in Deutschland 1919–1933', in Manfred Heinemann (ed.), *Sozialisation und Bildungswesen in der Weimarer Republik* (Stuttgart, 1976) p. 167 ff. See also Harald Wirbals, 'Theorie und Praxis der sozialistischen Erziehung in der Kinderfreudebewegung von 1923–1933 in Deutschland' (Diploma thesis, Pädagogische Hochschule Dortmund, 1976).

54. Karl Scharmann, 'Das Erlebnis der Solidarität. Erinnerungen an die Reichsjugendtage in Bielefeld und Nürnberg', *JADJB*, X (1978) pp. 140–6.

55. Franz Hammer, *Traum und Wirklichkeit – Die Geschichte einer Jugend* (Rudolstadt, 1975) p. 100, recalls his days in this group.

56. Hägel, *Internationale Wissenschaftliche Korrespondenz zur Geschichte der deutschen Arbeiterbewegung*, XII, pp. 185–9, 191–2.

57. Schult, *Aufbruch einer Jugend*, p. 214.

58. Peter H. Merkl, *Political Violence under the Swastika. 581 Early Nazis* (Princeton, NJ, 1975) p. 240.

59. Richard N. Hunt, *German Social Democracy 1918–1933* (Chicago 1970 edn) p. 109.

60. Brian Peterson, 'The Politics of Working-Class Women in the Weimar Republic', *Central European History*, X (1977) pp. 96–8.

61. A vivid account of the economic and social deprivation afflicting many proletarian youths in Weimar is given by Ferdinand Brandecker, 'Notizen zur Sozialisation des Arbeiterkindes in der Weimarer Republik', in Heinemann (ed.), *Sozialisation und Bildungswesen*, p. 39 ff.

62. Kindt, *Die Bündische Zeit*, pp. 1014–15.

63. Schult, *Aufbruch einer Jugend*, p. 187.

64. Kindt, *Die Bündische Zeit*, p. 1011.

65. Cf. Hugo Sieker, 'Erinnerung an die "Freie Proletarische Jugend"', *JADJB*, III (1971) pp. 64–74.

66. Willy Brandt (as Herbert Frahm) was a member of the SAJ and led its Lübeck branch in 1928. In 1931 he left to join the splinter Sozialistische Arbeiter-Partei and became chairman of its youth group, the Sozialistische Jugendverband. See Hinrich Jantzen (ed.), *Namen und Werke. Biographien und Beiträge zur Soziologie der deutschen Jugendewegung*, II (Frankfurt a. M., 1974) pp. 44–7.

67. The youth section of the Reichsbanner. In 1931 the Jungbanner had 220,000 members aged fourteen to eighteen years and 485,000 aged eighteen to twenty-five years (Kneip, *Jugend der Weimarer Zeit*, p. 149).

68. The group existed in this form until 1925, when it was expelled from the Social Democratic movement. Nelson then reformed the group as the Internationaler Sozialistischer Kampf-Bund. A detailed history is given in Werner Link, *Die Geschichte des Internationalen Jugend-Bundes (IJB) und des Internationalen sozialistischen Kampf-Bundes (ISK)* (Meisenheim, 1964).

69. See the reminiscences of an FSJ leader, Fritz Globig, in his book . . . *aber*

verbunden sind wir mächtig (East Berlin, 1954) pp. 281—2.

70. Otto Braun, 'In der Münchener FSJ', in Arlt, *Deutschlands Junge Garde*, pp. 163—8.

71. Kurella, *Unterwegs zu Lenin*, pp. 32 ff., 78 ff., 147.

72. Richard Cornell, 'The Origins and Development of the Communist Youth International 1914—1924' (Doctoral dissertation, Columbia University, 1965) pp. 108, 294 ff., 333 ff.

73. Details in Peter Hauck, 'Von der Autonomen Jugendorganisation zur Parteijugend — Der Spaltungsprozess der FSJD unter besonderer Berücksichtigung des Linkskommunismus 1919—20' (Dissertation, University of Mannheim, 1978) p. 77 ff.

74. Horst Pietschmann, 'Zum Prozess der Entwicklung der Freien Sozialistischen Jugend zu einem kommunistischen Jugendverband (1918—21)', *Beiträge zur Geschichte der deutschen Arbeiterbewegung*, XVII (1975) P. 1049.

75. See the obituary in *Die Junge Garde*, 1919, no. 8; repr in Arlt, *Deutschlands Junge Garde*, p. 162.

76. In 1918 Liebknecht wrote the famous words 'The revolutionary youth of the proletariat is the most passionate and purist flame of the German Revolution to date; they will be the brightest, most venerable, inextinguishable flame of the new Revolution, which must and will come . . .'. In *Zur Geschichte der Arbeiterjugendbewegung in Deutschland. Eine Auswahl von Materialien und Dokumenten aus den Jahren 1904—1946* (East Berlin, 1956) p. 73.

77. Jahnke *et al.*, *Geschichte der deutschen Arbeiterjugendbewegung*, p. 249.

78. Ibid., p. 269.

79. Pietschmann, in *Beiträge zur Geschichte der deutschen Arbeiterbewegung*, XVII, p. 1056.

80. Jahnke et al., *Geschichte der deutschen Arbeiterjugendbewegung*, p. 281.

81. Membership was increased to some degree late in 1922 when pro-Communist elements of the Sozialistische Proletarierjugend refused to join the SAJ and instead joined the KJD — Cornell, 'Origins and Development', p. 219. Also, the disbandment of small radically leftist groups such as the Entschiedene Jugend in the early 1920s often benefited the KJD — Hans-Harald Müller, *Intellektueller Linksradikalismus in der Weimarer Republik* (Kronberg, 1977) pp. 48—51.

82. Jahnke *et al.*, *Geschichte der deutschen Arbeiterjugendbewegung*, pp. 297—8.

83. Christoph Zimmermann, 'Die Arbeiterjugend- und Kindergruppenbewegung in Dortmund von 1918—1933' (Diploma thesis, Pädagogische Hochschule Ruhr, 1976) p. 62 ff.; Jahnke *et al.*, *Geschichte der deutschen Arbeiterjugendbewegung*, pp. 283—4, 302—9; Gerhard Roger, *Die pädagogische Bedeutung der proletarischen Jugendbewegung Deutschlands* (Frankfurt a. M., 1971) p. 143. The group was renamed Roter Jungpioniere in 1930; a junior section for six-to ten-year-olds called Rote Jungschar was then added.

84. Cf. Willi Perk, 'Antimilitäristische Aktion 1923 im Ruhrgebiet', in Arlt, *Deutschlands Junge Garde*, pp. 203—6; Manfred Uhlemann, *Arbeiterjugend gegen Cuno und Poincaré. Das Jahr 1923* (East Berlin, 1960).

85. Wolfgang Döke, 'Zur den freundschaftlichen Beziehungen zwischen Ernst Thälmann und der sowjetischen Jugend', in *Wissenschaftliche Zeitschrift der Wilhelm-Pieck-Universität Rostock*, XXVI (1977) p. 22; J. Chawanow, 'Zur Zusammenarbeit zwischen dem Lenischen Komsomol und KJVD', ibid., p. 17.

86. Institut für Marxistische Studien und Forschungen, *Dokumente und Materialien – Aus der Geschichte der deutschen Arbeiterjugendbewegung 1904–1945* (Frankfurt a. M., 1975) p. 18.

87. Kurt G. P. Schuster, *Der Rote Frontkämpferbund 1924–1929. Beiträge zur Geschichte und Organisationsstruktur eines politischen Kampfbundes* (Düsseldorf, 1975) p. 123 ff.

88. Werner Bramke and Kurt Finker, 'Die Rote Jungfront – Verkörperung der Wehrhaftigkeit der revolutionären deutschen Arbeiterjugend (1924–1929)', *Zeitschrift für Militärgeschichte*, XI (1972) pp. 73–4.

89. Wolfgang Döke, 'Zum antimilitärischen Kampf der revolutionären deutschen Arbeiterjugend 1924 bis 1928', *Wissenschaftliche Zeitschrift der Wilhelm-Pieck-Universität Rostock*, XXVI (1977) p. 194.

90. Herbert Schwabe, 'Zur wehrerzieherischen Arbeit der Roten Jungfront', *Zeitschrift für Militärgeschichte*, XIII (1974) pp. 181–9, prints two documents outlining this policy.

91. A KJVD circular of 17 November 1925 urgently called for closer co-operation between the two groups (BA, NS26/816).

92. Jahnke *et al.*, *Geschichte der deutschen Arbeiterbewegung*, p. 340; Schuster, *Rote Frontkämpferbund*, p. 240.

93. Bramke and Finker, in *Zeitschrift für Militärgeschichte*, XI, p. 74.

94. Jahnke *et al.*, *Geschichte der deutschen Arbeiterbewegung*, p. 403, gives 22,000. Hertha Siemering, *Die deutschen Jugendverbände* (Berlin, 1931) p. 280, gives 19,000 for 1929.

95. *Zur Geschichte der Arbeiterjugendbewegung*, p. 208.

96. Jahnke *et al.*, *Geschichte der deutschen Arbeiterbewegung*, pp. 403–6.

97. Fritz Grosse, 'Aus der Massenarbeit des KJVD', in Arlt, *Deutschlands Junge Garde*, p. 211; and Ella Rumpf, 'Wie die Kommunistische Jugendverband in Berlin agitiert', ibid., p. 216.

98. Jahnke *et al.*, *Geschichte der deutschen Arbeiterbewegung*, p. 463. A figure of 60,000 is given in Arlt, *Deutschlands Junge Garde*, p. 16. What these figures do not reveal is the very number of personnel in the KJVD, as happened also in the party.

99. Karl Heinz Jahnke, 'Ernst Thälmanns Beziehungen zur Arbeiterjugend', *Beiträge zur Geschichte der deutschen Arbeiterbewegung*, XVIII (1976) pp. 321, 324.

100. *Zur Geschichte der deutschen Arbeiterjugendbewegung*, p. 270.

101. A useful survey of anarchist thought and development in Germany is given in Ulrich Linse, 'Die Transformation der Gesellschaft durch die anarchistische Weltanschauung. Zur Ideologie und Organisation anarchistischer Gruppen in der Weimarer Republik', *Archiv für Sozialgeschichte*, XI (1971) pp. 289–372.

102. Ulrich Linse, *Die anarchistische und anarcho-syndikalistische Jugendbewegung 1919–1933* (Frankfurt a. M., 1976) p. 7 ff.

103. Ibid., pp. 11–12.

104. Ibid., pp. 49, 61, 93.

105. Stachura, *Nazi Youth*, pp. 37–8.

106. Ibid., p. 27 ff.

107. Peter D. Stachura, 'The Ideology of the Hitler Youth in the Kampfzeit', *Journal of Contemporary History*, VIII (1973) pp. 155–67.

108. Stachura, *Nazi Youth*, p. 50.

109. Ibid., p. 58 ff. Secessions of a radical socialist character from the Hitler Youth are discussed in Chapter 4.
110. Peter D. Stachura, 'The Hitler Youth in Crisis: The case of Reichsführer Kurt Gruber, October 1931', *European Studies Review*, VI (1976) pp. 331—56.
111. Stachura, *Nazi Youth*, pp. 97—99.
112. Ibid., p. 180 ff.
113. Daniel Horn, 'The National Socialist Schülerbund and the Hitler Youth, 1929—1933', *Central European History*, XI (1978) pp. 358, 371 ff. Horn exaggerates the extent to which NSS influence produced a more bourgeois HJ in 1932. By his own account, only 30 per cent of the 14,000 NSS members in mid-1932 took up membership of the HJ when given the opportunity. Yet between October 1931 and January 1933 the HJ more than doubled its membership, from 26,198 to 55,365. If the NSS supplied only about 4500 of the new recruits (29,167), where did the remainder come from? Available evidence must lead to the conclusion that in the last fifteen months before Hitler's appointment as Chancellor, the HJ continued to attract most of its ordinary members from among young workers. Horn's assertion (p. 375) that the educated *Mittelstand* dominated the HJ by 1933 is patently false.
114. Stachura, *Nazi Youth*, p. 110.
115. Ibid., p. 185 ff.

CHAPTER 5

1. Speech of 28 July 1936, quoted in H. H. Dietze, *Die Reichsgehalt der Hitler-Jugend* (Berlin, 1939) p. 233.
2. *Wille und Werk, Pressedienst der deutschen Jugendbewegung*, Apr 1933.
3. Werner Haverbeck, 'Aufbruch der Jungen Nation. Ziel und Weg der nationalsozialistischen Volksjugendbewegung', *Nationalsozialistische-Monatshefte*, Feb 1933, p. 56.
4. Schirach, *Hitler-Jugend*, pp. 188—9.
5. Reichsjugendführung der NSDAP, *HJ im Dienst. Ausbildungsvorschrift für die Ertüchtigung der deutschen Jugend* (Berlin, 1940) p. 28.
6. See memorandum from Reich Minister of Interior, Wilhelm Frick, of 8 November 1933 to provincial government officials reminding them that the police were duty-bound to act against HJ rowdyism — Bayerisches Hauptstaatsarchiv, Allgemeines Staatsarchiv (BHSA, ASA), Staatsministerium des Innern 71799.
7. BA, NS26/355 — Reichsjugendführung report of 1 June 1934.
8. *Das Junge Deutschland*, Apr—May 1933, p. 97.
9. *Wille und Werk, Pressedienst der deutschen Jugendbewegung*, Oct 1933.
10. Peter D. Stachura, 'The National Socialist *Machtergreifung* and the German Youth Movement: Coordination and Reorganisation, 1933—34', *Journal of European Studies*, V (1975) p. 257.
11. Paetel, *Jugend in der Entscheidung*, p. 141.
12. BA, NS26/334 for details of the group's formation.
13. See letter from Hitler to Hindenburg of 15 July 1933 in BA, Reichskanzlei 43II/523. See further von Trotha's letter to Hitler of 29 April 1933 and von Trotha's correspondence with von Hindenburg of May/June 1933 in BA, NS 26/334.

14. BA, NS26/334. von Trotha statement of 28 June 1933 to his group.
15. *Das Junge Deutschland*, Apr–May 1933, p. 129.
16. Gerhard Rossbach, *Mein Weg durch die Zeit. Erinnerungen und Bekenntnisse* (Weilburg, 1950) p. 110. The HJ embraced a number of constituent groups within its organisation. Boys aged ten to fourteen were organised in the Jungvolk; girls of the same age were in the Jungmädel; youths aged fourteen to eighteen were in the HJ proper; and girls aged fourteen to twenty-one years were in the BdM. In 1938 a special formation called Glaube und Schönheit (Faith and Beauty), for girls aged seventeen to twenty-one, was added to the BdM. Transfer from the Deutsches Jungvolk to the HJ took place every year on 20 April (Hitler's birthday) and from the HJ to the NSDAP on 9 November (the anniversary of the 1923 *Putsch*).
17. G. Mögling, 'Bündische Jugend ist heute Bolshevismus', *Wille und Macht, Führerorgan der Nationalsozialistischen Jugend*, 1935, no. 16 (Aug) p. 17 f.
18. The Adler und Falken remained legal until April 1935 and the Bund der Artamanen, the long-standing pro-National Socialist group, until October 1934. On this date the Artamanen was incorporated into the HJ.
19. Priepke, *Evangelische Jugend*, pp. 50–2. A regional reaction is analysed in D. von Lersner, *Die Evangelischen Jugendverbände Württembergs und die Hitler-Jugend 1933–34* (Göttingen, 1958); and the reaction of one particular group is discussed in Dieter Toboll, 'Evangelische Jugendbewegung im Dritten Reich, dargestellt am Bund deutscher Jugendvereine (BDJ)', *JADJB*, IV (1972) pp. 128–34.
20. *Reichsjugendpfarrer* Karl Friedrich Zahn put the case for coming together in his book *Kirche und Hitlerjugend* (Berlin, 1934).
21. Riedel, *Kampf um die Jugend*, p. 68 ff., gives details of Protestant protests.
22. Heinrich Roth (ed.), *Katholische Jugend in der NS-Zeit. Unter besonderer Berücksichtigung des Katholischen Jungmännerverbandes. Daten und Dokumente* (Düsseldorf, 1959) pp. 59–60 – statements of the National Committee of the KJMV, 2–3 May and 17 June 1933.
23. Müller, *Katholische Kirche und Nationalsozialismus*, pp. 177, 182–3.
24. Guenter Lewy, *The Catholic Church and Nazi Germany* (London, 1964) pp. 104–5.
25. Article 31 is given in full in Lawrence D. Walker, *Hitler Youth and Catholic Youth 1933–1936: A Study in Totalitarian Conquest* (Washington, 1970) p. 58.
26. International Council for Philosophy and Humanistic Studies and UNESCO, *The Third Reich* (London, 1955) p. 808.
27. Schirach, *Hitler-Jugend*, p. 37. See also Schellenberger, *Katholische Jugend*, pp. 160–1.
28. BA, Reichskanzlei 43II/524, Memorandum of March 1934 relating to clashes in Hennigsdorf.
29. Roth, *Katholische Jugend*, p. 56.
30. It is significant that von Schirach still thought it necessary to issue a secret circular to his top leaders on 28 September 1939 warning them to be on their guard against 'the internal enemy', by which he meant the Catholic youth groups (BA, NS28/30).
31. Reichsjugendführung der NSDAP, *Aufbau, Gliederung und Anschriften der Hitler-Jugend* (Berlin, 1934) p. 12. In June 1935 the *Abteilungen* were converted

into *Ämter* (Offices), of which there were fourteen. In 1940/1 they were reduced to six.

32. Günter Kaufmann, *Das kommende Deutschland. Die Erziehung der Jugend im Reich Adolf Hitlers* (Berlin, 1940) p. 37.

33. Baldur von Schirach, *Revolution der Erziehung. Reden aus den Jahren des Aufbaus* (Munich, 1938) p. 8.

34. BA, NS26/336 – von Schirach directive dated March 1933.

35. Stachura, in *Journal of European Studies*, v, pp. 265–6.

36. Cf. Rainer Schnabel, *Das Führerschulungswerk der Hitler-Jugend* (Berlin, 1938).

37. BA, NS26/342. See various directives for instruction in the schools.

38. Cf. Jürgen Schultze, *Die Akademie für Jugendführung der Hitlerjugend in Braunschweig* (Brunswick, 1978).

39. Arno Klönne, *Hitlerjugend. Die Jugend und ihre Organisation im Dritten Reich* (Hanover, 1956) p. 42.

40. Melita Maschmann, *Account Rendered: A Dossier on My Former Self* (London, 1964) p. 147.

41. Kaufmann, *Das kommende Deutschland*, pp. 41–2.

42. Ibid., p. 44. In 1939 there were 765,000 HJ leaders, male and female.

43. Ibid., p. 45.

44. Ibid., p. 39. These figures include all branches of the HJ. The specific HJ element (fourteen- to eighteen-year-old youths) was 786,000 and 1,168,734 respectively.

45. BHSA, ASA, Staatsministerium des Innern 73437/22, Hess directive of 24.8.1935, under title 'Beitritt von Kindern der Beamter zu den Jugendorganisationen der NSDAP'.

46. *Frankfurter Zeitung*, 29 Sep 1935.

47. Hans-Christian Brandenburg, *Die Geschichte der HJ. Wege und Irrwege einer Generation* (Cologne, 1968) p. 175.

48. BA, Reichskanzlei 43II/513 – memorandum dated 10 May 1935 of *Kreisamtsleiter* Müllner of Viersen-Kempen.

49. BA, NS26/358 – Die Mitgliederentwicklung der Hitler-Jugend im Jahre 1935, Stand vom 28. März 1936.

50. BA, Reichskanzlei 43II/513.

51. BA, NS26/361 – report of HJ *Gebiet* Saarpfalz of (probably) late 1935 on 'sexual criminality' in its ranks.

52. See next chapter for details.

53. Schirach, *Hitler-Jugend*, p. 72.

54. He gives a misleading and incomplete account of his thoughts on this matter in his memoirs: Baldur von Schirach, *Ich glaubte an Hitler* (Hamburg, 1967) pp. 231–2.

55. BA, Reichskanzlei 43II/525. See Lammers-Schirach correspondence from October 1935–December 1936 concerning the draft law. Rust's objections are expressed in a letter of 18 April 1936 to Lammers and others.

56. Ibid.

57. Ibid. – letter from von Schirach to Lammers, 12 November 1936.

58. See a characteristically pedantic letter from Lammers to von Schirach on 1 July 1937, informing him of the limits of his legal powers in the new office (BA, Reichsministerium des Innern 18/5317).

59. The full text of the law is in BA, Reichskanzlei 43II/525.

60. Schirach, *Revolution der Erziehung*, p. 49.
61. The text of the executive orders are available in BA, Reichskanzlei 43II/515.
62. Von Schirach's nationwide radio broadcast of 10 December 1936 — *Völkischer Beobachter*, 11 Dec 1936.
63. BA, Reichskanzlei 43II/515a. Von Schirach letter to Schwerin von Krosigk of 12 April 1937.
64. BA, Reichskanzlei 43II/512 — letters from von Schirach to Lammers of 16 June 1938 and 6 October 1938.
65. Kaufmann, *Das kommende Deutschland*, p. 39.
66. The problems of recruitment in East Prussia and Silesia, and in particular the counter-productive impact of the 1936 law, are related in an interesting HJ *Gebietsführer*'s report of 1 March 1937 (BA, Reichskanzlei 43II/515).
67. Edgar Randel, *Die Jugenddienstpflicht* (Berlin, 1942) pp. 106 f. With the introduction of the compulsory principle there was an ill-conceived attempt to divide the HJ into a so-called Stamm-HJ incorporating all those who had been members before April 1938, and an ordinary HJ, which was to be of somewhat inferior status. The experiment was finally discontinued in 1941.
68. BA, Reichskanzlei 43II/525a. See letter from Rust to Lammers of 12 April 1937.
69. Hans-Jochen Gamm, *Der braune Kult. Das Dritte Reich und seine Ersatzreligion* (Hamburg, 1962) p. 20.
70. Arno Klönne, *Gegen den Strom. Bericht über den Jugendwiderstand im Dritten Reich* (Hanover, 1958). Klönne overestimates the organisational cohesion and influence of the local opposition groups in Hesse on which this study is based, and relies too much on uncorroborated evidence. See also Hans Ebeling and Dieter Hespers (eds), *Jugend contra Nationalsozialismus. 'Rundbriefe' und 'Sonderinformationen deutscher Jugend'* (Frechen, 1968).
71. Daniel Horn, 'Youth Resistance in the Third Reich: a Social Portrait', *Journal of Social History*, VII (1973) pp. 26—50. Horn refers (p. 26) to 'something of a mass movement among youngsters' against the HJ, which is a totally erroneous assertion. A later comment, 'It stands to reason that working-class boys should not identify with National Socialism . . .' (p. 32), is simply fatuous. Horn provides skimpy material for his wildly false generalisations about small locally based groups such as the Kittelbach Pirates (p. 34). He contradicts himself on several points of his 'argument' and generally fails to show that the activities he describes were politically motivated.
72. For example, Karl-Heinz Jahnke, *Entscheidungen. Jugend im Widerstand 1933—1945* (Frankfurt a.M., 1970).
73. Hans Heindl, *Die totale Revolution oder die neue Jugend im Dritten Reich. Ein Bericht* (Augsburg, 1973). The unhappiness of a former HJ member is recorded, somewhat dubiously, in Hans Siemsen, *Die Geschichte des Hitlerjungen Adolf Goers* (Düsseldorf, 1947).
74. Brandenburg, *Die Geschichte der HJ*, pp. 189—227; Klönne, *Hitlerjugend*, pp. 87—97; Werner Klose, *Generation im Gleichschritt. Ein Dokumentation* (Oldenburg, 1964) pp. 215—36.
75. See report by the HJ on the d.j.1.11. of 9 May 1935 (BA, NS12/82).
76. Paetel, *Jugend in der Entscheidung*, p. 178; Ebeling and Hespers, *Jugend contra Nationalsozialismus*, p. 28.
77. Karl-Heinz Jahnke, *Jungkommunisten im Widerstandskampf gegen den*

Hitlerfaschismus (East Berlin, 1977) pp. 247–8. The Berlin unit of the KJVD had only 370 members in early 1936 (p. 173).
78. Franz J. Heyen (ed.), *Nationalsozialismus im Alltag. Quellen zur Geschichte des Nationalsozialismus* (Boppard, 1967) pp. 220–2.
79. Jahnke, *Entscheidungen*, p. 179 ff.
80. Quantitative evidence for this type of subjective judgement is virtually impossible to produce, but it is worth noting that a number of critical observers of the HJ have stressed its popularity. See Heer, *Revolutions of Our Time*, p. 108; and William L. Shirer, *The Rise and Fall of the Third Reich: A History of Nazi Germany* (London, 1960) p. 256.

CHAPTER 6

1. Schirach, *Revolution der Erziehung*, p. 35.
2. Schirach, *Die Hitler-Jugend*, p. 130.
3. This is the final line of the HJ anthem, 'Forward! Forward!'
4. Every HJ training camp carried this above its entrance.
5. Cf. Baldur von Schirach, *Die Fahne der Verfolgten* (Berlin, 1933), a collection of his offerings. His idealisation of Hitler is discussed in David O. White, 'Hitler's Youth Leader: A Study of the Heroic Imagery in the Major Public Statements of Baldur von Schirach' (Doctoral dissertation, University of Oregon, 1970). White concludes (p. 317) that Schirach was 'a heroic schizophrenic'. Fest, *The Face of the Third Reich*, is rather contemptuous of his 'boyish concept of loyalty' (p. 228).
6. Schirach, *Revolution der Erziehung*, pp. 45–6.
7. David Schoenbaum, *Hitler's Social Revolution: Class and Status in Nazi Germany 1933–1939* (London, 1967) p. 287.
8. Cf. Jean B. Neveux, 'La Jeunesse et les luttes politiques dans "Der Hitlerjunge Quex" de K. A. Schenzinger', *Revue Allemagne*, VIII (1976) pp. 431–48.
9. For the use of youth literature as propaganda, see the study by Peter Aley, *Jugendliteratur im Dritten Reich. Dokumente und Kommentare* (Hamburg 1967) pp. 25 ff., 142–3.
10. Gottfried Griesmayr, *Wir Hitlerjungen. Unsere Weltanschauung in Frage und Antwort* (Berlin, 1936).
11. Refer to Chapter 5 for details.
12. C. Dörner, *Freude, Zucht, Glaube: Handbuch für die kulturelle Arbeit im Lager* (Potsdam, 1937).
13. The hostel movement was founded in 1907 by Richard Schirrmann and taken over by the HJ in 1933. See Karl Hartung, *Richard Schirrmann und Wilhelm Münker. Die Gründer und Gestalter der deutschen Jugendherbergen* (Hagen, 1953); and Franz Pöggeler, 'Die Politisierung der Jugendarbeit, dargestellt am Beispiel der deutschen Jugendherbergen von 1933 bis 1945', paper at the Conference of the Historische Kommission der deutschen Gesellschaft für Erziehungswissenschaft in Bielefeld, Autumn 1978.
14. Erich Blohm, *Hitler-Jugend. Soziale Tatgemeinschaft* (Witten, 1977) pp. 161–82.
15. *Das Junge Deutschland*, July 1939, p. 344.

16. Günter Kaufmann, *Der Reichsberufswettkampf. Die berufliche Aufrüstung der deutschen Jugend* (Berlin, 1935) p. 16 ff.

17. Michael H. Kater, 'The Reich Vocational Contest and Students of Higher Learning in Nazi Germany', *Central European History*, VII (1974) p. 231.

18. Ibid., pp. 226—8.

19. Artur Axmann, *Der Reichsberufswettkampf* (Berlin, 1938) p. 28.

20. Richard Grunberger, *A Social History of the Third Reich* (London, 1974) p. 324. A critical (Marxist) assessment of the HJ attitude to young workers is provided by Fritz Petrick, *Zur sozialen Lage der Arbeiterjugend in Deutschland 1933—1939* (East Berlin, 1974) pp. 54 ff., 91—5

21. Ibid., p. 78, estimates that in 1939 42 per cent of the membership was working-class.

22. Hugh R. Trevor-Roper (ed.), *Hitler's Table Talk 1941—1944. His Private Conversations* (London, 1973) pp. 428 (entry of 12 Apr 1942), 461 (entry of May 1942).

23. Klönne, *Hitlerjugend*, pp. 23—4, 57—8, 61.

24. BA, NS26/364. See HJ reports covering 1934—7 period.

25. Maschmann, *Account Rendered*, p. 142.

26. BA, NS28/30. See confidential memorandum issued by von Schirach to his leading officials on 4 September 1939. In all, 649 youths lost their lives on HJ service between 1933 and 1939, mostly in traffic accidents.

27. Robert J. O'Neill, *The German Army and the Nazi Party 1933—39* (London, 1968) pp. 246—7.

28. BA, Reichskanzlei 43II/522a. HJ-Army treaty of August 1939 concerning the military instruction of the HJ-full text given.

29. BA, Reichskanzlei 43II/522b. See Schirach letter to Lammers of 28 January 1939, and Führer-Verfügung of 19 January 1939 on the new powers alloted to the SA in the sphere of pre-military training.

30. The Patrol Service was set up in 1934 as a kind of internal HJ police force. Its duties were to maintain discipline in the ranks, report on illegal youth activities, supervise parades and such like. Definitive regulations for the group were not issued until 1938. At the outbreak of war it had about 50,000 members (BA, NS26/338 Vorläufige Dienstvorschrift für den HJ-Streifendienst of 15 May 1936)

31. Gerhard Rempel, 'The Misguided Generation: Hitler Youth and SS, 1933—45' (Doctoral dissertation, University of Wisconsin, 1971) pp. 111 ff, 274—80, 427—8.

32. Richard Ernst Schroeder, 'The Hitler Youth as a Paramilitary Organisation' (Doctoral dissertation, University of Chicago, 1975) pp. 154 ff., 171. In 1939 the Flight HJ had 78,000 members, the Naval HJ about 50,000, the Motorised HJ 90,000 and the Signals HJ nearly 29,000.

33. Cf. Tracy Hutchins Koon, 'Believe, Obey, Fight: Political socialisation of Youth in Fascist Italy 1922—1943' (Doctoral dissertation, Stanford University, 1977); and Julius Gould, 'The Komsomol and the Hitler Jugend', *British Journal of Sociology*, II (1951) p. 310 ff.

34. Helmut Stellrecht, *Glauben und Handeln. Ein Bekenntnis der jungen Nation* (Berlin, 1938) p. 24. See also his *Die Wehrerziehung der deutschen Jugend* (Berlin, 1936).

35. As argued in Klönne, *Hitlerjugend*, p. 23 f.

36. E. Huber, 'Aufgaben der Jugenderziehung in nationalsozialistischen Staat', in Otto Borst (ed.), *Schulung des Erziehers im nationalsozialistischen Staat* (Esslingen, 1934) p. 48.
37. BA, Reichskanzlei, 43II/513 – speech of 6 July 1933 to *Reichsstatthaltern*
38. Kurt-Ingo Flessau, *Schule der Diktatur. Lehrpläne und Schulbücher des Nationalsozialismus* (Munich, 1977) p. 13.
39. Friedrich Hiller (ed.), *Deutsche Erziehung im neuen Staat* (Berlin, 1934) p. 25 f.
40. Trevor-Roper, *Hitler's Table Talk*, pp. 524 (entry of 8 June 1942), 356 (entry of 3 Mar 1942) – 'When I think of the men who were my teachers, I realise that most of them were slightly mad.' See also pp. 168, 674, 697.
41. Adolf Hitler, *Mein Kampf* (London 1969 edn), p. 120 ff.
42. Speech at the 1935 Party Rally, quoted in Norman H. Baynes (ed.), *The Speeches of Adolf Hitler, 1922–1939* (London, 1942) p. 542.
43. John Caruso, 'Adolf Hitler's Concept of Education and Its Implementation in the Third Reich' (Doctoral dissertation, University of Connecticut, 1974) pp. 73–6.
44. William E. Pulliam, 'Political Propaganda in the Secondary School History Program of National Socialist Germany, 1933–1945' (Doctoral dissertation, University of Illinois, 1968), p. 35. See also Dietrich Klagges (the principal theoretician of National Socialist history teaching), *Geschichtsunterricht als nationalsozialistische Erziehung* (Frankfurt a. M., 1937).
45. Hitler, *Mein Kampf*, pp. 388–9.
46. Karl Christoph Lingelbach, *Erziehung und Erziehungstheorien im nationalsozialistischen Deutschland* (Weilheim, 1970) pp. 36 ff., 47 ff.
47. Flessau, *Schule der Diktatur*, pp. 53, 66.
48. Schirach, *Die Hitler-Jugend*, p. 130.
49. See Chapters 1 and 2.
50. For a local example, see William S. Allen, *The Nazi Seizure of Power: The Experience of a Single German Town 1930–1935* (London, 1966) p. 224.
51. Peter D. Stachura, 'Das Dritte Reich und Jugenderziehung: die Rolle der Hitlerjugend 1933–1939', in Manfred Heinemann (ed.), *Erziehung und Schulung im Dritten Reich, Teil I. Schule, Jugend, Berufserziehung (Stuttgart, 1980)*, p. 49. For the NSS, see Horn, in *Central European History*, XI (1978) pp. 355–75.
52. The law stated, 'The highest task of the school is the training of youth for service to nation and State in the National Socialist spirit. The Hitler Youth completes this work by tempering the character, demanding self-discipline, and physical training. The school and the Hitler Youth, however, have to pay full regard to the co-operation of parents in education and to the preservation and care of family life' – quoted in K. Sloan, 'Education in Nazi Germany (1933–45)' (M. Phil. thesis, University of Leeds, 1972) p. 32.
53. Charles Francis Daigh, 'The Role of Literature and the Education of Youth in the Third Reich' (Doctoral dissertation, University of Illinois, 1967) p. 84.
54. A. Möller, *Wesen und Forderung der Hitler-Jugend* (Breslau, 1935) p. 71.
55. *Statistisches Handbuch von Deutschland 1928–1944* (Munich, 1944) p. 622.
56. BA, Reichskanzlei 43II/513. See reference to newspaper reports in September 1934 regarding the possible transformation of the Reichsjugendführung into a Reichsjugendministerium.
57. Stachura, in Heinemann, *Erziehung und Schulung im Dritten Reich*, p. 50.

58. Schirach, *Die Hitler-Jugend*, pp. 169—73. See also Michael H. Kater, Hitlerjugend und Schule im Dritten Reich; *Historische Zeitschrift*, 228 (1979) Heft 3 (June) p. 595.

59. Schirach, p. 173.

60. BHSA, ASA, Staatsministerium des Innern 71799. Rust order to HJ of 26 August 1933, and Frick circulars of 18 and 23 December 1933, 30 January 1934.

61. BA, Reichskanzlei 43II/1154a — memorandum of 3 November 1938 by Dr Otto Wacker, one of Rust's colleagues.

62. BA, Reichskanzlei 43II/524. Treaty signed by von Schirach and Dr. Stuckart of 7 June 1934 is given in full here. See also F. Mushardt and H. Tietjen, *Staatsjugendtag. Idee und Gestaltung* (Leipzig, 1934).

63. BA, Reichskanzlei 43II/513. Statement of 30 April 1935 concerning the *Landjahr*, his statement of 6 May 1935 on 'Jugenflege und körperliche Erziehung' and his 'Grundsätze für die körperliche Erziehung der Jugend ausserhalb der Schule' of 6 May 1935.

64. BHSA, Geheimes Staatsarchiv (GSA) 450. See von Schirach's speech in Königsberg, January 1935.

65. Rolf Eilers, *Die nationalsozialistische Schulpolitik. Eine Studie zur Funktion der Erziehung im totalitären Staat* (Cologne, 1963) p. 16. The State Youth Day had broken down in practice before being formally abandoned in December 1936, when the 1936 HJ Law came into force.

66. Michael H. Kater, 'Die deutsche Elternschaft in ihrem Verhältnis zu Hitlerjugend und Schule im Dritten Reich', Paper presented to Conference organised by the Historische Kommission der Deutschen Gesellschaft für Erziehungswissenschaft, Bielefeld, Autumn 1978.

67. The title was changed in 1938 to *HJ-Vertrauenslehrer*. See Hans-Jochen Gamm, *Führung und Verführung. Pädagogik des Nationalsozialismus* (Munich, 1964) pp. 137—8.

68. Daniel Horn, 'The Hitler Youth and Educational Decline in the Third Reich', *History of Education Quarterly*, 16 (1976) p. 435.

69. BA, Reichskanzlei 43II/956a. See letters from Rust to Ley of 21 January 1937 and 25 January 1937, and from Ley to Rust of 22 January 1937. Von Schirach found Rust's point of view 'incomprehensible' (letter of 22 Jan 1937).

70. Ibid. See Lammers's letter of 26 January 1937 to all parties concerned.

71. BA, Reichskanzlei 43II/514 — Rust decree of 21 January 1937.

72. BA, R21/73 — decree of 28 May 1937.

73. BA, NS26/358. Report entitled, 'Kriegsjugend Adolf Hitlers' (1944), p. 202 f. All pupils were male. See Hans Peter Bleuel, *Strength Through Joy: Sex and Society in Nazi Germany* (London, 1973) p. 121.

74. Schirach, *Revolution der Erziehung*, p. 101.

75. Harald Scholtz, *NS-Ausleseschulen. Internatsschulen als Herrschaftsmittel des Führerstaates* (Göttingen, 1973) p. 162.

76. A detailed analysis is given by Horst Ueberhorst (ed.), *Elite für die Diktatur. Die Nationalpolitischen Erziehungsanstalten 1933—1945. Ein Dokumentarbericht* (Düsseldorf, 1969) esp. pp. 9 ff, 41 ff, 180 ff. See also Scholtz, *NS-Ausleseschulen*, pp. 29—92, 324 ff.

77. Cf. Harald Scholtz, 'Die "NS-Ordensburgen"', *Vierteljahrshefte für Zeitgeschichte*, xv (1967) p. 269 ff.

78. Dietrich Orlow, 'Die Adolf-Hitler-Schulen', ibid., XIII (1965) p. 279 ff; Scholtz NS-Ausleseschulen, pp. 162–253, 377–8.
79. Albert Speer, Inside the Third Reich (London, 1971) pp. 58, 183–4. But Orlow, in Vierteljahrshefte für Zeitgeschichte, XIII, p.278, notes a later improvement in academic standards, a point endorsed by Scholtz in NS-Ausleseschulen, pp. 377–8.
80. BA, Reichskanzlei 43II/945 – letter from Bormann to Lammers of 3 February 1937.
81. Alfred Baeumler, Politik und Erziehung (Berlin, 1937) p. 103.
82. Janet M. McCauley, 'The Fate of the Catholic Schools in the Third Reich: A Case Study' (Doctoral dissertation, St Louis University, 1966) pp. 66–7. See also Jeremy Noakes, 'The Oldenburg Crucifix Struggle of November 1936: A Case Study of Opposition in the Third Reich', in Peter D. Stachura (ed.), The Shaping of the Nazi State (London, 1978) pp. 210–33.
83. Eilers, Die nationalsozialistische Schulpolitik, p. 126; Kater, 'Hitlerjugend und Schule', pp. 596 f, 607 ff.
84. BA, NS12/82. Letter from the NSLB Hauptamtsleitung, of 19 December 1935 to HJ Bannführer Kurt Fervers; letter from HJ Unterbannführer Fritz Helke of 6 March 1935 to the NSLB Reichsamtsleitung.
85. BA, NS26/245. Monatsbericht den NSLB Kreis Döbeln, February 1934; Bericht über die Arbeit der Abteilung Mädchenbildung im NSLB Sachsen, March 1934.
86. BA, Reichskanzlei 43II/515. See letter of 11 November 1939 from Herr Zschintsch of the Reich Education Ministry to Lammers.
87. Schirach, Revolution der Erziehung, p. 125.
88. National Archives Microfilm Collection (NA), T-81, 104/121. Report of the Teacher Training Institute at Darmstadt November 1943, p. 106 ff.
89. A. Kluger (ed.), Die Deutsche Volksschule im Grossdeutschen Reich (Breslau, 1940) p. 110.
90. BA, Reichskanzlei 43II/522b – letter from Lauterbacher to Lammers of 3 July 1939.
91. Horn, in History of Education Quarterly, XVI, pp. 433–4.
92. Stachura, in Heinemann, Erziehung und Schulung im Dritten Reich, p. 56.
93. See the revealing comments of Hitler youths in Die Junge Welt, Apr 1943, p. 10 ff.
94. Das Junge Deutschland, Sep and Nov 1942, pp. 250 and 316 respectively.
95. BA, Reichskanzlei 43II/943 – letter to Rust of 25 September 1940.
96. National Archives(NA): T-175/258, 259/2 – Dated 5 April 1940.
97. Grunberger, A Social History, p. 371.
98. NA, T-175/261/2, 754, Meldungen aus dem Reich, 10 July 1941, 16 February 1942.
99. BA, NS28/30.
100. NA, T-81 159/97 – circular to Hitler Youth Gebietsführer of 11 September 1939.
101. BA, Reichskanzlei 43II/515 – letter from Rust to Lammers of 11 November 1939.
102. The full title was 'Beauftragte des Führers für die Inspektion der HJ und Reichsleiter für die Jugenderziehung der NSDAP'.
103. BA, NS26/358. Accords of 31 January 1941 entitled 'Schule und Hitlerjugend'

and 'Übereinkommen über die Leibeserziehung'; BA, Reichskanzlei 43II/522a for other details.

104. Trevor-Roper Hitler's *Table Talk*, p. 675 (entry of 29 Aug 1942).

105. BA, NS26/358. Report entitled, 'Kriegsjugend Adolf Hitlers' (1944) p. 195 ff, reference to regulations of 9 September 1941 from the Reich Education Ministry.

106. Scholtz, *NS-Ausleseschulen*, pp. 280—1.

107. BA, Reichskanzlei 43II/956a. Letter from Rust to Lammers of 3 January 1942.

108. Ibid. — letter from Rust to Lammers of 3 January 1942. Rust made himself vulnerable in a way when, after visiting an AHS school in July 1941, he publicly expressed satisfaction with its educational work (BA, Reichskanzlei 43II/956a. Report of 10 July 1941 by Deutsches Nachrichtenburo).

109. NA, T-175/123/2, 648, 498. Report from SS-Hauptsturmführer to Himmler of 10 December 1941.

110. BA, R21/525, 526, 527 contain numerous details — see in particular report issued by the Oberkommando der Kriegsmarine, Berlin 1943, entitled 'Bestimmungen über den Kriegseinsatz der deutschen Jugend in der Kriegsmarine als Marinehelfer', in/526. Special arrangements were made for their schooling near to their service positions.

111. Trevor-Roper, Hitler's *Table Talk*, p. 673 (entry of 29 Aug 1942).

112. NA, T-81/7/14683 ff. Report by Paul Wegener 1942.

113. BA, NS22/739. Letter from Bormann to Ley of 5 January 1941.

114. NA, T-175/20/2 — correspondence from SS-*Brigadeführer* Gottlob Berger to Himmler, 2 September 1942.

115. Institut für Zeitgeschichte, Fa. 91, 7 Fasc., 19 Bl., 1482 — 'Vermerk für den Reichsleiter vom 3. Dezember 1943'. Alfred Rosenberg had similar ambitions: see his *Letzte Aufzeichnungen: Ideale und Idole der nationalsozialistischen Revolution*, ed. H. Härtle (Göttingen, 1955) p. 149.

116. *The Trial of the Major War Criminals before the International Military Tribunal* (Nuremberg, 1947—9) XIV, pp. 367, 431—2.

117. Klönne, *Hitlerjugend*, pp. 30, 82.

118. Scholtz, *NS-Ausleseschulen*, p. 286.

119. BA, NS28/38 — details of the programme in HJ circulars of 22 February and 18 June 1941.

120. BA, NS26/358. Report 'Kriegsjugend Adolf Hitlers' (1944) p. 63 ff.

121. BA, R21/723, Report of KLV-camp Inspectors, 1944. One camp, at Bad Podiebrad, was so chaotically run that it was closed down in 1944.

122. BA, NS26/358, Report 'Kriegsjugend Adolf Hitlers', p. 70 ff; BA, NS26/241, report on 'Die Deutsche Gemeinschaftschule', and article by Otto Freyer on 'Die KLV-Lager als neue Erziehungsform'.

123. BA, R21/510 — Sicherheitsdienst Report 1944.

124. BA, NS26/358. Report 'Kriegsjugend Adolf Hitlers' (1944) p. 204 ff. states that 26 per cent of pupils that year were working-class; see also Orlow, in *Vierteljahrshefte für Zeitgeschichte*, XIII, p. 277.

125. William Jannen, 'National Socialists and Social Mobility', *Journal of Social History*, IX (1976) pp. 352—4.

126. BA, NS26/358. Report 'Kriegsjugend Adolf Hitlers' (1944) p. 197 ff.

CHAPTER 7

1. Quoted in *Völkischer Beobachter*, 28 Mar 1945.
2. *Die Junge Welt*, Oct 1939, p. 63.
3. Reichsjugendführung der NSDAP, *Die Werkarbeit im Kriegseinsatz der Hitler-Jugend* (Berlin, 1942); M. Dargel (ed.), *Mädel im Kampf* (Berlin, 1941); Klose, *Generation im Gleichschritt*, pp. 237–66.
4. *Das Junge Deutschland*, XXXVII Jan (1943) p. 63.
5. Ibid., Oct 1942, p. 284 f.
6. BA, Reichskanzlei 43II/522a, quote from Völkischer Beobachter, 15 August 1942.
7. BHSA, GSA, *Reichsstatthalter* Epp 451 – 'Verordnung über die Heranziehung der deutschen Jugend zur Erfüllung von Kriegsaufgaben'.
8. BA, NS26/358. Report 'Kriegsjugend Adolf Hitlers' (1944) p. 88 ff.
9. Ibid. – HJ Report 1944.
10. Ibid. – Massnahmen zur totalen Kriegseinsatzes in der Hitler-Jugend', 5 Sep 1944.
11. Dietrich Orlow, *The History of the Nazi Party, 1933–1945*, II (Pittsburgh, 1972) p. 342.
12. BA, Reichskanzlei 43II/512 – Rust memorandum of 29 January 1940.
13. Reichsjugendführung der NSDAP, *Kriminalität und Gefährdung der Jugend. Lagebericht bis zum Stande vom 1. Januar 1941* (Berlin, 1941) pp. 15–17, 40–3, 187–9, 209 ff.
14. *Völkischer Beobachter*, 21 Mar 1940.
15. BA, R18/5317, Verordnung zur Ergänzung des Jugendstrafrechts vom 1940.
16. BA, NS26/358. Report 'Kriegsjugend Adolf Hitlers' (1944) p. 223 ff. The number of detentions under *Jugenddienstarrest* rose from 815 in 1940/1 to 3178 in 1942/3.
17. NA, T-175/20/2525 – letter from Axmann to Heydrich of 20 January 1942.
18. BA, NS26/358 – HJ Report 'Kriegsjugend Adolf Hitlers' (1944) p. 205 ff.
19. BA, R18/5317. See letter of 11 September 1941 from Hitler Youth Chief of Staff, Helmut Möckel, to the Reich Interior Ministry.
20. Cf. Christian Petry, *Studenten aufs Schafott. Die weisse Rose und ihr Scheitern* (Munich, 1968); Inge Scholl, *Die weisse Rose* (Frankfurt a. M., 1955).
21. Paetel, *Bild vom Menschen*, p. 49.
22. Ger van Roon, 'Wirkungen der Jugendbewegung im Deutschen Widerstand', *JADJB*, VI (1974) p. 36.
23. Hans Mommsen, 'Social Views and Constitutional Plans of the Resistance', in *The German Resistance to Hitler* (London, 1970) p. 100.
24. Rempel, 'The Misguided Generation', p. 396.
25. BA, NS26/358. Report 'Kriegsjugend Adolf Hitlers' (1944) p. 10 ff.
26. Ibid.
27. BA, NS26/336, HJ-Army agreement of December 1941 – details here.
28. *Das Junge Deutschland*, Dec 1940, p. 286.
29. Ibid., June 1942, p. 157.
30. BA, R21/511, see Hitler's order (1942) for the establishment of the training camps.
31. Cf. Ludwig Schätz, 'Luftwaffenhelfer – ein Kapitel zur Geschichte des deutschen Wehrmachtsgefolges im zweiten Weltkrieg' (Doctoral dissertation,

University of Munich, 1970); Paul Edmunds, 'Luftwaffenhelfer im Einsatz', *Das Parlament, Aus Politik und Zeitgeschichte*, xxvi (1976) B33–54.
32. Cf. Kurt Meyer, *Grenadiere* (Munich, 1965). Meyer was the division's commander in 1944; also private testimony given to the author by former Polish army personnel.
33. See copies of *Die Junge Welt*, 1944.

Bibliography

Unpublished sources

1. BUNDESARCHIV KOBLENZ

(a) *Hauptarchiv der NSDAP*

NS 26/ 241   NS Lehrerbund
245   NS Lehrerbund
259   NSV Jugendhilfe
334   Grossdeutsche Jugend
336   Das Werden der HJ
338   RJF
339   RJF – Stabsführung
342   Reichsjugendführerschule – HJ Schulung
346   HJ – Eingänge/Schulungsangelegenheiten
347   HJ – Terrorfälle
348   HJ Hilfe
349   Berichte der NPEA Plön
355   HJ Presse – Propaganda/Schulung
356   HJ Presse
357   HJ – RJF
358   HJ Presse – und Propagandaamt
360   HJ verschiedenes
361   'Hitler Youth' von Willy Koerber
364   HJ Südwest – Korrespondenz
366   HJ Gau München–Oberbayern
370   HJ Grenzlandamt (Allgemeines Korrespondenz)
423   Reichsparteitag 1936
816   KPD. Kommunistische Jugendverband Deutschlands
1264   B. von Schirach. Korrespondenz
1285   Die Artamanenbewegung
1366b   B. von Schirach

(b) *Reichskanzlei*

R43II/513	Nationalerziehung und Reichsjugendgesetz, Bd 1 (1933—5)
525	Bd 2 (1935—7)
525a	Bd 3 (1937—9)
512	Bd 4 (1936—42)
514	Bd 5 (1939—43)
515	Jugendführer des Deutschen Reiches Bd 1 (1937—44)
515a	Bd 2 (1937, 1942)
519	Jugendertüchtigung Bd1 (1930—5)
520b	Bd 2 (1936—44)
520c	Jugendgerichtsbarkeit und Fürsorgeerziehung 1934—5 and 1941—2
521	Soziale Jugendhilfe und Jugendwohlfahrt Bd 1 (1933—4)
522	Bd 2 (1936—9)
523	Jugendverbände, insbesondere Hitlerjugend Bd 1 (1933—5)
524	Bd 2 (1934)
522a	Bd 3 (1936—41)
522b	Bd 4 (1938—44)
943 ⎫ 945 ⎭	NSDAP, Beamtenpolitik
956a	Adolf-Hitler-Schulen
956b	Napola Bd. 1 Bd 1 (1937—42)
956c	Bd 2 (1941—4)
1154a	Reichspropagandaministerium

(c) *Hauptamt für Erzieher/Reichsverwaltung*

NS 12/82	Schriftwechsel — Reichsjugendführung 1934—5
532 ⎫ 533 ⎭	KLV — Kosten
539	Bekleidung von Erziehers (KLV-Lagern)

(d) *Hitler-Jugend*

NS 28/30 Geheime Rundschreiben 1939, RJF
  31 RJF – Stabsführung: Geheime Rundschreiben
  32 RJF – BdM: Geheime Rundschreiben
  33 RJF – Amt für Gesundheitsführung: Geheime Rundschreiben
  34 RJF – Der MOB Beauftragte: Geheime Rundschreiben
  35 RJF – Sozialamt
  36 RJF – KLV
  38 RJF – Befehlsstelle IV
  41 Gebiet Mittelelbe
  42 Gebiet Mark Brandenburg
  43 Gliederung und Aufbau der HJ
  44 HJ Gebiet Thüringen

(e) *Reichsministerium des Innern*

R18/5025 }
 5317 } NSDAP, Gliederungen und Verbände

(f) *Reichsministerium für Wissenschaft, Erziehung und Volksbildung*

R21/ 73 Jugenderziehung – Massnahmen
 510 Schliessung von Schulen
 511 Vormilitärische Ausbildung in WEL
 525 Kriegseinsatz der Jugend
    Bd 1
 526 Bd 2
 527 Bd 3
 528 Bd 4
 529 Bd 7
 530 Bd 8
 723 Vermerke, KLV-Angelegenheiten

(g) *Stellvertreter des Reichskanzlers*

R 53/92 }
 93 } HJ und katholische Jugendorganisationen
 94 }

(h) *Der Reichsorganisationsleiter der NSDAP*

NS22/739   Parteikanzlei-Schriftwechsel

2. BAYERISCHES HAUPTSTAATSARCHIV: ALLGEMEINES STAATSARCHIV, MUNICH

(a) *Akten des Staatsministeriums des Innern*

71799	NS Sportbewegung Hitlerjugend 1928—36
71800	HJ, Jugenddienst — Verordnung
73003	RJF 1938—9
73437/22	HJ, Beitritt Beamtenkinder 1933—8

(b) *Sonderabgabe I: Akten des Generalstaatskommissars*

1542	NSDAP, BdM, NSS
1544	NSDAP, HJ Bayern
1555	NSDAP, Auflösung der HJ

3. BAYERISCHES HAUPTSTAATSARCHIV: GEHEIMES STAATSARCHIV, MUNICH

Reichsstatthalter Epp:
450   HJ 1933—8
451   HJ 1938—45

4. INSTITUT FÜR ZEITGESCHICHTE, MUNICH

Fa 91, 7 Fasc., 19 Bl., 1482

5. *National Archives Microfilm Collection*

T-81/7, 159, 104	Adolf Hitler Kanzlei; Oberste SA-Führung
T-175/20, 123, 258, 261	NSDAP, Parteikanzlei

Published sources

1. PERIODICALS AND NEWSPAPERS

Das Junge Deutschland, amtliches Organ der Reichsausschuss der deutschen Jugendverbände (pre-1933)
Das Junge Deutschland, amtliches Organ der Jugendführer des deutschen

Reiches (post-1933)
Der Feldmeister
Der Führer
Der Junge Bolschewik
Deutsche Freischar
Die Freideutsche Jugendbewegung
Die Junge Garde
Die Junge Front
Die Junge Welt
Die Kommenden
Frankfurter Zeitung
Freideutsche Jugend
Junge Anarchisten
NS— Monatshefte
Quickborn
Süddeutsche Monatshefte
Völkischer Beobachter
Wandervogel, deutscher Bund
Wandervogelmonatsschrift
Wille und Macht, Führerorgan der NS-Jugend
Wille und Werk, Pressedienst der deutschen Jugendbewegung

2. SECONDARY WORKS – A SELECT LIST

The broad range of books and articles used for this study are indicated in the footnotes. Limitations of space do not permit their reproduction in full here. The following list has been restricted, therefore, to those works which were found to be of particular value for understanding the youth movement, and to a number of works which readers might wish to note for further reading.

Ahlborn, Knud, *Kurze Chronik der Freideutschen Jugendbewegung 1913 bis 1953* (Bad Godesberg, 1953).
Arlt Wolfgang (ed.), *Deutschlands Junge Garde. 50 Jahre Arbeiterjugendbewegung* (East Berlin, 1954).
Aufmuth, Ulrich, Die deutsche Wandervogelbewegung unter soziologischem Aspekt (Göttingen, 1979).
Becker, Howard, *German Youth: Bond or Free?* (London, 1946).
Bers, Günter (ed.), *Arbeiterjugend im Rheinland – Erinnerungen von Wilhelm Reimes und Peter Trimborn* (Wentorf, 1978).
Blohm, Erich, *Hitler-Jugend. Soziale Tatgemeinschaft* (Witten, 1977).

Blüher, Hans, *Wandervogel, Geschichte einer Bewegung*, 2 vols (Jena, 1912).

Blum, Emil, *Die Neuwerk-Bewegung 1922−1933. Kirche zwischen Planen und Hoffen* (Kassel, 1973).

Bohnenkamp, Hans, 'Jugendbewegung und Schulreform', in E. Korn, O. Suppert and K. Vogt (eds), *Die Jugendbewegung, Welt und Wirkung. Zur 50. Wiederkehr der Freideutschen Jugendtages auf den Hohen Meissner* (Düsseldorf, 1963).

Borinski, Fritz, and Milch, Werner, *Jugendbewegung: The Story of German Youth 1896−1933* (London, 1945).

Borinski, Fritz; Grimn, Horst; Winkler, Edgar; and Wolf, Erich (eds): *Jugend im politischen Protest. Der Leuchtenburgkreis 1923−1933−1977* (Frankfurt a. M., 1977).

Bramke, Werner and Finker, Kurt, 'Die Rote Jungfront − Verkörperung der Wehrhaftigkeit der revolutionären deutschen Arbeiterjugend (1924−1929)', *Zeitschrift für Militärgeschichte*, 11 (1972) pp. 72−9.

Brandenburg, Hans-Christian, *Die Geschichte der HJ. Wege und Irrwege einer Generation* (Cologne, 1968).

Brandenburg, Hans-Christian, and Daur, Rudolf, *Die Brücke zu Köngen. Fünfzig Jahre Bund der Köngener 1919−1969.* (Stuttgart, 1969).

Bühler, Karl, 'Arbeitsdienst als Erziehungsaufgabe in frühen Theorien der zwanziger Jahre', *JADJB*, 7 (1975) pp. 41−65.

Cornell, Richard, 'The Origins and Development of the Communist Youth International, 1914−1924' (Doctoral dissertation, Columbia University, 1965).

Croon, Helmuth, 'Jugendbewegung und Arbeitsdienst', *JADJB*, 5 (1973) pp. 66−84.

Dehnkamp, Willy, 'Zum Bildungshunger der Arbeiterjugend', *JADJB*, (1978) pp. 59−69.

Döke, Wolfgang, 'Zum antimilitarischen Kampf der revolutionären deutschen Arbeiterjugend', *Wissenschaftliche Zeitschrift der Wilhelm-Pieck-Universität Rostock*, XXVI (1977) pp. 191−8.

Dougherty, Richard W., 'Eros, Youth Culture and Geist: The Ideology of Gustav Wyneken and Its Influence Upon the German Youth Movement' (Doctoral dissertation, University of Wisconsin, 1977).

Eberts, Erich, *Arbeiterjugend 1904−1945. Sozialistische Erziehungsgemeinschaft − politische Organisation* (Frankfurt a. M., 1979).

Eilers, Rolf, *Die nationalsozialistische Schulpolitik. Eine Studie zur Funktion der Erziehung im totalitären Staat* (Cologne, 1963).

Elzer, Hans-Michael, 'Reformpädagogik und Jugendbewegung', *JADJB*, (1975) pp. 6—15.

Eppe, Heinrich, and Uellenberg, Wolfgang, *70 Jahre Sozialistische Jugendinternationale. Zur Geschichte der internationalen sozialistischen Kinder — und Jugendorganisationen* (Bonn, 1976).

Esler, Anthony (ed.), *The Youth Revolution: The Conflict of Generations in Modern History* (Lexington, Mass., 1974).

Feuer, Lewis S., *The Conflict of Generations: The Character and Significance of Student Movements* (New York, 1969).

Fishman, Sterling, *The Struggle for German Youth: The Search for Educational Reform in Imperial Germany* (New York, 1976).

Flessau, Kurt-Ingo, *Schule der Diktatur. Lehrpläne und Schulbücher des Nationalsozialismus* (Munich, 1977).

Frobenius, Else, *Mit uns zieht die neue Zeit* (Berlin, 1927).

Gamm, Hans-Jochen, *Führung und Verführung. Pädagogik des Nationalsozialismus* (Munich, 1964).

Geissler, Wilhelm, *Kunst und Künstler in der Jugendbewegung*, 1 (Burg Ludwigstein, Witzenhausen, 1975).

Gerber, Walther, *Zur Entstehungsgeschichte der deutschen Wandervogelbewegung. Ein kritischer Beitrag* (Bielefeld, 1957).

——, *Der Hamburger Wandervogel 1907—1919. Drei Chroniken* (Wunstorf, 1969).

Giesecke, Hermann, *Die Jugendarbeit* (Munich, 1971).

Gillis, John R., *Youth and History: Tradition and Change in European Age Relations 1770—Present* (New York, 1974).

Glaser, Hermann, and Silenius, Axel (eds), *Jugend im Dritten Reich* (Frankfurt a. M., 1975).

Grau, Helmut, *d. j. l. ll.* [Deutsche Jungenschaft] — *Struktur und Wandel eines subkulturellen jugendlichen Milieus in vier Jahrzehnten* (Frankfurt a. M., 1976).

——, 'Bündische Jugend — Spielweise der "Bourgeoisie"? Aspekte des Wandels der Sozialstruktur bündischer Gruppen vor und nach dem II. Weltkrieg', *JADJB*, (1972) pp. 63—74.

Greiff, Walter *et al.* (eds), *Gespräch und Aktion in Gruppe und Gesellschaft 1919—1969* (Frankfurt a. M., 1970).

Griesmayr, Gottfried and Würschinger, Otto, *Idee und Gestalt der Hitlerjugend* (Munich, 1979)

Grunberger, Richard, *A Social History of the Third Reich* (London, 1974).

Hägel, Helmuth, 'Die Stellung der sozialdemokratischen Jugendorganisationen zu Staat und Partei in den Anfangsjahren der Weimarer Republik', *Internationale Wissenschaftliche Korrespondenz zur Geschichte der deutschen Arbeiterbewegung*, 12 (1976) pp. 166–216.

Hall, Alex, 'Youth in Rebellion: The Beginnings of the Socialist Youth Movement 1904–1914', in Richard J. Evans (ed.), *Society and Politics in Wilhelmine Germany* (London, 1978) pp. 241–66.

Hargasser, Franz, 'Der Einfluss der Jugendbewegung auf die Erwachsenenbildung', *JADJB*, 7 (1975) pp. 29–40.

Hastenteufel, Paul, *Jugendbewegung und Jugendseelsorge. Geschichte und Probleme der katholischen Jugendarbeit im 20. Jahrhundert* (Munich, 1962).

Hauck, Peter, 'Von der Autonomen Jugendorganisation zur Parteijugend – der Spaltungsprozess der FSJD unter besonderer Berücksichtigung des Linkskommunismus 1919–1920' (Doctoral Dissertation, University of Mannheim, 1978).

Heer, Friedrich, *Revolutions of Our Time: Challenge of Youth* (London, 1974).

Held, Joseph, 'Embattled Youth: The Independent German Youth Movements in the 20th Century' (Doctoral dissertation, Rutgers State University, 1968).

——, 'Die Volksgemeinschaftsidee in der deutschen Jugendbewegung: Tätigkeit und Weltanschauung einiger Jugendvereine zur Zeit der Weimarer Republik', *Jahrbuch des Instituts für Deutsche Geschichte*, 6 (1977) pp. 457–76.

Henrich, Franz, *Die Bünde katholischer Jugendbewegung. Ihre Bedeutung für die liturgische und eucharistische Erneuerung* (Munich, 1968).

Horn, Daniel, 'Youth Resistance in the Third Reich: A Social Portrait', *Journal of Social History*, 7 (1973) pp. 26–50.

——, 'The Hitler Youth and Educational Decline in the Third Reich', *History of Education Quarterly*, 16 (1976) pp. 425–47.

——, 'The National Socialist Schülerbund and the Hitler Youth, 1929–1933', *Central European History*, XI (1978) pp. 355–75.

Hüser, Fritz, 'Kultureller Aufbruch junger Arbeiter. Zur Dichtung der Arbeiterjugend', *JADJB*, 10 (1978) pp. 70–85.

Institut für Marxistische Studien und Forschungen, *Dokumente und Materialien. Aus der Geschichte der deutschen Arbeiterjugendbewegung 1904–1945* (Frankfurt a. M., 1975).

Jahnke, Karl-Heinz, *Entscheidungen. Jugend im Widerstand 1933–45* (Frankfurt a.M., 1970).

——, *Jungkommunisten im Widerstandskampf gegen den Hitlerfaschismus* (East Berlin, 1977).

Jahnke, Karl-Heinz *et al.*, *Geschichte der deutschen Arbeiterjugendbewegung 1904–1945* (Dortmund, 1973).

Jannen, William, 'National Socialism and Social Mobility', *Journal of Social History*, 9 (1976) pp. 339–66.

Jantzen, Hinrich, *Jugendkultur und Jugendbewegung. Eine Studie zur Stellung und Bedeutung Gustav Wynekens innerhalb der Jugendbewegung* (Frankfurt a. M., 1963).

—— (ed.), *Namen und Werke. Biographien und Beiträge zur Soziologie der deutschen Jugendbewegung*, vols I–IV (Frankfurt a. M., 1972 1974, 1975, 1977).

Jantzen, Walter, 'Die soziologische Herkunft der Führerschicht in der deutschen Jugendbewegung. 1900 bis 1933', in *Führungsschicht und Eliteproblem. Konferenz der Ranke-Gesellschaft* (Frankfurt, 1957) pp. 127–37.

Jovy, Michael E., 'Deutsche Jugendbewegung und Nationalsozialismus. Versuch einer Klärung ihrer Zusammenhänge und Gegensätze' (Doctoral dissertation, University of Cologne, 1952).

Karl, Willibald, *Jugend, Gesellschaft und Politik im Zeitraum des Ersten Weltkriegs. Zur Geschichte der Jugendproblematik der deutschen Jugendbewegung im ersten Viertel des 20. Jahrhunderts unter besonderer Berücksichtigung ihrer gesellschaftlichen und politischen Relationen und Entwicklungen in Bayern* (Munich, 1973).

Kater, Michael H., 'Die Artamanen – völkische Jugend in der Weimarer Republik', *Historische Zeitschrift*, 213 (1971) pp. 577–638.

——, 'The Reich Vocational Contest and Students of Higher Learning in Nazi Germany', *Central European History*, VII (1974) pp. 225–261.

——, 'Bürgerliche Jugendbewegung und Hitlerjugend in Deutschland von 1926 bis 1939', *Archiv für Sozialgeschichte*, XVII (1977) pp. 127–74.

——, 'Die deutsche Elternschaft in ihrem Verhältnis zu Hitlerjugend und Schule im Dritten Reich', paper presented at Conference organised by the Historische Kommission der Deutschen Gesellschaft für Erziehungswissenschaft, Bielefeld, Autumn 1978.

——, 'Hitlerjugend und Schule im Dritten Reich', *Historische Zeitschrift*, 228 (1979), Heft 3 (June) 572–623.

Kaufmann, Günter, *Das kommende Deutschland. Die Erziehung der*

Jugend im Reich Adolf Hitlers (Berlin, 1940).

Kindt, Werner (ed.), *Grundschriften der deutschen Jugendbewegung* (Düsseldorf, 1963).

—— (ed.), *Die Wandervogelzeit. Quellenschriften zur deutschen Jugendbewegung, 1896−1919* (Düsseldorf, 1968).

—— (ed.), *Die deutsche Jugendbewegung, 1920 bis 1933. Die Bündische Zeit. Quellenschriften* (Düsseldorf, 1974).

Klönne, Arno, *Hitlerjugend. Die Jugend und ihre Organisation im Dritten Reich* (Hanover, 1956).

——, *Gegen den Strom. Bericht über den Jugendwiderstand im Dritten Reich* (Hanover, 1958).

Klose, Werner, *Generation im Gleichschritt. Ein Dokumentation* (Oldenburg, 1964).

Kneip, Rudolf, *Wandervogel − Bündische Jugend. 1905−1943. Der Weg der sächsischen Jungenschaft zum grossen Bund*, new edn (Frankfurt a. M., 1976).

—— (ed.), *Jugend der Weimarer Zeit. Handbuch der Jugendverbände 1919−1938* (Frankfurt, 1974).

Kneip, Rudolf *et al.*, *Jugend zwischen den Kriegen. Eine Sammlung von Aussagen und Dokumenten über den Sachsenkreis im Freideutschen Konvent* (Heidenheim, 1967).

Elizabeth Korn, Otto Suppert, Karl Vogt (eds), *Die Jugendbewegung: Welt und Wirkung. Zur 50. Wiederkehr der Freideutschen Jugendtages auf den Hohen Meissner* (Düsseldorf, 1963).

Korth, Georg, *Der Wandervogel 1896/1906. Quellenmässige Darstellung nach Karl Fischers Tagebuchaufzeichnungen von 1900* (Frankfurt a. M., 1967).

Krebs, Gilbert, 'Was bleibt heute von der Jugendbewegung − von aussen gesehen?', *JADJB*, 6 (1974) pp. 58−72.

Kupffer, Heinrich, *Gustav Wyneken* (Stuttgart, 1970).

Kurella, Alfred, *Unterwegs zu Lenin. Erinnerungen* (East Berlin, 1967).

Laqueur, Walter Z., *Young Germany: A History of the German Youth Movement* (London, 1962).

Lersner, D. von, *Die evangelischen Jugendverbände Württembergs und die Hitler-Jugend 1933−34* (Göttingen, 1958).

Lindstaedt, Erich, *Mit uns zieht die neue Zeit. Fünfzig Jahre Arbeiterjugendbewegung* (Bonn, 1954).

Lingelbach, Karl Christoph, *Erziehung und Erziehungstheorien im nationalsozialistischen Deutschland* (Weinheim, 1970).

Linse, Ulrich, *Die Kommune der deutschen Jugendbewegung. Ein Versuch des Überwindung des Klassenkampfes aus dem Geiste der bürgerlichen*

Utopie. Die 'kommunistische Siedlung Blankenburg' bei Donauwörth 1919/1920 (Munich, 1973).

———, 'Die Jugendkulturbewegung', in Klaus Vondung (ed.), *Das Wilhelminische Bildungsbürgertum. Zur Sozialgeschichte seiner Ideen* (Göttingen, 1976) pp. 119−37.

———, *Die anarchistische und anarcho-syndikalistische Jugendbewegung 1919−1933. Zur Geschichte und Ideologie der anarchistischen, syndikalistischen und unionistischen Kinder- und Jugendorganisationen 1919− 1933* (Frankfurt a. M., 1976).

———, 'Lebensformen der bürgerlichen und der proletarischen Jugendbewegung', *JADJB*, 10 (1978) pp. 24−58.

Loewenberg, Peter, 'The Psychohistorical Origins of the Nazi Youth Cohort', *American Historical Review*, 76 (1971) pp. 1457−502.

Luban, Ottokar, 'Die Auswirkungen der Jenaer Jugendkonferenz 1916 und die Beziehungen der Zentrale der revolutionären Arbeiterjugend zur Führung der Spartakusgruppe', *Archiv für Sozialgeschichte*, XI (1971) pp. 185−223.

Lüth, Erich, 'Jugendbewegung vor den Forderungen der Politik. Grenzen und Gemeinsamkeiten zwischen freier und gebundener Jugendarbeit', *JADJB*, X (1978) pp. 90−103.

Mahr, Gerhard, *Romano Guardini* (Berlin, 1976).

Maoz, Eliyahu, 'The Werkleute', *Year Book of the Leo Baeck Institute*, IV (1959) pp. 165−82.

Markel, Richard, 'Brith Haolim. Der Weg der Alija des Jung-Jüdischen Wanderbundes (JJWB)', *Bulletin des Leo Baeck Instituts*, 9 (1966) pp. 119−89.

Maschmann, Melita, *Account Rendered: A Dossier on My Former Self* (London, 1964).

Mau, Hermann, 'Die Deutsche Jugendbewegung. Rückblick und Ausblick', *Zeitschrift für religiöse Geistesgeschichte*, I (1948) pp. 135−49.

Meier-Cronemeyer, Hermann, 'Jüdische Jugendbewegung', pts 1 and 2, *Germania Judaica*, VIII (1969) pp. 1−56, 57−118.

———, 'Gemeinschaft und Glaube. Reflexionen über die Deutsche Jugendbewegung', *Jahrbuch des Instituts für Deutsche Geschichte*, VI (1977) pp. 421−55.

Messerschmid, Felix, 'Bilanz einer Jugendbewegung. Quickborn und Rothenfels von den Anfängen bis 1939', *Frankfurter Hefte*, 24 (1969) pp. 786−97.

Mogge, Winfried, 'Bündische Jugend und Nationalsozialismus. Probleme der Forschung, illustriert am Beispiel Eberhard Koebels und der Deutschen Jungenschaft', Paper presented at Conference organised by the Historische Kommission der Deutschen Gesellschaft für Erziehungswissenschaft, Bielefeld, Autumn 1978.

Mosse, George L., *The Crisis of German Ideology: Intellectual Origins of the Third Reich* (New York, 1971).

Müller, Jakob, *Die Jugendbewegung als deutsche Hauptrichtung neukonservativer Reform* (Zurich, 1971).

——, 'Über die zukünftige und vergangene soziale und politische Bedeutung der Jugendbewegung', *JADJB*, VI (1974) pp. 13–21.

Nicklis, Werner S., 'Tendenzen zeitgenössischer Pädagogik und die Ideale der Jugendbewegung', *JADJB*, 7 (1975) pp. 16–28.

Orlow, Dietrich, 'Die Adolf-Hitler-Schulen', *Vierteljahrshefte für Zeitgeschichte*, 13 (1965) pp. 272–84.

Paetel, Karl O., *Das Bild vom Menschen in der deutschen Jugendführung* (Bad Godesberg, 1954).

——, *Jugend in der Entscheidung 1913–1933–1945* (Bad Godesberg, 1963).

——, 'Die deutsche Jugendbewegung als politisches Phänomen', *Politische Studien*, 8 (1957) pp. 1–14.

Paul, Wolfgang, *Das Feldlager. Jugend zwischen Langemarck und Stalingrad* (Esslingen, 1978).

Petrick, Fritz, *Zur sozialen Lage der Arbeiterjugend in Deutschland 1933–1939* (East Berlin, 1974).

Pietschmann, Horst, 'Zum Prozess der Entwicklung der Freien Sozialistischen Jugend zu einem kommunistischen Jugendverband (1918–21)', *Beiträge zur Geschichte der deutschen Arbeiterbewegung*, 17 (1975) pp. 1045–60.

Priepke, Manfred, *Die evangelische Jugend im Dritten Reich 1933–1936* (Hanover, 1960).

Pross, Harry E., *Jugend, Eros, Politik. Die Geschichte der deutschen Jugendverbände* (Berne, 1964).

——, *Die Zerstörung der deutschen Politik: Dokumente 1870–1933* (Frankfurt a. M., 1959).

Raabe, Felix, *Die Bündische Jugend. Ein Beitrag zur Geschichte der Weimarer Republik* (Stuttgart, 1961).

Reichsjugendführung der NSDAP, *Kriminalität und Gefährdung der Jugend: Lagebericht bis zum Stande vom 1. Januar 1941* (Berlin, 1941).

Rempel, Gerhard, 'The Misguided Generation. Hitler Youth and SS, 1933–1945' (Doctoral dissertation, University of Wisconsin 1971).

Rheins, Carl J., 'The Schwarzes Fähnlein, Jungenschaft 1932–1934',

Yearbook of the Leo Baeck Institute, XXIII (1978), pp. 179–97.

Riedel, Heinrich, *Kampf um die Jugend. Evangelische Jugendarbeit 1933–1945* (Munich, 1976).

Rinott, Chanoch, 'Major Trends in Jewish Youth Movements in Germany', *Yearbook of the Leo Baeck Institute*, XIX (1974) pp. 77–95.

Roessler, Wilhelm, *Jugend im Erziehungsfeld. Haltung und Verhalten der deutschen Jugend in der 1. Hälfte des 20. Jahrhunderts* (Düsseldorf, 1957).

Roger, Gerhard, *Die pädagogische Bedeutung der proletarischen Jugendbewegung Deutschlands* (Frankfurt a. M., 1971).

Rosenberg, Alwiss, 'Die Artamanen und der Arbeitsdienst', *JADJB*, IX (1977) pp. 230–41.

——, 'Bäuerliche Siedlungsarbeit des Bundes Artam. Ein agrarpolitischer Versuch bündischer Jugend', *JADJB*, 9 (1977) pp. 199–229.

Rosenbusch, Heinz S., *Die deutsche Jugendbewegung in ihren pädagogischen Formen und Wirkungen* (Frankfurt a. M., 1973).

Rosenstock, Werner, 'The Jewish Youth Movement', *Yearbook of the Leo Baeck Institute*, XIX (1974) pp. 97–105.

Roth, Heinrich (ed.), *Katholische Jugend in der NS-Zeit. Unter besonderer Berücksichtigung des Katholischen Jungmännerverbandes. Daten und Dokumente* (Düsseldorf, 1959).

Rüegg, Walter (ed.), *Kulturkritik und Jugendkult* (Frankfurt a. M., 1974).

Saul, Klaus, 'Der Kampf um die Jugend zwischen Volksschule und Kaserne. Ein Beitrag zur "Jugendpflege" im Wilhelminischen Reich 1890–1914', *Militärgeschichtliche Mitteilungen*, 10 (1971) pp. 97–143.

Schatzker, Chaim, 'The Jewish Youth Movement in Germany between the Years 1900–1933' (Doctoral dissertation, Hebrew University, Tel Aviv, 1969).

——, 'Martin Buber's Influence on the Jewish Youth Movement in Germany', *Yearbook of the Leo Baeck Institute*, XXIII (1978), pp. 151–71.

Schellenberger, Barbara, *Katholische Jugend und Drittes Reich. Eine Geschichte des Katholischen Jungmännerverbandes 1933–1939 unter besonderer Berücksichtigung der Rheinprovinz* (Mainz, 1975).

Schirach, Baldur von, *Die Hitler-Jugend. Idee und Gestalt* (Leipzig, 1934).

——, *Revolution der Erziehung. Reden aus den Jahren des Aufbaus* (Munich, 1938).

——, *Ich glaubte an Hitler* (Hamburg, 1967).

Schlicker, Wolfgang, 'Die Artamanen-bewegung. Eine Frühform des Arbeitsdienstes und Kaderzelle des Faschismus auf dem Lande', *Zeitschrift für Gesichtswissenschaft*, XVIII (1970) pp. 66–75.

Schmidt, Ulrike, 'Über das Verhältnis von Jugendbewegung und Hitlerjugend', *Geschichte in Wissenschaft und Unterricht*, XVI (1965) pp. 19–37.

Schneider, B., *Daten zur Geschichte der Jugendbewegung* (Bad Godesberg, 1965).

Scholtz, Harald, *NS-Ausleseschulen. Internatsschulen als Herrschaftsmittel des Führerstaates* (Göttingen, 1973).

Schroeder, Richard E., 'The Hitler Youth as a Paramilitary Organisation' (Doctoral dissertation, University of Chicago, 1975).

Schult, Johannes, *Aufbruch einer Jugend. Der Weg der deutschen Arbeiterjugendbewegung* (Bonn, 1956).

Schultze, Jürgen, *Die Akademie für Jugendführung der Hitlerjugend in Braunschweig* (Brunswick, 1978).

Schwabe, Herbert, 'Zur wehrerzieherischen Arbeit der Roten Jungfront', *Zeitschrift für Militärgeschichte*, XIII (1974) pp. 181–9.

Seidelmann, Karl, *Bund und Gruppe als Lebensformen deutscher Jugend* (Munich, 1955).

——, 'Das Bündische in unserer Existenz – vom Jugendbund zum Lebensbund', *JADJB*, 5 (1973) pp. 52–65.

——, 'Die Pfadfinder in der deutschen Jugend-Geschichte der zwanziger Jahre', *JADJB*, 6 (1974) pp. 107–26.

——, 'War die Jugendbewegung präfaschistisch?', *JADJB*, 7 (1975) pp. 66–74.

——, *Die Pfadfinder in der deutschen Jugendgeschichte, Teil I. Darstellung* (Hanover, 1977).

—— (ed.), *Die deutsche Jugendbewegung (pädagogische Quellentexte)* (Bad Heilbrunn, 1966).

—— (ed.), *Jugend und Ideologie. Eine Sammlung von Aufsätze* (Frankfurt a. M., 1978).

Siefert, Hermann, *Die Bündische Aufbruch 1919–1923* (Bad Godesberg, 1963).

Speiser, Heinz, *Hans Breuer-Wirken und Wirkungen* (Burg Ludwigstein, 1977).

Stachura, Peter D., 'The Ideology of the Hitler Youth in the Kampfzeit', *Journal of Contemporary History*, 8 (1973) pp. 155–67.

——, *Nazi Youth in the Weimar Republic* (Santa Barbara and Oxford, 1975).

——, 'The National Socialist Machtergreifung and the German Youth Movement: Coordination and Reorganisation, 1933–34', *Journal of European Studies*, 5 (1975) pp. 255–72.

——, 'The Hitler Youth in Crisis: The Case of Reichsführer Kurt Gruber, October 1931', *European Studies Review*, 6 (1976) pp. 331–56.

——, 'Das Dritte Reich und Jugenderziehung: die Rolle der Hitlerjugend 1933–1939', in Manfred Heinemann (ed.). *Erziehung und Schulung im Dritten Reich*, Teil I, *Schule, Jugend, Berufserziehung* (Stuttgart, 1980) pp. 37–59.

——, Deutsche Jugendbewegung und Nationalsozialismus: Interpretationen und Perspektiven, JADJB, XII (1980).

Stählin, Otto, 'Der Begriff "deutsche Jugendbewegung"', *JADJB*, 9 (1977) pp. 161–85.

Steinbrinker, Henrich, 'Der Geist der Gemeinschaft. Wechselwirkungen zwischen Arbeiterjugendbewegung und "bürgerlicher" Jugendbewegung bis 1933', *JADJB*, 10 (1978) pp. 7–23.

Strauss, Herbert, 'The Jugendverband. A Social and Intellectual History', *Yearbook of the Leo Baeck Institute*, VI (1961) pp. 206–35.

Toboll, Dieter-Horst, 'Evangelische Jugendbewegung 1919–1933, dargestellt an dem Bund deutscher Jugendvereine und dem Christdeutschen Bund' (Doctoral dissertation, Bonn University, 1971).

Ueberhorst, Horst (ed.), *Elite für die Diktatur. Die Nationalpolitischen Erziehungsanstalten 1933–1945. Ein Dokumentarbericht* (Düsseldorf, 1969).

Vesper, Will (ed.), *Deutsche Jugend, 30 Jahre Geschichte einer Bewegung* (Berlin, 1934).

Völpel, Christiane, *Hermann Hesse und die deutsche Jugendbewegung* (Bonn, 1977).

Vollmer, Antje, *Die Neuwerkbewegung 1919–1935* (Doctoral dissertation, Free University Berlin, 1973).

Walker, Lawrence D., *Hitler Youth and Catholic Youth 1933–1936: A Study in Totalitarian Conquest* (Washington, DC, 1970).

Wandruszka, Adam, 'Die deutsche Jugendbewegung als historisches Phänomen', *Quellen und Forschungen aus italienischen Archiven und Bibliotheken*, 51 (1972) pp. 514–38.

Wangelin, Helmut, 'Der Wandervogel und das Völkische', *JADJB*, 2 (1970) pp. 43–77.

Wilhelm, Theodor, 'Der geschichtliche Ort der deutschen Jugendbewegung', in Werner Kindt (ed.), *Grundschriften der deutschen Jugendbewegung* (Dusseldorf, 1963).

Wolf, Hans, 'Von Wandervögeln, Scouts und Pfadfindern', *JADJB*, 3 (1971) pp. 26–39.

——, 'Fahrt in den Böhmerwald – Sommer 1911', *JADJB*, 8 (1976) pp. 114–23.

——, 'Der Alt-Wandervogel als Traditionsbund der Jugendbewegung', *JADJB*, 5 (1973) pp. 27–41.

Ziemer, Gerhard, 'Begriff und Grenzen der Jugendbewegung', *JADJB*, 1 (1969) pp. 7–17.

——, 'Die Übergangszeit zwischen Wandervogel und Bündische Jugend', *JADJB*, IV (1972) pp. 54–62.

——, 'Die deutsche Jugendbewegung und der Staat', *JADJB*, V (1973) pp. 42–51.

——, 'Hans Blühers Geschichte des Wandervogels. Die erste Deutung der deutschen Jugendbewegung', *JADJB*, 9 (1975) pp. 186–98.

Ziemer, Gerhard, and Wolf, Hans, *Wandervogel und Freideutsche Jugend* (Bad Godesberg, 1961).

Verlag Neues Leben, *Zur Geschichte der Arbeiterjugendbewegung in Deutschland. Eine Auswahl von Materialien und Dokumenten aus den Jahren 1904–1946* (East Berlin, 1956).

Index